ROUGH DIAMOND
The life story of
Bill Gilvear

Bill Gilvear

Sheana Brown

Christian Focus

© Sheana Brown
ISBN 1 871 676 851

Published in 1996 by Christian Focus Publications,
Geanies House, Fearn, Ross-shire, IV20 1TW, Great Britain.
Reprinted 1997
Cover design by Tom Windsor

Printed and bound in Great Britain by
The Guernsey Press Co. Ltd, Guernsey, Channel Islands

Contents

MILESTONES

1930 Birth
1939 Gallowgate to Dennistoun
1941-43 Evacuation
1944 Beatties. The Stick-It
1946 Tent Hall
1949 National Service. Sick Bay Attendant training
1951 Glasgow Western District Hospital, Oakbank
1955 Rob Royston Sanatorium
1956 Bible Training Institute
1958 Paris
1959 Antwerp
1960 Tent Hall. Belgian Congo gains independence
1961 Congo
1964 Massacre in N.E. Province
1965 Return to Congo
1967 Evacuated to Glasgow
1968 Yorkhill Hospital
1969 Car accident
1970 Wedding. Return to Zaire
1971 Glasgow. Surgery to arm
1973 Glasgow Medical Mission
1974 Royal Sailors Rest, Faslane
1978 Royal Sailors Rest Deputation Work
1985 Africa Inland Mission
1987 Ill health. Unemployment
1990 Scripture Gift Mission

1

Willie

'Hey! Willie!,' a small boy was running up the street shouting as loud as he could. 'Willie, whaur are ye? It's a cairt. Come oan!'

These last words echoed down the close of Number 42 as Tommy Young came to a halt outside the tenement where he and his friend both lived. The close was a dingy, concrete corridor which led from the street to the back courts of the tenements. There many of the children played amongst the rubbish which lay in midden heaps, running in and out of the washing which hung on improvised lines.

Just as Tommy was preparing to shout again, a high-pitched squawk came from the far end of the close. 'Comin'!' it yelled, and a moment later out of the darkness flew a dishevelled tornado of a boy. Thinly-soled shoes slapped against the stone floor of the close and skidded to a halt as Willie Gilvear careered wildly into his friend.

'Hey, watch it!' cried Tommy.

'Ach, Ah've nae grips on these shoes,' returned Willie. 'Whaur's the cairt? Ur ye gonnie go an' catch a hudgie?'

Catching a free ride on the back of any passing vehicle was one of their favourite pastimes. They turned to look down the street at the approaching horse-drawn cart.

Standing together, the two boys were like any others playing in the streets around them. Both wore long, grey shorts which came down to their scarred and grubby knees. These were topped by knitted pullovers – long in the sleeve and short in the body with too much washing. And both wore scuffed shoes. Willie's toe poked through the end of his right shoe and he either wore no socks at all, or they had disappeared in a crumpled ball

7

inside his shoe. Certainly none could be seen.

Both boys also had very short hair. It was shaved round the back of their necks, leaving them with a tousled thatch on top. Willie's blonde hair stood up on end like the bristles on a brush and pointed in all directions – no two ways the same.

But it was Willie's smile which really differentiated him from other boys. His face was long and pale and streaked with the dirt of the streets where he played. Yet when it broke into a smile everything was transformed. A huge, toothy grin appeared which seemed altogether too big for his face. As if he had suddenly too many teeth to fit in behind his lips, they beamed out, happy to be free.

And the rest of his face crumpled up to make room: his eyes, his ears, his cheeks, and even his voice was altered. It was a face made for smiling, and Willie's happy nature meant that he did more than his fair share of it.

Tommy Young was unimpressed, however, with the set of Willie Gilvear's features. He was more concerned with the approaching cart.

'Here it comes,' he breathed as it rumbled up, loaded high and covered with an old tarpaulin. The two boys flew round the back before the driver could see them. Then, with a great leap, they grabbed the tail-gate and hauled themselves up, wriggling and squirming until they achieved a sitting position. Then they sat there, swinging their legs as the carter continued unknowingly up the street.

Willie and Tommy felt like kings as they bumped over the cobbles of Comleypark Street. They waved to the other children playing in the street as they passed. Some were floating paper boats and leaves in the water-clogged gutters, while others were poking at the open drains with sticks, trying to jab at the rats which lurked there. A group of girls played at hop-scotch, marked out in chalk on the pavement. Others raced around playing 'tig' or 'kick the can'. The boys had a good vantage point from which to survey their world.

One or two mothers stood at the end of their closes while others leaned out from windows, deep in conversation: these 'hingie oots' were the main means of swapping gossip and relaxing. If a particularly long session was planned, some even put a cushion on the window sill before settling down there for a long 'natter' with passers-by or neighbours.

The boys then passed two women wheeling their families' washing in big prams. They were heading round the corner to the 'Steamie' in Whitevale Street. A piece of rope tied over each huge pile held it in place.

Small groups of men, young and old, stood at the corners or leaned against a wall, well away from the playing children, enjoying a smoke. Too many men and too few jobs meant some were always idle. The boys had heard it all and let it wash over them many times before.

They passed a small woman out with her message bag. She was the wee woman from Number 31 and she lived just opposite Willie and Tommy. She was well known to all the children of the street for she was the 'puff-candy wifie'. This was an orange, sticky sweet which she made. She would then wrap up little bits of it in newspaper and sell it to the children for a penny a piece.

'Mebbe she's bin oot buyin' some sugar fur the puff-candy,' said Willie hopefully.

'Aye,' approved Tommy, 'that'd be smashin!'

Soon the carter drew in the reins to halt at the end of their street. 'Whoa!' he bellowed to the horse and the steady clip-clop of the hooves slowed slightly.

'Come oan,' said Willie and taking their chance, the two boys flung themselves off the tail-gate and landed unceremoniously on the cobbles. Laughing and shoving one another, they scrambled away before the driver could spot them and wave his fist at them. Then, striding out proudly as if they had just stepped out of their own private limousine, the two boys turned back up Comleypark Street again. Catchin' hudgies – there was nothing like it!

2

The Gilvears

That night round the table in the Gilvears' kitchen there was the usual squash as the family sat down to their tea. Daddy sat at the end, keeping the high spirits of his offspring under control. Just one look from under those heavy brows was enough to still even Willie's chattering tongue.

Kenneth Gilvear was a big man, tall and straight. To all his friends he was known as 'Big Kenny'. He was not a native Glaswegian having been born and brought up in Stirling-shire, in the country. Even now as he went off to work each morning it seemed he would be more at home heading out to farm the country fields rather than to plough up and down the streets of Glasgow as he did each day with his fruit and vegetable cart.

For Willie's father was a carter and he worked from the Fruit Market near Barrowland. Each morning he would go off to work dressed in the same clothes: a jacket tied across his broad chest, old trousers and a flat cap pulled down over his ears. His great feet were clad in heavy and what seemed to Willie, huge shoes.

Willie had never seen his father at work. He had never seen the horse and cart he drove. He just knew that he left early in the morning to tackle up the horse and that he came home from the stables after his work, having bedded the animal for the night.

Willie thought then for perhaps the first time about his Daddy at work. Did wee boys like him jump on the back of his cart? And did those wee boys have to be quick before his Daddy saw them in case he chased them off like most of the other carters did? Willie suspected that they did for although he knew that his father could sometimes laugh and joke, he also knew him to be strict. Like the rest of his family, Willie respected his father greatly and took his word as law.

Yet for all his size and seeming healthiness, Kenneth Gilvear was unwell periodically. As a young man working in the Glasgow market, Kenneth had been kicked by a cart-horse. Ever since then he had suffered from epileptic convulsions. They struck him without warning and left him weak and feeble. It was a terrible sight to witness and it was hard for the big man to rise above his uncontrolled and stigmatized illness.

Willie's mother, Lily, was by any comparison a small woman. Standing next to her tall husband, she seemed tiny. Yet what she lacked in height, she made up for in personality. Willie had always been told that although he looked like his father and took his height from him, he had nevertheless inherited his mother's happy-go-lucky attitude to life.

Dressed in her apron, she presided over her home with warmth and kindness and worked hard to make her husband's wage go as far as possible to feed and clothe her large family. At least there was usually plenty of fruit and vegetables to make a meal go further as her husband brought home bits and pieces left at the end of the day on the cart.

Willie's mother also went out to work part-time to help financially. Early in the morning she would head off to Campbell's the Bakers in Argyll Street. Only when she got home could she see to her house and children.

It was a busy, hard life for her although there were some perks which went with the job. Sometimes she would come home from work with leftovers – tasty cakes and buns her family never normally saw.

'Ah'll huv tae plank these,' she would say and attempt to hide the titbits. Her favourite 'plank' or hiding place was a deep shelf above the recessed bed in the wall of the kitchen. In such a small house as theirs, however, nothing could be hidden for long. Soon Willie and his brothers had found the hoard and raided it.

'Ah'll sort yous!' called their father, pretending to chase them but it was half-hearted as he shared their sweet tooth – and he knew the hiding place too!

Every penny coming into the Gilvear household helped, however, for there were seven of them at that time in the room and kitchen which was the flat, two flights up in 42 Comleypark Street. Sitting opposite Willie across the table were Cathy and Lily. Willie's eldest sister, Ellen, had not lived at home for some time. She had been 'given' to Willie's grandparents in Blythswood Street. The reason ostensibly was to give more room to the others still at home. But, in truth, she was placed there to help keep the peace in what was a violent, strife-ridden home.

Cathy and Lily who were still at home were both older than Willie too and they had little to do with him. Their activities at school and their plans for the future were of little concern to him. His head was too full of games and nonsense to pay much attention to their girls' talk.

But as the eldest boy, Willie felt a certain responsibility, particularly to his younger brothers, Kenneth and Jim. Playing out in the street and further afield he would try, young as he was, to take care of them. He stood up for them in the fights and brawls that went on inevitably amongst the children. And when it was time to call them in for meals or bed, Willie usually knew where they could be found and he would go and round them up for his mother.

The kitchen in which they sat seemed hardly big enough to contain them all as they sat round the table. And when they all got up from their meal, the room seemed to shrink even further. A single chair sat by the big, black range which took up a large part of the wall. Their father sat down there after the meal and having tossed some wood onto the grate in the middle of the range, he picked up the paper and began to read. Willie's mother took up position at the sink and started to wash up.

On the opposite side of the room was a small dresser which

held all the plates. Other than that there was only the bed in the wall recess where Willie's parents slept. This left the one other room for all the children who slept head to toe in the big bed there. It was very cramped, yet with so many mouths to feed, it was all the Gilvears could afford.

The boys usually went out again after tea to play until bedtime. Nobody in their street could afford a radio or any other form of entertainment so all the children spent their lives outside. Tonight, however, was the dreaded bath night so they would have to be in early.

Not having a bathroom in the house, merely the stair toilet, the boys were bathed one after another in the tin bath which was placed in front of the fire. The last one in had to sit in the coldest, dirtiest water. Yet even so, no one wanted to be first.

The bottom of the tin bath was ridged and uncomfortable to sit on. And the carbolic soap left a smell which stayed on the skin and hung in the air. Their mother would scrub at their knees and their faces with the big, pungent smelling bar.

'How come you boys aye git so manky?' she would ask. 'Playin' oot in a' that muck up the backclose, nae doot! Ye widny think wan wee yin could git this dirty!'

Then, after their bath, their hair was combed with a narrow bone comb. This was to scrape out any nits which might be lurking in their hair. So filthy were the places that they got to through the day that a small boy's head was perfect breeding ground for any self-respecting bug. The boys would fidget and twist under the comb but Mrs Gilvear was persistent. They would hear her cracking the nits between her fingers to kill them as she found them in the comb.

These undignified toiletries over, it was time for bed and the boys would tumble between the blankets, exhausted from the day's play. Huddled together, they would jostle for position for a while, laughing and joking in the darkness, until one by one they would drift gently off to sleep.

3

Comleypark Street

In those days in the Gallowgate, Willie's life seemed full of little but play. School was there to be endured, but once it was over, he was as free as a bird.

There were so many children in the street that there were always companions for every adventure. Sometimes they kept to the back courts, jumping the dykes which separated the tenements, or playing in the little boiler houses where some of the women did their washing. On other occasions they ventured further afield, perhaps as far as Gypsy Hill where the travelling people gathered, or perhaps just into the other streets nearby.

One of Willie and Tommy's favourite games was 'girders'. These were thin, metal hoops which they tossed along with an iron rod which had a hook at the end. The best place to race these was on the bridge in Thompson Street, parallel to Comleypark Street. There they could chase the home-made girders along the long, flat tarmac without interruption – until a rare vehicle came along and they all scattered before the driver's roar.

There were other times when fast legs were necessary too, like when the police would find the boys playing football on a Sunday. This was a serious offence and if the big, black police van came into view the shout would go up: 'It's a black Mariah! Leg it!'

Then the boys had to run and hide where they could – in the middens or up the stair. And pity the boy who was left carrying the ball. For if they were caught, they were bundled into the back of the police van and taken to Tobago Street Police Station! There they would wait for their parents to pick them up – and then there would be trouble!

So seldom did Willie and his friends go indoors, that even if they became hungry they would shout on their mothers from the street.

'Aw, Mammy, a jeely piece!' Willie would shout below her window and a few minutes later his mother would fling down a small parcel – a jam sandwich wrapped up in an old bit of paper.

As Mrs Gilvear went out to work, Willie found himself often calling on his 'Auntie' Sadie for his 'piece'. Sadie Thompson was an old friend of the family and she lived in the same tenement as the Gilvears. Married late in life, Sadie had no family of her own but she loved children nevertheless. Indeed she later adopted two children herself.

Willie loved the kindly Sadie with her beaming red cheeks and her generous heart. She became a second mother to him, as well as to other children in the street. And it was always better to ask Sadie for a bite to eat anyway, rather than his mother – the Gilvears were two flights up while Sadie was only one, so Willie had a better chance of catching his 'piece' as it came flying out of the window!

With no extra pennies in the families to spare to give to the children, Willie and his friends often set about trying to earn some money for themselves. One of the favourite ways was to scour the middens and back courts for empty, discarded bottles. Once they had a few they would march down to the shop and show them to the grocer.

'Here's some ginger bottles, mister – empties,' they would demand and the shopkeeper would lean over and count them carefully before passing over the few ha'pennies to the eager, grubby hands.

Any means was used to earn a few coppers, however, and sometimes Willie and his pals would be given some by the local MP, Campbell Steven, for helping him.

Campbell Steven was with the Independent Labour Party and he would come through the Gallowgate, knocking on doors and talking to people in the streets. Given their penny, the children would form an 'electioneering band' and parade behind him down the street, singing 'his' song in the back courts and up the closes, wherever he went. Any political opposition, like Mr Murphy from another party, were shown no mercy once the children's allegiance had been bought! And so they would sing:

> 'Vote, vote, vote fur Campbell Steven,
> Here comes Murphy at the door.
> An' we'll bang wur penny drum –
> An' we'll make ol' Murphy run
> An' we'll nivir see ol' Murphy ony more!'

Although the streets saw little in the way of traffic, they were always noisy with the children's ringing voices with the usual wails and cries. Young boys' squeaky cries echoed up to the chimney pots; younger children danced and sang as they played; little girls were 'falling out' and making friends again with the usual taunts and tears. And during these regular tiffs, the finger-pointing rhyme would often be heard, floating down the street like some religious chant:

> 'Tell-tale tit,
> Yer Mammy canny knit
> Yer Daddy canny go to bed
> Withoot a dummy tit!'

There was one night when children's and adults' voices mingled together in the street. Boys and girls were up late; dance halls emptied and the dancers were on the cobbles; men were out on the pavement, cheering and congratulating one another.

For it was a night of celebration: Benny Lynch, a local, Glasgow boy, had won the World Flyweight Boxing Champion-ship, at Shawfield, the home of Clyde Football Club. He had won it for Scotland, and had won it for Glasgow – on Glasgow soil.

And not only that, but he was coming round to visit his Auntie after the fight and she just lived in the next street! They could hardly believe it! It seemed that the entire male population of the Gallowgate, and some of the women too, were out in force.

Never had there been such excitement. Willie and Tommy rushed about in the crowd, trying to be the first to see the hero arrive.

'Ah hud tae jook doon the stair before ma Mam could git me,' said Willie.

'Aye, me too,' agreed Tommy.

'But Ah widny miss this fur ony'hing!' Willie added.

'Me neither,' puffed Tommy as the two boys 'ducked and dived', throwing mock punches at one another.

And then the new champion was spotted coming up the street. What a row went up. Men and boys rushed onto the cobbles to greet the little man who bore the scars of his battle that night.

'Guid on ye, Benny!' came the cries.

'Ye banjoed him guid an' proper. Ye really clobbered him!'

One voice merged into another around the champion: 'Ye wur smashin', 'Yon fight wis a belter!', 'Gaun yersel', wee barra!', 'Ya beauty!'

The more sentimental or inebriated were near to tears: 'The wee man's done it fur Glesga – an' he's jist a punter like the rest o' us.'

Everyone wanted to shake Benny Lynch's hand or say a word of praise to him, so he made slow progress up the street. Some of the women were hanging out of their windows watching, while others were less interested:

'Whit's the rammy fur? Wan wee guy's knocked the lights oot o' anither! So whit?'

Some were so incensed by the noise and kerfuffle that they resorted to throwing buckets of water out of their windows to scatter the crowds!

Willie and Tommy danced off the pavements with the others

to dodge the deluge and laughed at those who were caught. What
a night of excitement it was!

But such occasions were the exception in the street. It was
during the day, generally, that the street was at its noisiest. Apart
from the playing children, tradesmen plied their wares as they
passed. Their raucous cries intimated their arrival on the street.

'Co-al!' shouted the dusty-faced driver as he heaved the
blackened bags onto his shoulders and dumped the contents
round the back in the bunkers in the back close.

The ragman was a special favourite with the children. Although
most were dressed virtually in rags themselves, still he would
come collecting the very worst of their clothes and toss them up
into his cart.

But the children would wait for him to finish when he would
stand at the back of his cart and look down at the growing crowd
of eager, young faces.

'Who's fur candy rock?' he would shout, and delving into his
deep pocket, he would pull out a fist-full of pink boiling sweets
and throw them high into the air. The delighted, waiting children
would scramble to get their share.

Occasionally, Willie would miss these rare treats by being sent
on an errand. By the time he was eight he was old enough to be
sent as far as Appin Road across the city to the 'Shan Shop'
where the baker's seconds were sold at cut-down prices.

'Ach, dae Ah huv tae go,' Willie would moan. It was a long
way there in his thin shoes and it would feel a lot further on the
way home, carrying all the bread and rolls for the family.

'Ur ye wantin' ma boot up yer backside?' Willie's Daddy
would reply. 'Ye go doon that road, or else!'

So there was nothing for it but to go. Clutching the few pennies
given him by his father, Willie would trudge off reluctantly
through the streets.

Yet at that time, Willie was noticing a change in his father. No
longer was he as stern as he had been but he was becoming more

gentle with the children. He would talk to them and take out his big, new Bible and tell them what was inside.

Willie remembered the night his father had come home with the Bible. There was a man who worked near his father in the Fruit Market known as Black Peter. He came from the Gorbals in Glasgow but was originally from the West Indies. He was always asking their father to go with him to somewhere called the Tent Hall.

This night, Kenneth Gilvear had agreed to go with Black Peter to a special meeting, a big gathering at St George's Cross in Maryhill Road. When his father came home he told them all about it – how there had been singing and how a man called Pastor Findlay had got up and begun to speak. Willie listened to his father's rich voice: 'He telt us that God loved us, an' that Jesus died fur us.' His father spoke warmly, describing it all.

'An' whit's this ye've goat, Daddy?' asked Willie.

'That's a Bible, son. Ah'm gonnie learn a' aboot the Saviour I trustit the night.'

Willie did not understand the words his father spoke but he saw his glowing face. And from that night Kenneth Gilvear read to his family from the big book.

'Here's ma favourite verse,' he would say, and then recite Isaiah 55:1: 'Ho, every one that thirsteth, come ye to the waters, and he that hath no money; come ye, buy, and eat; yea, come, buy wine and milk without money and without price.'

He also taught the children to say a prayer before they ate at the table and another before they went to bed at night. It was all a great novelty to them at first. But they were just doing what they were told. Yet this was the beginning of any Christian influence in young Willie Gilvear's life.

4

The Tent Hall

Willie's father began immediately to attend the Tent Hall with Black Peter. This was a big building on Steel Street. The name had come from its beginnings as a huge tent, erected on Glasgow Green where evangelistic meetings had once been held. The American evangelist, D L Moody, had led the campaign from the canvas 'church'. When these first 'tent meetings' were over, the organisers and new converts wanted to continue to reach out to the people of Glasgow, particularly the poor. It was then that they moved into the meeting place in Steel Street opposite Glasgow Green and gave the building its anachronistic title.

The Tent Hall's frontage and door looked quite unprepossessing but once inside the building seemed to open out with galleries round three sides. High up on the walls were Bible verses written out in coloured paint. There was a huge stage at the front of the hall. Graduated tiers of choir seats rose up from the stage on both sides. Seats filled the main part of the 'church', so that in total it could hold up to 2200 people. There were also two additional halls: the North Hall and the Back Hall. They were often in use to house the overflow congregation. You had to be early to claim a Main Hall seat!

This was true particularly at the Saturday night meetings. Willie went with his father regularly and while his father took up the position he had been given of greeting people at the door, Willie sat nearby with Granny Slaven.

Granny Slaven was an old woman who was a Tent Hall regular and known to everyone there. She sat just inside the door and she wore a long, black dress with a woollen shawl round her shoulders. After the singing, Willie would creep onto Granny Slaven's knee and snuggle down inside that shawl. There he would sleep peacefully until his father came for him at the end of the night.

But Willie tried to be awake for the hymns. He loved the singing at the Tent Hall. Mr Troup, the Superintendent, would stand at the front and wave his hymn book vigorously to keep the beat. Another man at the piano played the tune while the choirs at the front made the rafters ring with song. Willie filled his chest full and sang as loud as he could. It was a great feeling.

The police station next door in Turnbull Street often shook with the noise as 2,000 people stood up and began to sing. The roughs and toughs of Glasgow's East End jailed in its cells perhaps wondered if their time had come!

Willie's father also started going to the early Sunday morning prayer meetings and he would take Willie with him. After the praying, there was a free breakfast for the poor and the down and outs, many of whom slept rough on Glasgow Green. Willie and the rest – sometimes as many as nine hundred people – sat down eagerly at the long tables and had a good 'tuck in'.

On Sunday at 2 o'clock there was also a free dinner for the poor children of Glasgow. The big kitchen in the Tent Hall would fill with steam as huge urns of water boiled and the ladies of the Tent Hall hurried to and fro, serving up hot food to hundreds of hungry, clamouring children.

For the Tent Hall was always full of children. Some were the children of members like Willie, and others just came in off the streets.

It was in the Tent Hall that Willie's father first met the homeopathic doctor who tried to help the big man control the epilepsy which dogged him. Conventional doctors were too expensive and had never been able to help before. But this was a new concept and Kenneth Gilvear willingly received the treatment and herbal remedies this doctor provided.

It seemed at first that the new medicines were having some success and Willie's father came to rely on them. Yet they did not control the life-threatening seizures which still came upon him.

Willie was still a little boy when he first witnessed one of his father's convulsions. He had fallen in the street and ran into their flat with blood running down his leg.

'Daddy,' he sobbed, 'Ah fell aff the dyke.'

Willie's father got up and was soon washing the cut knee, trying to clean the dirt from the wound.

'Ye're an awfy laddie,' he murmured. 'Ayeways up tae somethin' – tearin' aboot like a bull in a china shop. An',' he added emphatically, looking at Willie's clothes, 'ye would land in the midden!'

Suddenly Kenneth Gilvear's whole body was violently racked by a convulsion. He jerked up from his stooping position over Willie's knee. His eyes rolled up into his sockets. His mouth opened, moving noiselessly and he fell heavily to the floor.

Willie looked down in horror as his father lay jittering and shaking at his feet. He froze to the spot in terror. What was happening? What had he done? Finally, he found his voice and shouted frantically for his mother.

'Mammy, Mammy, come here! It's Daddy – Oh come!'

Crying and frightened, Willie watched as they held his father's jerking body till it stopped. When it was still, they carried him carefully over to his bed.

Kenneth Gilvear lay there, still and grey. It would be a few hours before he would feel able to get up again. In fright, Willie ran to his mother's skirts and sobbed away his shock and fear.

Nothing, however, would induce Willie's father to see a doctor. 'Ah'll jist use ma own medicines,' he insisted. 'They've done the trick fur me before, ye know. Ah feel a wee bit wabbit the minute. But ah'll soon be as right as rain.'

Although there did not seem to be any reduction in the number of Willie's father's seizures, or in their severity, they did not keep

Kenneth Gilvear from carrying on a normal life. Indeed, he seemed quite fit – even, to Willie's delight, coming second behind Jock Troup in the adults' race at the Tent Hall Sunday School Picnic.

The Sunday School Picnics to Rouken Glen Park were always exciting occasions. To the children who only went as far distant from their homes as they could walk, a tram ride – and one to a picnic – was a real adventure.

Willie and his pals looked forward eagerly to the chosen day. And when it came they piled onto the waiting tram cars and sang all the way to the picnic spot. To get on a tram was novelty enough; to get a ride *for nothing* was a cause for celebration and hymns and choruses floated out of the tram car windows as they went.

The big park at Rouken Glen gave ample space for the children of all ages to run around. The Tent Hall workers soon set up games of football and rounders while others prepared the picnic food and drinks. Three-legged races, sack races, and the egg and spoon all brought great hilarity. And when Jock Troup won a big doll and Willie's father a doll's bath set for their efforts, everyone enjoyed a good laugh.

With the attractions of the picnics and the hymn singing, as well as the joy of being amongst so many happy people, Willie was always keen to go to the Tent Hall with his father. His sisters joined the choir there and Willie's brothers would come too. But Willie was the real regular with his father. And he was the only early riser in the family so he was the only one to benefit often from the Tent Hall breakfasts. He knew too that it pleased his Daddy if he went and that would have been incentive enough. To be stepping down the cold streets on a grey, smoggy morning, stride for stride, just Willie and his Dad, was a great feeling. Two men together. Then Willie's big grin would be stuck firmly and proudly all over his face.

5

Ballindalloch Drive

Back home it was becoming apparent that it would not be possible for the Gilvears to continue living in the tiny room and kitchen in the Gallowgate.

'It's gettin' ridiculous,' Willie's father would say. 'Wur packed in here like sardines, ye know.' And if the Gilvears children could be seen, all lying head to toe in the one bed, that is just what they looked like – sardines in a tin!

Round the table it was no better. Elbows and knees knocked together and the children squirmed and squashed one another to get more room. And it was not going to get any easier – Mrs Gilvear was expecting her seventh child.

'Naw, we'll huv tae git somethin' a bitty bigger,' decided their father.

Nothing more was said until Willie heard his parents discussing the move. They were speaking in low tones at the table and Willie could hear snippets of the conversation. It all sounded very exciting.

'It's brand new, Lily! Can ye believe that? Wan o' thay new council blocks in Dennistoun. Naeb'dy's lived there before – naeb'dy!'

Willie sat very still listening. He would have jumped up and asked his father all about it but something about their whispering voices stopped him. Was the move going to be a secret, then? Willie listened all the harder.

The murmuring at the table continued. It was difficult to make anything out. Then Willie heard his normally mild mother raise her voice.

'We'll, Ah'm nae huvin' a' ma faimily's worldly goods

gauk'd at fae the windies, ye know. It'd be the talk o' the Steamie fur days. Ah can jist hear them noo!' Willie's mother mimicked her neighbours: ' "Did ye see yon wee foutery table, an thae chairs – Ah widny pay a penny piece fur the whole jing-bang!" An' whit about the new folk at the ither end? Naw!' she said vehemently, reverting to her own voice, 'It'll huv tae be at night!'

A moonlight flit! Willie was so excited he could hardly keep himself from shouting out. He had heard of such night-time removals but had never expected to be in one.

His father, however, was not so keen.

'Ah dinna like this kinda caper – wi' a' the weans too. Who's carin' whit the neighbours think?'

'Ah do,' exclaimed his wife – so that was that.

Yet when it actually came, the midnight move lost much of its appeal. The night it happened, Willie and his brothers were wrapped up in bed, fast asleep. When their father came in to wake them he hustled them out of bed and into the cold kitchen where they dressed with fumbling fingers and bleary eyes. Then they trooped in a long column down the stairs, past the stair toilet and out into the close and then the dark street. The wind nipped at Willie's legs and he clutched feebly at the box of odds and ends he had been given to carry. There did not seem to be much fun in this.

All the previous day, Willie's father had been trying to get hold of a small lorry in which to transport their few belongings. He had found one at last and out in the dark street it was piled high with the few bits of furniture and other possessions the Gilvears owned.

The table was strapped on with ropes and boxes of dishes and blankets sat between its legs. And Daddy's armchair looked very out of place perched on top of it all.

Willie and the others clambered onto the lorry as well as they could while their mother sat in the front with their father. And then they were off.

But if the flit was not proving to be as exciting as Willie had hoped, worse was to come. For the Gilvears in their borrowed lorry did not get far. A few streets away they came rattling and shuddering to a halt. The lorry would go no further!

What were they to do? It was the middle of the night and they were stuck with all their worldly possessions in some unknown street!

The only solution was to get out and walk, carrying what they could with them. What a pathetic sight they made – seven shadowy figures, shivering and stumbling along the streets to their new home.

By the time they arrived, however, the walk had woken and warmed Willie up. He had never been in this street before. It was called Ballindalloch Drive and although it was a relatively short distance from their old room and kitchen in the Gallowgate, this was in Dennistoun and was worlds apart.

'Look at us – livin' in a *Drive,* ye know!' they laughed. 'Is that no' jist dead posh!'

'It's goat a gairden!' breathed Cathy as they walked up the path. And so it had. Being on the ground floor, the garden was theirs.

The children explored the new house by the light of the moon streaming in through the curtainless windows.

'There's no' even a wee bit o' lino' on the floors,' exclaimed young Lily as they passed from room to room on the bare floorboards.

'But look at a' this space,' replied their mother, gazing round in wonder. 'It's like a hotel! Ah've nae furniture tae put in ony o' these rooms! Ah'll just huv stuff fur the kitchen, an' that'll be it, end o' story!' For the new house seemed palatial. It had *three* bedrooms, a kitchen *and* a living room, and *a bathroom*!

'A bathroom! Imagine!' came the cry.

'Aye but,' called back Willie, 'the lavvy's broke!'

'Haud yer wheesht!' was all their father would say, 'or ye'll

huv the hale neighbourhood roon' before wur here a minute.
Settle doon.'

The meagre amount they had managed to carry from the lorry
sat mournfully on the floor and soon the whole family had to lie
down beside it. The bed had been left on the lorry so there was
nothing but bare boards to lie on. They curled up together to keep
warm, tossing and turning against one another in an attempt to get
more comfortable. What a welcome this was to their new home!

Willie lay awake for a while trying not to think of his sore bones
on the hard floor, and trying instead to think of this as his new
home. It was all so strange and sudden he could hardly believe
they were here. Maybe he would wake up the next morning in his
own bed in their old room. Maybe he would have a kick-about
with Tommy before school. Maybe he would ... maybe ... mmm.

Willie drifted slowly and restlessly off to sleep, and so began
the Gilvears' life in their new home.

6

War

At that time the talk amongst the grown-ups was all of war. 'War was coming' they said and they talked of 'Glasgow being a German target'. It was just as the Gilvears moved to Dennistoun that all the rumours became reality.

When war was declared, Willie's sisters found work at Singer's in Clydebank. This was a sewing machine factory which was turned into a munitions factory with the onset of war. By that time Cathy was married and Ellen and Lily were soon to follow her. But they were often back at home. Cathy's husband, Jimmy Burnet, in particular, had long been like one of the family. Cathy and Jimmy often came to stay in the Gilvear's big Dennistoun house.

To the children, war only became real when shelters began to be built in the back courts and near the schools. Soon they were issued with gas masks and drilled on how to use them. Even the new Gilvear baby, Violet, had to be put in a wooden 'gas box' when the sirens went.

Fitting on the gas masks in those early days and running for cover was treated by the children and Willie, aged eight, as fun and just another game. They made up songs and ditties to sing while they sat waiting for the sirens to stop in the little corrugated iron shelter at the back of the house. They would sing,

'An aeroplane, an aeroplane,
Away up in the sky.
We a' run helter-skelter
But don't run aifter me,
Fur Ah'll be in ma shelter
An' it's faur too wee!'

It was in the shared shelters that the Gilvears got to know their new neighbours. They had already met the Watsons who lived directly above them, mainly because 'Big Watty', as the children called Mr Watson, was a notorious drunkard.

Often the Gilvears would hear the fights that went on upstairs with dishes flying and doors slamming. Even the light shades in the ceiling would shake and bits of plaster fall down as Big Watty roared and stamped around his house. Willie and his brothers would be in bed wondering if he was about to crack the ceiling from side to side and land up in bed beside them!

In the shelters, however, Willie befriended the Clarke boys who lived on the top floor. They went to the Tent Hall also but the families had never really known each other.

Mr Clarke was a tiny man, the smallest Willie had ever known. It always made Willie laugh to know that wee Mr Clarke drove one of the biggest cranes in the whole of the Clyde shipyards. What a size of a man for a job like that!

Mr Clarke, for all his lack of height, was a strict disciplinarian and he rarely let his five sons away from their studies indoors to play. But once the friendship was formed, Gordon and Willie in particular became inseparable.

Whenever possible, the boys roamed the area together and explored Willie's new surroundings. One of their best finds was the Mollindina Burn where they could go fishing, 'catchin' baggie minnies in a jeelie jaur'. With a piece of cane and a little net, they enticed the tiny minnows into their jars. A length of string sufficed as a handle and the boys proudly showed off their 'baggie minnies' to their friends.

Trains crossed the Mollindina Burn by a stone bridge, slowing up as they did so before entering Alexandra Park Station nearby. With the war on, troop trains packed with soldiers often chuffed over the bridge. They rolled by above the boys' heads as they sat fishing or playing about in the water.

'Here's anither o' them trains,' Willie would cry as one came into view. 'An' it's a Yankie wan!'

American soldiers in their distinctive uniforms and short hair leaned precariously out of the loaded trains as they slowed up for the station. Willie and Gordon waved energetically to them.

'Goat ony gum, chum?' Willie always ventured boldly and sometimes he was rewarded with a little packet of chewing gum, tossed down from the passing train.

Soon Willie was to be found regularly up in the Clarkes' flat. He certainly made sure he was there on Friday nights, for that was Monopoly night. To Willie who had no such games in his house, apart from toys they had made themselves, board games were great fun. The fact that the boys usually ended up fighting over the outcome was no deterrent to the exuberant Willie.

Gordon Clarke was similarly to be found often in Willie's company, playing on the stair, much to Mr Clarke's wrath. Together with young Alex Keys who lived in the other middle flat, they would gleefully ring doorbells and tie door handles together before running away. It was as well that Mrs Clarke was so soft-hearted or they might have got into more trouble than they did!

Mrs Dennison who lived opposite the Gilvears on the ground floor, was not so soft-hearted, however, and was often the butt of the boys' practical jokes. She was a small, dark woman (though not as small as Mr Clarke) and she had been left a widow for some years. She guarded her clean close jealously and checked the boys' high spirits whenever she saw them. And she always watched to see that her son – another Alex – did not become caught up in Willie's mischief with his pals. To tie Auld Denny's door handle to the Gilvears opposite was no feat for the faint-hearted!

The boys were as keen to keep clear of Auld Denny as she was of them. For she always seemed to know exactly what was going on, especially wrong-doing. If their laughter was heard, she would be out on the stair ranting at them. If a young girl was saying a fond farewell in the back close to a boyfriend, for instance, Auld Denny would have her head round the corner and be there on top of them before they knew it.

She seemed to believe that she was a bit above the rest of the occupants of Ballindalloch Drive and that somehow it was her job to ensure that nothing of which she disapproved ever took place in her street. Rarely was she seen in the stairwell to do anything other than complain.

'Keep aff her,' the boys would say as they passed her door. 'Auld Denny'd huv the Polis aifter us as sure as guns!'

Mrs Dennison seemed to have a particular knack of catching Willie at some misdemeanour. Perhaps it was that he seemed often to be the ring-leader in whatever forbidden game they were playing. But Mrs Gilvear had little time for their tell-tale neighbour, so Willie missed some of the punishment he regularly earned.

For Willie was a restless, happy-go-lucky boy. Always ready with a quick quip or up to some mischief, he entered into every activity headlong, and at full speed. He was an insuppressible scallywag whose cheeky, wide grin seemed to welcome trouble. Yet he was one to whom most people (Auld Denny excluded) could not help but feel drawn.

Willie's favourite game was football and there was a green area where they played near Ballindalloch Drive. After a game one day, Willie ran all the way home with a terrible thirst. So thirsty was he that he outpaced the other boys from his stair.

He rushed to their flat and into the kitchen. There by the sink was a glass bottle, half-full with some copper coloured liquid.

'Aw, Irn Bru,' Willie gasped, taking a huge mouthful.

Immediately, he began gagging at the unexpected foul taste. Hearing his coughing and spluttering, his mother came through into the kitchen.

'Whit is it, William?' she demanded, leaning over his bent back. Seeing his red, contorted face she asked all the more urgently, 'Whit huv ye done?'

'It wis that Irn Bru, Ma,' he croaked. 'Ah took a big slug o' it, but it tasted honkin'.' Again he began to gag at the sink.

'Im Bru?' shrieked his mother. 'That wis ammonia ye wee...!
Aw, come oan. We'll huv tae git ye doon tae the Green Ladies.'

The Green Ladies were the Public Health Sisters of Glasgow.
Whenever some accident occurred these nurses in their starched,
green uniforms were the first port of call in their Crail Street Clinic
at Parkhead.

So Willie and his mother walked as quickly as they could all
the way to the Clinic, Willie still retching and coughing all the way.

Willie's only other experiences with the Green Ladies up to
this point had been unpleasant ones when they had painted the
children's skin with some strong-smelling, stinging ointment
which was the kiss of death to any lingering bug or bacteria.

But on this visit he became truly grateful for their help. Soon
he was made to feel comfortable again and his throat became
easier. Then he only had to listen to his mother's remonstrations.

'Huv ye nae sense in that heid, William Gilvear,' she scolded.
'Ye nivir stop tae think fur a minute, do ye? Aw, gi' me strength!'

It seemed that the accident-prone Willie was to become a
regular visitor at the Crail Street Clinic for it was soon afterwards
that he fell outside and split his head open. He and his friends had
been playing tig in the back-courts, jumping over the railings
which separated the Dennistoun houses. In his excitement, Willie
had slipped and the spike of the railing had gone right into his
head!

There was blood everywhere. Willie lay inert on the ground.
Gordon and Alex looked from one to the other fearfully before
running to get help. Soon he was carried all the way to the Clinic
where the Green Ladies quickly set about repairing the damage.

When Willie came round again he sat up quickly but cried out
with the pain.

'Not so fast, wee man,' they said, easing him back down onto
the bed. 'Don't you be in such a hurry.'

And Willie was very grateful to lie quietly and listen to their low-pitched, kindly voices. He tried to give a little smile but every time he even moved his face, his head seemed ready to burst.

A doctor came to see Willie too and the Green Ladies told Willie of how the doctor had been needed to patch him up after his accident. Willie was very impressed and there and then decided that when he was big, he wanted to be a doctor too.

'Ah'll mak' people better. Ah want tae look aifter people like yous Ladies an' the doctor are doing.'

The Green Ladies joked gently with him: 'Well, you'll need all your brains if your going to be a doctor. You can't be leaving wee bits of yourself on every playground you know! And have you paid the council for that railing yet, my boy?'

But nothing would shake Willie from his future plan. He was thrilled by their ability to heal the sick and to make people better from illnesses and accidents like his own. It was perhaps his first thought too for those caught up in the continual bombing raids which hit the city.

For the initial novelty of war was soon overshadowed by the true nature of the fighting, even for the youngsters. Everyone was shocked when a huge land mine was dropped on the Gallowgate, not least the Gilvears who had only just left those very streets.

When the bombing Blitz began on the shipyards of Clydeside, the whole city was in mourning. Willie's sisters came home from Singer's one day weeping and stunned by the horror of it all. Through tears and hysteria they told how they had stumbled home past burning, half-demolished buildings and even clambered over broken bodies in the rubble to escape the raids. It was a shocking, frightening time.

They stayed at home the next day but then had to return, frightened and sickened with it all, yet needed in the fight to maintain the war effort.

Kenneth Gilvear

Although so much was happening in the world outside, the Gilvears were soon wrapped up in troubles of their own. It happened one evening when Kenneth Gilvear took to his bed, feeling a bit unwell; he felt tired and weary. So, taking young Jim with him, he disappeared through to the bedroom.

'Ah'm no sick, like. Jim and me'll jist huv a wee lie down – Ah'll see if he'll no drop off so's Ah can put him in wi' the ither two, ye know.'

A while later, Cathy's husband slipped in to see how his father-in-law was feeling. Finding both Jim and his father awake still, Jimmy asked, 'D'ye fancy a cuppa, Mr Gilvear, jist where you are, ye know?'

Soon Jimmy came back with a cup of tea and left them there, father and son wrapped up in bed.

It was some time later that Jimmy returned to the bedroom. The scene that met his eyes horrified him. He stood fixed to the spot in the doorway, trying to take it all in.

Wee Jim was sitting up in bed, still and white. He was staring down silently at his father on the bed. Kenneth Gilvear himself lay contorted on the bed, stiff and straight. His eyes were open but did not focus. His lips were apart and his teeth bared. It was if they were frozen in some unvoiced scream. And his whole face was blue – a dull, steely blue.

Willie and Ken in bed heard the commotion but they had no idea what was happening. Scraping chairs on the lino; rushing feet; their mother's cry; the front door banging and running footsteps; wee Jim, shaking now and frightened, bundled into bed with them: what was happening? Neither Willie or Kenneth dared to go and see and no one came to tell them. All they had missed was Jimmy's first hoarse whisper to those gathered in the kitchen: 'Yer da – he's deid, he's deid in there! Come quick!'

It was in the morning when the boys emerged to see solemn faces and eyes puffy from weeping that they were told their father was gone. He had died suddenly in his bed. The epilepsy which had plagued him for twenty years had finally claimed him. Kenneth Gilvear had suffered a seizure while drinking his tea and had choked to death, his young son helpless there beside him. 'Death by asphyxiation' the death certificate read.

The cold truth of the explanation could not help them understand. Willie and his brothers were stunned by it. Their strong, vigorous Daddy was gone? Ken and Jim looked instinctively to Willie to show them how to grasp this terrible thing – but Willie could not help. He trailed from room to room, hearing the crying and weeping; he could not stay clinging to his mother's skirts. But it made no sense. He could not seem to piece it all together. The house, although full of people, seemed empty without his Daddy. Where was he?

Being the eldest of the boys although he was barely even ten years old, Willie was asked to go to the funeral. Willie had never been to a funeral before. But when he got there it did not seem like a funeral should to him.

It was to be a short service, not held in a church but just round the graveside at Riddrie Cemetery. It was November and the wind whipped around the headstones. The damp air seemed to steal silently amidst the huddled group of mourners. Rain fell and from time to time great gusts of wind within the rain blew sharp needlepoints of wetness into their faces.

Yet the men who came from the Tent Hall seemed unaware of the chill and the dark clouds chasing across the sky. To Willie's amazement they played their instruments and seemed to him to be *happy*. Their concertinas wheezed cheerfully and their faces smiled. Locked in his own fragile shell of grief, Willie could not understand it. His world had just fallen in on him. Happiness had disappeared. The boundaries had all been changed. He could not see, did not want to see what was ahead.

Yet these men were singing of 'the land that is fairer than day'. They talked of Kenneth Gilvear going to be with the Lord. Inside, Willie's heart was crying out: he did not want his Daddy to be with the Lord; he wanted him to be back at home.

It was then that Willie wept and wept. He cried as if his heart was cut in two. Sobbing and shaking he could no longer see or hear what was happening. The pain felt like it would crush him; he was lost; alone.

Gently, two arms gathered him into themselves and his tears melted into some soft, warm material. Willie closed his eyes and the darkness was soothing – but the heavy sobbing did not stop. Cradled there in a stranger's arms, Willie did not see his father's body being lowered into the ground. Jock Troup said a few words and prayed. Then, in the biting wind, the shabby coffin disappeared from view.

Kenneth Gilvear's body was laid to rest in a borrowed plot – Cathy's husband, Jimmy, had given it to them when he realised they had none. And there would be no headstone. In years to come, no one would know where Kenneth Gilvear's body lay.

When it was all over the chief mourners returned to Ballindalloch Drive for the funeral tea, prepared by Willie's mother. Willie sat by his father's brother, Uncle Willie, after whom he learnt, he was named. All Willie's uncles were there although he had not noticed them even at the cemetery.

Gently, Uncle Willie helped his namesake use the knife and fork which were put out on the table for the occasion. His big hands folded over Willie's own, clutching the unaccustomed utensils. And all the time Willie could hear what his Daddy would be saying: 'Jist stick it in yer mooth, son, an' be done wi' it. None o' this knife and fork malarky!'

Later, when all the relatives had gone, Jock Troup came and prayed over them. It was a subdued and frightened family that listened as he commended them to God. After he left, their mother gathered them to herself. And looking down at them she said, 'Well, ye know yer Daddy wis the only real bread-earner in this hoose. Ah'll huv tae go oot and find work noo.'

So that is what she did. The next morning she set out to find a full time job and with the war on, she was able to come home with one that night.

But it was the beginning of a different life for the Gilvears. They had never had much money. They had always just managed to scrape by. But now all their mother could do was to give the children something to eat and pay the factor the rent. There was no money spare to clothe them even. All their clothes had to be given them by the Public Assistance Board – in other words, the Gilvears were 'on the Parish'.

To make matters worse, with the war on, rationing was introduced. Soon every man, woman and child was granted a ration book which entitled them to certain meagre amounts of basic foods and clothing: 2 ozs of butter a week; 2 ozs of sugar....

Scarcity became common and the Gilvears found it particularly hard to get fuel. As winter approached, the coal man's loud cry was seldom heard out in the street. The Gilvears' coal bunker was empty all too often. Each sliver was scraped out of the metal box in the back close. But eventually they had to do without. Then, despite the number of rooms they now had, the whole family would gather in the kitchen or living room to keep warm. Woollen jumpers, long johns and vests were all worn to keep out the cold.

It was during one of these spells in January when there was no coal to be had, that further tragedy hit the Gilvears.

Willie, Kenneth and Jim were sitting through in the living room as usual that evening with their mother. It was too cold to go out, even for them. Lily was still at home but she had braved the cold weather and was out. Both Ellen and Cathy were married although they came in to see their mother often, especially after their father's death. But not tonight.

To pass the time the boys had the new radio on. It was a great novelty and they turned the volume up high, twiddling the knobs and fighting over which station to choose. Their mother sat with little Violet cradled on her lap, trying to get the baby to sleep amid all the boisterous noise.

'Whit a racket yer makin', boys!' their mother complained. 'The wee wan'll nivir sleep wi' yous lot. Ah'll jist pop her into the pram fur some peace an' quiet.'

So Lily Gilvear took her baby through to the end room across the hall and wrapped her up for a sleep.

Some time later while the three boys were still tinkering with the radio and play-fighting, more to keep warm than out of any grievance, their mother left her sewing and went through to check on Violet. Willie had barely noticed his mother leaving till he heard a strange screech and she appeared again at the living room door. What was wrong with her? She was wailing and waving her arms. Her whole body was shaking – 'Oh ma daughter, ma wee daughter.' Willie jumped up in fright. 'Shut off that radio,' his mother screamed. 'Ma baby, oh ma baby.' She staggered around the room as if she could not see. Willie was scared to touch her, she seemed so strange, so out of control.

He turned out of the room and down the corridor. What was so bad? Surely nothing could have happened to ... Willie could hardly bring himself to think of Violet's name. Terrified, yet needing to know, he crept into the far room and up to the pram. There she was – but Violet was just a little still body. Foam was coming out of her mouth. She was chilled blue with the cold. Willie jumped back in fright and horror. Shaking, he sprinted back to the others.

Following on so soon after their father's death, a mere two months, it seemed to Willie that a dark, heavy cloud had descended over their home. Tears throbbed from every eye. Weeping and pain were everywhere he turned. For another coffin was to be filled – a tiny, white one this time – that seemed too small to hold even a doll. Willie's mother remained utterly distraught by her baby's death, and the manner of it, for weeks. Nothing would placate her. Willie was glad when Ellen and Lily were around. For he was completely at a loss. He was frightened by his mother's face, her tears, her distress. And his inability to help dug deep into his heart.

The next time the coal man called, Willie's mother greeted him reproachfully and tearfully on the stair. And the big man was stunned by what had happened.

Yet what could he do if he had no coal to deliver? And was it all his fault that a poor widow with a large family was not a priority for delivery? But nothing would bring little Violet back to them: a silent, unknown victim of a war in other countries, before she was old enough even to understand.

8

Upper Skelmorlie

Only weeks after Violet's death, the day came which every family in the city had both dreaded and longed for since the war began. It was evacuation: every child at risk was to be sent from the bombed city to areas of rural Scotland where they would be safe. Each family struggled over the painful decision to send the children away or to keep them at hand. For no one knew who or what would be left when the children returned; no one knew if anyone would survive to see the outcome if they stayed where they were in Glasgow.

On the morning of the big day, Willie's mother had the three boys up early. Usually an early-riser, Willie had to be cajoled and nagged to get dressed and washed. Even as they sat at the kitchen table, the tears were flowing.

'Dae we huv tae go, Mammy?' Kenneth asked, repeatedly.

'We want tae stay wi' you,' Willie muttered, looking at his mother, pleadingly. But he knew it was no use. It was all arranged. Their clothes were washed and pressed; their packed lunches were ready; their few belongings were tied up in three little boxes; their gas masks were hanging by the door. Nothing was going to stop it happening now.

They were all to congregate at Alexandra Parade School. When Willie, Kenneth and Jim arrived with their mother, the playground was swarming with children and parents. Willie could almost enjoy the confusion and excitement of it all, if only it was not so unknown; if only Mammy were coming too. He worried about leaving her so soon after Violet had been taken from her too.

After what seemed like an age the children were all grouped

in long lines of pairs. Each child was given a badge with their name and a number on it. They seemed to be constantly counted and recounted. Then they were marched out of the school grounds, a long curling tail of children, marching round to Alexandra Park Railway Station. Behind came the parents, bunched in moving, grieving groups like a mourning procession along the street.

Finally on the station platform the last goodbyes were to be said. The noise of crying filled the air. Mothers and fathers wept over children; boys and girls clung fiercely to their mother's skirts before being prised away. Willie thought he had never seen so many tears in all his life. He heard his mother's voice over the noise.

'Now, Willie, Ah'm relyin' on you tae tak' care o' yer brothers. Ye're a big boy noo.' Yet even as the words passed her lips, she pulled him to her and wept over him. Kenneth and Jim held onto her as if they would never let go.

But, of course, they had to at last. The final moment came when they were loaded onto the train – hundreds of unhappy boys and girls, watched by hundreds of unhappy parents. Willie tried desperately to catch a last look at his mother – but too many others were doing the same thing. It was no use. So he pulled Kenneth and Jim towards him and gripped them hard – they did not know if they were being wrestled or hugged. Then slowly and inevitably the train chuffed out of the station. It was the saddest day in Glasgow of the entire war.

The Gilvear boys were bound for Upper Skelmorlie which lies on the Ayrshire coast south of Glasgow between Wemyss Bay and Largs. Once out of the city, the train steamed through open countryside such as the boys had never seen. The Firth of Clyde flowed past on one side for much of the journey while fields rolled by on the other. Towns and villages flashed passed their wide-eyed gaze. They seemed to arrive at their destination all too quickly.

The little station of Skelmorlie soon thronged with children.

Willie kept a tight grip of Kenneth and Jim lest they get separated and lost in the crowd. But they soon found that they were all bound for the same place – a big mansion of a house in Upper Skelmorlie.

Getting off the transfer bus in Upper Skelmorlie, the children were herded together once again and the Gilvears and about twenty others were led up a long, leafy drive, through the vast, grassy grounds of their new home.

And a mansion is what it seemed like to the children. They stopped as the house came into view, all turrets and towers, balustrades and balconies.

'Is it a palace, like?' they breathed.

'Yon's nivir fur us, is it?' Awe and wonder were written all over their faces.

But there was no mistake; this was where they would live. Several houses like it, scattered in this small area, were to house the scores of other Glasgow evacuees who had spilled off the train.

The houses had been handed over by a Lady Fleming. She was a local dignitary who had made available this exotic accommodation for the use of the children from the streets and tenements of war torn Glasgow.

The children were soon placed in dormitories with a bed each. Every child's meagre possessions were stored beside their beds and they were told how they must keep themselves clean and tidy. Willie was glad his brothers were with him. But he knew no others in their group.

Looking after Willie and the others were two ladies from nearby villages. Theirs was to be no easy task. They had a regime and a timetable to impress upon these unknown children. Discipline was to be enforced. Yet the children soon discovered that these two lovely ladies were no match for them. Away from home, with no parents to check them, the children let their wildness run free.

There was certainly freedom to run off some of their wild

exuberance in the grounds of the great house. Initially, Willie found the wide open space of the lawns disconcerting, compared with the boxed-in streets and closes of home. But soon he and the others were running free amongst the trees of the orchard, climbing and chasing or burrowing into the bushes to make dens and hide-aways. Even the air felt different: no more were there smog-ridden skies overhead obscuring the feeble sun. Here there were no smoke-belching chimneys and factory fumes: it tasted sweet and fresh on their lips.

Another treat which they soon discovered was to be given to the evacuee children was a weekly free cinema ticket. Every Saturday afternoon the huge band of excited children was marched down the few miles into the town of Largs to the Viking Cinema.

There a fare of Western films with frenzied cowboy and Indian chases and red-hot battles was fed weekly to the children. 'Hop Along Cassidy' and 'Bill Boyd' became well-known heroes. And each time they appeared on the screen the pent-up excitement of the children would spill over, uncontrollably. Even as the lights were lowered and the name of the film was emblazoned on the cinema backdrop, greet cheers and shrieks would echo through the auditorium – pandemonium would break out. Boys and girls ran up and down the aisles with excitement. 'Hi-ho, Silver!' they yelled, calling to the figures on the screen. Small gun battles and skirmishes would break out all over the cinema; over seats, down steps, under chairs. The poor ushers had never experienced anything like it. They were accustomed to a more refined clientele. Saturday afternoon duty for them was one to be avoided whenever possible.

Nor did the people of Largs and Wemyss Bay know what had hit them. Both towns were respectable, fashionable holiday resorts, peopled by the well-to-do, the middle classes of South West Scotland.

Suddenly they were invaded by hundreds of wild uncontrollable, Glasgow children, unrestrained 'urchins from the city slums'. The people of Largs would roll their eyes and sigh: if this was doing their bit for the war effort, it was a heavy price to pay!

Yet the beautiful surroundings and the free cinema visits were no compensation to Willie for all that he had left behind. Willie, the happy-go-lucky joker with the infectious grin, had been too badly battered in recent months by all the trauma and loss in the family, to take this upheavel and turmoil of separation in his usual manner.

Ordinarily, Willie would have dived into the play and freedom headfirst. He would have been the ring-leader in all the schemes and pranks. But now he was more subdued. He did not know anyone; he did not know really where he was; the classes at school were large and strange; the house provided no haven of homeliness where he could be himself; he worried about his mother and if she would be the same again after all that had happened; and he wished he could see his Daddy.

Indeed, Willie found increasingly that he felt unsure and nervous. He had been taken out of the world he knew, to a world he did not know and one in which he could never relax. And he was lonely; so very, very lonely.

To increase Willie's woes, a boy in his house, Frank Reid, seemed determined to fight and bully his way through his time there. At school or at the house, Frank was a constant threat. Willie like the rest had to stand their ground against him in turn. Yet the antagonism with which Frank lived unsettled Willie as it never would have done in the streets at home.

9

Visits

Every month Willie's mother came to visit for a day. Bright and early the three boys set off from the big house and down the drive to the Upper Skelmorlie lift. This was a strange contraption in the form of a short, steep railway which ferried a small number of passengers down from the heights to the village below. It was the quickest way to descend and the children soon became accustomed to it. Initially, however, it had been a great novelty.

'Is it like a tram, Miss?' they had asked.

'Why's it makin' that racket, Miss?'

'Whit if it gets stuck, ye know?'

Several were frightened and had refused to go in. But as one of the older ones, Willie had to help lead the way.

Today, on this red letter day in the month, the three Gilvears stepped aboard. Once inside, the doors banged shut behind them and they were shunted down the steep slope in their peculiar electric lift.

Having reached the Skelmorlie bus stop, Willie, Kenneth and Jim stood in a line. They did not talk much, each intent on being the first to see their mother's bus appear round the bend. Each month it was the same; as soon as Mrs Gilvear came down the bus steps the three boys clambered round her, hugging her and holding her as if they would never let her go.

On the first few visits there had been so much to show her: the house, their beds, the school, the funny lift, the sea. And as the boys were never good letter writers, there was plenty always to tell.

But as the months went on, Willie in particular was more interested in what was happening at home.

'Whit's goin' on in the street, Mammy?' he asked, repeatedly. 'An' how aboot Big Watty?' This always made the two younger ones laugh for Mr and Mrs Watson's domestic rows were legendary on the street. 'An' whit aboot Auld Denny? Is she still as crabit?'

Mrs Gilvear always tried to frown on Willie's cheeky remarks, but as she had no fondness for her troublesome neighbours she found it hard not to smile.

But behind Willie's impertinence was the yearning to be home again. His homesickness and loneliness often became too much and he would beg her to take him away.

'Please, Mammy, Ah' canny stick it. Ah jist want tae be home again – like it was before.'

Mrs Gilvear could not tell him how different it all was; how faces were missing from the street; how the Glasgow bombing was intense and so destructive; how terrified she was as she crossed town to work; and how nothing could ever be the same again anyway without their father.

Instead she just hushed him gently: 'Wheesht, William, see how yer settin' the other two aff noo. It'll no' be long noo surely.'

To prevent or at least reduce these outbursts, Mrs Gilvear tried to make their short time together as happy as possible. They walked into Largs together, or sat on the promenade, looking out across to the islands. And she always tried to bring good, happy news of happenings at home: funny tales from work or what their sisters were up to. Occasionally, however, the news could not be bouyant and happy, such as the time she told the three boys that Ellen's young husband, Steven, who was in the Navy, had been killed.

Steven Richardson had been a favourite with the boys as soon as he began coming round to Ballindalloch Drive. He would talk to them and wrestle with them, always interested in their chat and their games. He had even made scarves for the boys at the weaving loom where he worked.

Hearing this news the boys were all upset. In addition, other deaths were too near the surface for them not to be reminded all over again. His death too made the war seem much more real. Somewhere out at sea Steven's boat had been hit. He was dead. It was because of all this bombing that they were here in Upper Skelmorlie. It made some sense – but it did not make it easier to bear.

To help cheer them up, Mrs Gilvear would try sometimes to bring some treat with her. One day Mrs Gilvear's tears of frustration joined those of the boys when she found she had left a special parcel which she had made up for them on the bus. She realised only minutes after the bus had pulled away.

'Aw, naw, yer parcel,' she cried, 'Ah've left it oan the seat. Ah jist put it by me an'...' She could not believe her forgetfulness. And it had contained lots of specially gathered odds and ends as well as precious sweets and a jersey each which she had spent the evenings knitting. Willie and the boys just gulped and tried not to be too disappointed. Their mother was distressed enough, and they just wanted to be with her anyway.

Such was Willie's anxiety and unhappiness during these months that he began inadvertently to do again what he had not done for years. Much to his humiliation and horror, he began to wet the bed. It started suddenly one night when he woke up to find himself lying in cold, wet sheets. He had tossed and turned and the sheets were all tangled round him and clinging to his legs. He did not know what to do. What had happened to him?

The other children left no doubt in his mind. 'Weet-yer-breeks-Willie' they called after him on the way to school and in the playground. Willie was so ashamed. He hid his red, blotchy face under his arm and ran away from them. His whispered pleas of 'Ah canny help it' went unheeded and unheard.

Each night he would will himself not to do it again. But the more he tried, the worse it seemed to become. Morning after morning his pyjamas would be clinging to him and nothing could disguise the damp sheets.

'Aw, look, the kiddy's at it again!' the boys in the dormitory would cry mercilessly. The two ladies in their house did their best but they too scolded and cajoled the embarrassed and tortured Willie. It gave them so much more work, they said. Something would have to be done.

The solution, it seemed was to send Willie away to the Cunningham Home in Irvine, several miles away. There they were 'accustomed to such things' and they would 'sort him out'. So Willie was parcelled off to the Home.

There in Irvine began more torment for Willie. Alone, without his brothers even and the faces he now knew, he was subjected to a strict night-time regime. He was put to bed with a thick undersheet which made him hot and uncomfortable. Then every half-hour, a surly porter would prod Willie awake and push him through to the bathroom. It seemed to Willie as if he was sleep walking. No sooner would he drop off than he would be whisked up and propelled reeling with sleep and tiredness along the cold corridor.

Apart from the humiliation and fatigue it caused him, especially with all the other children knowing just why he was there, the strict programme did not work. The porter did not wake him up at the right times, it seemed; every morning he was wet. Standing before his would-be curers, Willie was rebuked and reviled. Ashamed and alone and bowed down with guilt, he was truly miserable – just the saddest wee fellow you ever met in your life.

As the treatment was not working, discussions were held and it was decided that living with a large crowd of children was not suiting Willie. Instead he should be moved again and sent to live with a family in Largs. Willie's cries to his mother became more urgent: 'Aw, Mammy, tak' me home. Dinna leave me, please, Mammy. Dinny let them move me again.'

Tears flowed down his cheeks and hers but his mother was powerless to grant his wish.

So Willie left Kenneth and Jim behind at the big house and was shunted on again to Largs. The couple who were to care for Willie were pleasant enough but Willie was too unhappy and nervous to settle. His loneliness became worse without the company of the other children and he cried himself to sleep at night, still bed-wetting one way or another.

The final straw came during one of Mrs Gilvear's visits to the boys. She tried to get Willie to tell her about his new home and about the family.

'Well, they're a' right, Ah suppose,' said Willie, miserably. 'An' Ah git tae see Ken and Jim at the weekends.' They tak' us to an awfy funny church, though, Mammy,' he added. 'It's goat statues, an' candles, an' things, and it smells right funny, an' ye huv to bend doon when ye go in.'

'Whit!' cried his mother. 'They're nivir left-footers? Feinians! Well, if that's no' the absolute limit? Ma boys goin' to the chapel. Right, well, we wull see aboot this.' The boys watched with alarm as their mother pulled herself up to her full meagre height before marching them up to the house.

'These boys are Protestants!' she declared to the shocked man on the doorstep. 'An' Ah'll no huv him here anither minute!'

And so, to Willie's delight and bewilderment, the Gilvears boys' banishment from Glasgow and home was abruptly over. There were few murmurings against their departure, especially as Willie's bed-wetting was a continuing, bothersome problem. In addition, the war was moving now even to Ayrshire, with air raid warnings and dashes to the shelters becoming more and more common. So after two, long, unhappy years, Willie, Kenneth and Jim were going home.

10

Return to Dennistoun

Back in Glasgow and back in Ballindalloch Drive much had changed. Even as the boys returned on the train from Largs they could see the damage the war was doing in the city. Buildings were blackened shells without roofs reaching up into the sky; windows were darkened by black sheeting; grey barrage balloons hung elephant-like in the sky.

On their street it had changed too. Most of the children were still evacuated or living with relatives far beyond the city. And many of the men were missing too. There had been those who had volunteered at the beginning of the war but now conscription was in force. Most of the men therefore were either serving out in Europe or had given their lives already on the same battlefields. Only those with good medical reasons or necessary work to do were left behind.

So the Gilvears' was certainly not the only home without a father in it. Yet it was still strange to live in the house and not have their big Daddy there too. As Mrs Gilvear had to work to keep the family in food, the boys were left often to look after themselves. Indeed, with the boys back home, and Ellen and Lily there much of the time, Willie's mother had to take any extra work whenever she could get it. So the boys amused themselves. They made toys and created games as they had always done; carties and catapults and kick the can.

Now Willie was older he felt a little removed from Kenneth and Jim's more childish games. He would walk in on them and find them dressed up in rags playing cowboys and Indians as they had seen in the cinema at Largs.

'Whit' re ye two sissies doin' in thae skirts and tassles?' Willie would joke and his brothers would fly into a rage at being found out in silly games dressed in even sillier clothes.

Willie preferred to visit his old haunts and playgrounds like the football green and the Mollindina Burn – or just wander off restlessly round the streets to see what was going on.

He began also to do more and more for his mother. Willie soon realised that every single penny earned was precious and he concocted various schemes for earning some. First of all he began carrying the strips and boots and balls for the local football team, Dennistoun Waverley, on Saturday afternoons. The carrying and cleaning were no hardship for football-mad Willie, for in addition to the few coppers he earned, he was allowed to watch the game.

But this was not enough. When he saw his mother's willing acceptance of this weekly pittance, Willie began job-hunting in earnest. Soon he was delivering milk in the morning and newspapers at night, and during the day he would be on the look-out for ways to earn more. A well-tried method was to ask for the empty wooden crates from Massey and Galbraith's Fruiters and Grocers and chop them up. Then he would parcel the bits into small bundles with string and sell them round the doors for tuppence or threepence a time.

Through no fault of his own, therefore, Willie was seldom at school. Indeed the only person he knew very well at school was the School Board Attendance Officer. He seemed never to be away from the Gilvears' door, wondering what Willie was up to. He would stand on the door step in his green suit waving Willie's attendance card and usually a severe letter too from the school authorities. If Willie was actually in the house during one of these calls he would hear only a muffled conversation. For Willie would be hiding in the cupboard inside!

For these were hard times and schooling seemed immaterial compared to the day-to-day need to have enough money in the jar to eat and pay the factor. It was always bad when the big, severe man who was their factor came banging on their door. He carried a large register in which every copper was noted down and totted up. It was no use hiding in the cupboard when he came and he would have little sympathy with Mrs Gilvear's hardship. At least once Willie began to contribute his meagre earnings he did not feel so helpless about it all. He did not mind the cheaply manufactured 'parish' clothes so much or having to get a ticket for the hand-out shoes for the poor. He did not even mind the long trek to the Shan Shop for the cut-price bread.

That year as Christmas approached the boys all knew that it would be a day much the same as any other.

'Dinny bother wi' a stocking, you two,' Willie advised his brothers. 'A' ye'll git wull be a hole in it!'

Extras for fancy food and toys were just not available.

It was all the more exciting therefore when a worker from the Tent Hall turned up on their doorstep one day before Christmas. Initially embarrassed because they had not been to the big building since their father's death two years before, the boys were soon dancing and shrieking round the house. For the man had given them three tickets for the Children's Christmas Treat. A Christmas Treat! It was for all the poor children of Glasgow from the Gallowgate to the Gorbals – all for free.

Soon the buzz of excitement was everywhere.

'Huv ye heard?' the word went round, 'if ye go doon tae the Tent Hall, they'll gi'e ye a wee ticket fur the Christmas Do! Ye'll huv tae run like the clappers, though,' came the warning. 'They're gaun' like snaw aff a dyke!'

Certainly with so many children in the area, tickets were scarce. Willie and his brothers hugged their tickets to their chests. Their's were special. Their's had been hand delivered!

So they were first among the happy throng of children on the day of the Christmas Treat. They ran the whole way, hundreds of boys and girls of all ages. They swooped like a great wind down the Gallowgate, through the Saltmarket and into Steel Street

where they arrived red-faced and excited at the door. Willie stood
puffing in the great queue which stretched right round the Tent
Hall, clutching his ticket like grim death!

When the doors opened, Willie piled into the Tent Hall with
all the other children, seven hundred in all. They took their seats,
boys on the left, girls on the right. Then, like the others, he listened
excitedly to all the Christmas carols played by the Springburn
Salvation Army Band.

Willie's broad grin was never off his face. The shiny instruments gleamed under the lights and the noise of the trombones
and the trumpets filled the hall. Willie's feet tapped to the rhythm
thumped out by the big bass drum.

Then he listened as they were told the Christmas Story of the
baby born in a manger who was worshipped by angels, by
shepherds and by the men from the East. Yet the wise men could
have come from the East End of Glasgow for all Willie understood or even heard. He was too engrossed in staring at the
baskets and baskets of TOYS!

They sat on the platform on the tiered choir seats – baskets
of toys for girls and basket of toys for boys, graded as to age.
Willie did not know that so many toys existed. His eyes grew
bigger and wider by the minute – he did not want to blink in case
he missed something!

After the Christmas Story came the Christmas feast. What a
spread! Each child was given a bag of goodies to eat. Ladies in
aprons stood at the end of each row of children with great trolleys
covered with the bags. There were twenty ladies for the girls and
twenty for the boys. And inside each bag was a sausage roll, a
big pie and a great slice of cake. Willie and the others ate till they
felt fit to burst!

Then, just as they thought it would soon be over, the lights
went out. There were 'oohs' and 'aahs' of anticipation. Then, up
on the balcony, out of a little house constructed there, came Santa
Claus. Dressed in his red suit and with a thick, white beard, he

carried a heavy sack over his shoulders.

'Hurray!' shouted Willie with all the others and Santa came down into the hall. What a clamouring and yelling there was! The Tent Hall workers had struggled to contain the joyful children from the start, but now the hundreds of youngsters gave their thrilled excitement voice!

Santa walked right round all the children as well as he could. He was blowing his bugle and shaking his rattle, and calling 'Hello' to the boys and girls. Bright, shining eyes followed the red-caped figure as he walked all the way to the front. Then he went right up to Mr Troup and gave him a big hug!

Standing there he called out to the children: 'Boys and girls, when you go out the door, tonight, I'm going to give you all a present.' Again cheers and shrieks went up from his young listeners.

'And not only that,' he added, 'I'm also going to give you a slice of my Granny's cloutie dumpling!'

So the boys and girls all left the Tent Hall, brimming over with the excitement of their treat, full from the party food, and tightly clutching a toy in one hand and a big slice of dumpling in the other.

They stepped out along Steel Street as if they owned the place. Never had there been a Christmas like it!

It was through the Tent Hall some months later that Willie and the others received one of their biggest surprizes, one which was to prove a lasting, wonderful memory for all of them. It was during the summer holidays and they were all out on the street as usual. Willie was enjoying a welcome break from the attentions of the School Board Officers. Nobody ever went away during the holidays but for the children who had never known any other way, to be free from school was good enough.

But one day a man came up into Dennistoun to speak to the children. George I. Stewart was often seen there as he was the Children's Evangelist who worked in the Tent Hall. He often held meetings and clubs for the children and whenever he appeared, boys and girls gathered round him expectantly.

However, today he had the best news ever. Once a few were gathered Mr Stewart asked the children,

'How would you like to go on holiday?' A score of faces lit up.

'A holiday? Yer kidding, mister!' called a few of the more worldly-wise amongst them. 'We canny e' en afford the tram ride tae Rouken Glen!'

'No, No,' replied Mr Stewart. 'We have a Fresh Air Fortnight Fund to send all you children on holiday.'

'Fresh air, whit's that?' laughed the children, looking up at the heavy, smog-ridden skies. But soon they were dancing on the cobbles and the gutters, and clamouring at the poor man, eager not to miss such a wonderful chance.

Even until the day that George I. Stewart arrived in Dennistoun to pick them all up, Willie could hardly believe it was true. He was not sure if he could trust it all to actually happen. And what did you take 'on holiday'? It wasn't like being evacuated, was it? What did you *do*?

But sure enough, the smiling, white-haired gentleman turned up and took the wildly cheering boys and girls all the way to a big house in Shandon, near Helensburgh.

The great house seemed to groan with the scores of children packed inside its walls. But the weather was lovely and the parkland was theirs to explore and invade. It was like a holiday camp with games to play, fun to be had, and lovely food to eat.

One of the first things they all received after they arrived in the big house in Shandon was a set of lovely new clothes. All the ragged, second-hand and public hand-out shorts and jumpers were taken away. Soon everyone was dressed in the best!

Willie looked down happily at the belt Mr Stewart had handed him. It had a shiny snake buckle and the stretch fabric had a blue and white stripe.

'Here you are, Willie,' he had said. 'I don't suppose you

Rangers supporters would wear anything but blue and white.'

For the next two weeks, Willie and his two brothers who were with him had a wonderful time.

Mr Stewart and his helpers also told them more of what they heard in Sunday School all that time ago – of how God loved each one of them, that Jesus had given up everything for them, that they could be God's children if they would just ask Him.

Willie gazed up at Mr Stewart during those evening talks. It was as if the love of God came pouring out of the man. He did not know each child. But God told him to love each one in Jesus' name – and that is what he was doing.

Willie looked at the pure white hair which covered Mr Stewart's head like a snowy halo.

'He must be God's own angel,' he thought. 'A snaw-white, holy angel come doon frae heaven.' He thought again and changed his mind: 'Naw,' Willie decided happily, 'this must be heaven the noo!'

11

Off to Work

Over the rest of that summer the boys entertained themselves as they had always done. Other friends were trickling back from their war-enforced exile in the country although the war was still not over. But it meant there were more companions in the neighbourhood.

Willie's mother was still working all the hours she could. From early morning to late at night she worked at the bakers. It was a constant struggle to stay out of debt. Nevertheless, they were all together at least, with a home to live in and food to eat.

It was all the more heart-breaking therefore when someone reported Mrs Gilvear to the Prevention of Cruelty to Children Officers, for neglect. The two officers came to the door one day. Willie was alone in the house and when he opened the outside door, the two men barged right in on top of him.

They pushed him aside and stood in the middle of the living room floor staring round at the room. Willie was mystified and shocked. They fired questions at him.

'Where's your mother, boy. When will she be back? Are you here alone? And what age are you? How old are your brothers? Where are they?'

Willie tried to answer their questions but the two men seemed more interested in looking in all the cupboards and behind all the furniture. What were they expecting to find? No corner of the house was missed by the two officers who jotted down notes of all they saw. Willie trailed after them not trusting them out of his sight for he knew this was a terrible thing to happen. Finally, with a warning that action would be taken and reports compiled, the two men left as abruptly as they had arrived.

When his mother came home, Willie told her what had happened.

'Ah couldny keep them oot, Mammy!' he exclaimed, feeling guilty in case he had done something wrong.

For his mother's face was red and upset. Angry tears were in her eyes.

'An' whit dae they expect me tae dae? Neglect!' she exclaimed, her voice rising to a shout. 'Am Ah no knockin' ma pan in workin' day and night jist to provide fur us a', so Ah am?'

She threw herself down on a chair and put her head in her hands. 'Whit can Ah dae? How can we eat if Ah stay here at home?'

The threatened tears began to flow as her tiredness and frustration overcame her. She rocked to and fro quietly in the chair. The boys looked on in dismay. But her silence did not last long as she looked up suddenly with an even angrier and stronger look on her face.

'An' Ah dinna need two guesses to know who reportit me neither – an' she disny live far frae here!'

Willie mouthed the words 'Auld Denny' to his brothers. But their mother seemed better for this final outburst and Willie breathed a sigh of relief. He had seen his mother crushed and defeated by grief before and he could not face watching that again.

Instead Mrs Gilvear was walking purposefully round the room, deep in thought. Then she looked up at her young boys, standing there watching her every move, relying on her to come up with some solution. She smiled: 'Dinny worry, yersels, boys. Whit Ah'll dae is this. Ah'll git a lodger in and he can pay the rent, an' Ah'll stay here and look aifter yous, so Ah will.'

It seemed so simple; the answer to all their problems.

The man who came to live with them as their lodger was an Englishman named Harry Spendley. He was a tall, strong man and he worked at the Parkhead Forge in Glasgow. The boys had never seen him before but they were willing to let him come and go and have as little to do with him as possible. It felt peculiar to have a stranger in their home but they knew they just had to get used to it. And it was good to have their mother at home more too.

But the Gilvear family had been very unfortunate in the man they had taken into their home. It was not long before Harry Spendley began to teach Willie to gamble, sending him up a back close nearby to the 'bookies' to lay his bets for him. Willie became adept at hanging around there, keeping a look out for any police and laying the bets as he had been instructed. Soon Willie was laying his own with the little money he had.

Worse than that, however, was the discovery that Harry Spendley was a heavy and regular drinker. Spirits that had never been in the house for as long as Willie could remember were now there constantly. The weekends were worst when the lodger would get blindingly drunk. They would hear him coming up the garden, shouting and roaring and they would try to get out of sight as quickly as possible. For the lodger was often very violent, throwing furniture and smashing the few dishes they possessed.

The first time he hit their mother, the boys were aghast. Willie threw himself into the fray but he was tossed away like an irritating fly or pest. His mother begged him not to intervene.

That first time it was over in a moment. But never had there been anything like it before in their home. And once the violence had begun, there seemed no way to stop it.

It was at that time, Willie's School Board Attendance Officer finally washed his hands of Willie. Gambling was now added to his other offences. So on a final visit to Ballindalloch Drive the beleaguered man let his feelings be known.

'Look, Gilvear, we've both had enough of this, ' he sighed. 'You're fourteen now. You might as well beat it.'

Overjoyed, Willie soon heard of a job with Beatties Bread Factory in Dennistoun as a spare van boy. He headed down to the factory and after an interview with a Mr McGowan there, he was given the job. He would fill in as a delivery van boy when any of the others were sick. Willie walked home proud as a peacock; he had got his first real job.

It was not long before Willie was put on a regular round instead of just filling in for others and he was allocated to a driver named Jimmy Kerr.

The job began at 6 am so he was up at five o'clock every morning. He had always been an early riser so he did not mind too much. Once he got to the factory and had his card stamped, his first task was to harness the horse which would pull the van. The horses were stabled together, near the factory, each having a small enclosure with the horses' name written above.

Willie hated this job of creeping in beside the big horse and leading it out to the yard. And his was a nervous animal anyway, flinching and snorting when anyone approached.

Once out in the yard, he would hitch the horse to the van and then climb up beside his driver, Jimmy Kerr. Having loaded up with boards of bread and rolls and cakes, Jimmy would flick the reins and they would set off, rolling out of the yard on their great stone wheels to begin their particular round.

Jimmy and Willie's round was from Dennistoun to Kelvin Hall. It was a long trip, out past the Sandyford Henderson Memorial Church of Scotland, with many stops. At each stop, Willie would jump down and using the steps at the back of the big van, he would reach up and pull out the particular board or basket to be delivered. Then he would balance it precariously on his head and carry it in to wherever it was being delivered. It took Willie some time before he could walk without staggering under the full board. And it was not helped when the horse would back up suddenly and knock Willie off his perch on the steps. Then he would tumble down, unceremoniously onto the cobbles, bread board, loaves, cakes and all.

Willie soon got to know some of the other van boys. When they all arrived back from their rounds in the afternoon, they would stable their horses together and tell what had happened that day. Willie had some tale often to make the others laugh.

'Whit a time Ah had o' it, the morn!' he told his friend, Willie Russell, one day. Willie Russell was a small, fair-haired boy who was on the Maryhill run.

'Yon stupit horse!' he cried. 'Ah went in, ye know, an' the minute Ah took aff his harness, he was aff! He went ramming intae them ither wans and legged it oot intae the yard! The stable boy was doin' his nut, shoutin' and bawlin' at me! Ah jist scarpered! Jimmy Kerr was giving me fits a' the way up Paton Street this morning!'

For Jimmy Kerr was a wild man for whom to work. He had red, wavy hair and came from an area of Glasgow named Roystonhill. Willie often felt the sharp edge of his tongue when something went wrong! Jimmy loved to tease Willie whom he called Bill.

So Jimmy and 'Bill' would set off together and before long Jimmy would steer the great stone wheels of the van into the tram rails which criss-crossed the wide streets. Helpless beside him, Willie would be terrified a tram would come flying along towards them.

'Git aff the rails, Jimmy,' he would cry. But it would only make the driver worse. Then if a tram appeared coming straight at them, its driver would ring the bell furiously with his foot. Jimmy would look wilder than ever and stick rigidly to the rails. By the time they were yards apart, Willie would be shouting and screaming at Jimmy, scared out of his wits: 'Are ye tryin tae get us kilt? Get aff, get aff! Yank him oot.'

Just as Willie was sure the tram would smash into them, Jimmy would pull the horse over out off the path of the tram. The tram driver would shake his fist and yell at them. But Jimmy would just laugh – all the more loudly when he looked down at the poor, white face of his quivering van boy.

But it was not a good idea to get on the wrong side of Jimmy Kerr. One day, Willie arrived home to Ballindalloch Drive, tired after his heavy day. Just as he got in, however, he discovered he still had the payment for the last delivery in his pocket. He had forgotten to give the money to Jimmy when he came out of the last shop. It was four pounds – Willie looked down at it in dismay.

'Aw, Mammy,' he cried, 'Ah've still goat that money on me. Ah'll get skinned, the morn.' And he dashed out of the door. Running all the way, he stopped only at Roystonhill when he found Jimmy Kerr and handed the money over which he felt was burning a hole in his hand.

Willie, however, was not so scrupulously honest in all things. Jimmy would often be after him for stealing from the van.

'Ah saw that,' he would bellow, 'pinchin' them swiss rolls. Come back here till Ah sort ye, ye wee moron.'

Yet Jimmy was fair usually with Willie. Friday was pay day but after the Saturday run which was a double load, and which left the boys exhausted, the van drivers would give their boys a 'bung' or a tip. Jimmy would toss Willie a half a crown always which was a good amount – not to be sniffed at.

Jimmy let Willie away early on a Saturday too. For Willie kept up his job with Dennistoun Waverley, carrying the football gear. Jimmy would clear up for Willie therefore after the double run. Willie was often so tired at the end of the day's work, especially Saturday, that Jimmy would let him creep into the back and lie under the canvas for a sleep. He would snooze all the way back, past the Shan Shop where they off-loaded any damaged bread and cakes and round to the factory again.

If he was not rushing off, however, Willie enjoyed the company of the other boys. As home became less and less welcoming because of their surly, violent lodger, Willie would linger with the others. And as he spoke less about his job at home, he stayed chatting there in the factory stable yard. The other boys were the first to hear one day how he and Jimmy Kerr between them had brought Glasgow city centre to a stand-still.

It was during the winter and all the horses were fitted with special, studded horseshoes by the blacksmith to prevent them slipping on the icy cobbles. The winter shoes were some help but accidents still happened.

'It wis this mornin',' Willie explained. 'Jimmy wis drivin' doon St Vincent Street tae the crossroads in Hope Street. Ye know yon big crossin' right in the centre, like?' The other boys nodded, knowing the perils of that junction, one of the busiest in Glasgow.

'Well, Jimmy wis goin' like the clappers, ye know. He wis jist goin' tae go fur it, intae Bothwell Street. Ah was jist hingin' on fur grim death. An' then did the stupit horse no fa' – right over on its hunkers? It was flailin' aboot an' a' these vans and cars were slammin' on their brakes and ringin' and hootin' and gawn aff their heids! So, muggins here,' Willie prodded his chest, warming to his tale, 'muggins here hud tae git doon tae the daft animal. Ah hud tae pit ma knee right on its heid so's Ah cud git the harness aff. Ah wis sure it wis goin' tae take aff, ye know. By the time Ah hud fixed it up again tae the van, Jimmy wis gawn mental – as well as a' thae ithers. Ah thought Ah wis gonny be run right over, Ah really thought Ah wis a goner!'

'Aye, Ah did hear,' piped up Gordon Elliot, another of Willie's pals, 'Ah did hear there was a heap o' folk in Glasgow late fur work this mornin'!'

And so the boys broke up laughing to finish their allotted tasks.

12

'Gil'

The tales and fun that Willie shared with the boys at work were told less and less at home in these days. For a dark cloud had descended on the home again with the arrival of the lodger.

That first, short spurt of violence against Willie's mother had been the harbinger of others, more prolonged and of greater ferocity. On Saturday and Sunday mornings she was often blackened by the blows reigned upon her the night before. What seemed incredible, however, was that the lodger and his mother, Willie knew, were living now as man and wife. How could this be? How could this brute of a man be taking over everything from their father? Why did their mother let it happen?

It was not long before the family had their first trip in a 'black mariah' police van. They were taken off to spend the night at Tobago Street Eastern Police Station. As the boys had lain in their beds, shaking and flinching at the sound of every blow, they had been almost glad to hear the hammering on the door and the voices of the policemen demanding entrance. Even sleeping in the police cells was better than that.

For Willie was completely unable to do anything to prevent these violent outbursts. He and his brothers were sometimes locked into their bedroom to stop them interfering. Yet even if he could get out, Willie was no match for the big, drunken lodger. The alcohol seemed to give Spendley more strength than ever and he upturned and flung furniture around him as if it was feather-light. And each time, his mother was tossed around in the same way, or had crockery thrown at her. And ultimately punches reigned on her too.

Willie would lie in bed listening. Staring ahead intently he spat out the words, 'Ah'll kill him, Ah'll kill him!' over and over. Fists and teeth clenched, he fought against the hot, angry tears which stung his eyes. He must not cry. It was bad enough having Kenneth and Jim crying themselves to sleep beside him without him joining in too.

It was the helplessness which was worst; that old feeling he had known at this father's death and Violet's too, and all through his time in Upper Skelmorlie. He could do nothing. Nothing could change things. He was chained to inactivity and was left to burn inside with anger and resentment and fear.

Willie could feel it eating him up as he lay in bed, night after night listening to all the sounds of pain and rage through the thin walls. He would wake exhausted and be up early for his work and the feeling would burn through him again as he clambered over the devastation and wreckage in the living room. Shame and frustration stopped Willie even looking sometimes at his beloved mother's swollen, battered face.

Willie and the others began to avoid going home more and more, especially at weekends. They wanted to avoid Spendley's dark, surly presence and the bruising punches with which he was so free. In addition, Lily had joined up with the WRENs recently and Ellen had married again, so both sisters were away from home. But it was not enough for Willie to stay out of the house. What he needed was to find some release from this helplessness and pent-up rage. It left him angry and fearful at the power of his own feelings. He needed to find some way to respond to all the violence around and inside him.

It was at this time that Willie began to associate more with some of the wilder boys who worked at Beatties. There were two in particular whom he had avoided in the past – indeed they seemed to keep to themselves and be uncommunicative with the rest. Now, however, Willie was drawn to their hardness and aggression. As he began to speak with them, their violent speech and pugnacious attitude appealed to him more and more.

Although they were very secretive, Willie began to learn that they were both gang members on the East side of Glasgow. They belonged to the 'Stick-It Gang' which had grown up out of a gang called The South Side Stickers, on one side of the Gallowgate. The 'Stick-It' were based on the streets of Glenlyon, Glen Park and Glen Dale and were fiercely protective of their own patch. Indeed, there existed a state of bitter open warfare with the 'Santoi Gang' from the other side of the Gallowgate.

For the first time Willie began to hear real tales of the numerous street gangs which were found all over Glasgow. He had always known of the existence of gangs, he supposed, but never had he known there were so many. It was like another world. His new friends spoke of the Norman Conks from the Gorbals. They were Roman Catholics and were well organised as well as being extremely violent. They faced their arch rivals, the Protestant Billy Boys from Bridgeton, with weapons of all descriptions – hatchets, pickshafts, swords and knives.

The 'Stick-It', Willie learned, were equally violent. Their favourite weapon was a razor, split in two and then inserted into the edge of their compulsory peaked caps. Then, as soon as look at you, they would whip off their caps and slit your throat from ear to ear. Bicycle chains, often sharpened or with metal points between each link were carried also in deep, cavernous pockets inside each gang member's jacket. In addition, an arsenal of home-made and improvised weapons were held up sleeves or in belts.

The battles and fights for which these weapons were used were what interested and excited Willie most. The Stick-It's vendetta with the Santoi Gang was all about retaliation and revenge: one attack prompted another in return; no wrong was left unchallenged; violence brought forth yet more violence and vengeance was exacted.

These were values to which Willie could relate. Unable to respond or retaliate at home, now he had found a way. It was not long before Willie was asking if he too could run with the Stick-It Gang. Once they knew he was a possible recruit, Willie's friends told him more about the Stick-It and the gang environment in which it belonged.

There were various smaller, subsidiary gangs – it seemed, also in the area. Each side had its off-shoots, like the Parlour Boys who stood by the Stick-It. Then there was the Bridgegate Boys who were part of the larger Santoi. Allegiance to the gang and its head was paramount. Loyalty was the most important attribute the boys demanded, along perhaps with the ability to destroy. Was he still interested? Willie nodded excitedly. Of course he was.

There was always a rendezvous point for each gang – a street corner usually in their area. Once a week or more, the gang members would congregate there, the message of the meeting passed down through the ranks. It was to just such a rendezvous that Willie was brought first by his new friends at Beatties.

The boys in the Stick-It Gang were in their late teens mostly, with the small band of leaders being nearer twenty or over. Willie knew they were the ones who took responsibility for planning and organising the fights and raids, sometimes involving the faithful, smaller group, the Parlour Boys, sometimes not.

Standing amongst these boys, all dressed alike in jackets and peaked caps, he felt uncomfortable and young. His two new friends stood beside him sponsoring him to the group. But the others looked on suspiciously. He was clearly on trial to see how he would behave.

He was introduced as 'Gil' to the others: in the atmosphere of fear and criminality, no real names were allowed. No one would be able to inform on another even if they wanted to.

Soon, however, Willie was a regular known face in the Stick-It's gatherings. He bought his own peaked cap, and helped by the boys, forced the split razor right along the edge into the seam. He fitted out his jacket also with its deep inside pocket and soon had the bicycle chain to fit inside. Afraid yet excited, he dreamed how he would reign down on their rivals, swinging his chain into their startled faces.

He did not have to wait too long before his opportunity came. A raid was planned on the Santoi. It was another angry retaliatory attack for a previous ambush – a self-perpetuating cycle of violence and revenge.

That first battle was both thrilling and terrifying for Willie. Waiting in the darkness and silence with the others, his throat felt gripped tight as if in a vice. His heart was pounding so hard he felt if he opened his mouth the whole world would hear it. So, crouched behind a wall, on the edge of the waste ground which was the appointed battlefield, he clenched his teeth hard. He was clutching his bicycle chain in both hands. Most of the others had a broken bottle too, along with their ingenious arsenal of weapons: long metal bars which could be swung over the head with a leather strap; huge steel bolts with nuts at either end making a great, heavy dumbbell; a home-produced mace with sharp metal spikes.

Each was prepared to use these macabre weapons. For no one was going in to this with their eyes shut, least of all Willie. He knew someone might get killed. Many certainly would be hurt. And what was so terrifying was that that was why they were there – to see how many and how much they could maim and harm. Willie knew that he would have to perform. For he was being watched. Although too young to become an official member, this was to be the private initiation of 'Gil'.

In the silence that surrounded them, Willie clearly heard the signal to move. Immediately, two or three of the older boys launched forward into the night. Over the wall they leapt. They charged down on the barely seen Santoi at the far end of the wasteland. Behind them followed the rest with blood-thirsty cries and yells. And Willie was there too. Chain raised and head thumping, he thundered into the fray – it was a release, an outpouring of all the anger inside.

After that first fight, Willie was no longer scared. He had done it. He had not been hurt. But he had more than survived it – he had relished it. The terror, the screams in the darkness, the blood, the speed and frenzy of it all – he could almost taste it in his mouth so real was it all. And he craved more. The next meeting was a delighted pouring over of events: who had done what; who had drawn most blood; which side's casualties were the greater.

For the first time in months, Willie felt strong and capable. And he belonged. Although young and inexperienced, he had taken part and was one of them, one of the tight band who shared each other's guilt. He relied on their allegiance and they relied on his. It all felt very good. And so it began – a two year apprenticeship for Willie to one of the foremost razor gangs in Glasgow's East End.

In subsequent raids the allegiance of the Stick-It members was to be tested by the police. Sometimes police ambushes would descend upon them mid-fight, out of nowhere it seemed. Armed and caught in the act, the only option was to run and both sides would flee into the night. To be caught meant a heavy beating, for the police carried long, riot batons and would lay into them to surrender their weapons.

One of the best-known officers was a Sergeant they named 'Split-Lip' from the Tobago Street station. He was responsible for a number of ambushes and for herding large numbers of gang members over the years into the cells – including Willie. He was a hard, uncompromising officer and the boys learned respect for his harsh ways.

Yet none would let slip a word to 'Split-Lip' or any other officer. Loyalty was everything and the brotherhood which developed within the gang could never be broken. It was not an allegiance borne out of sentimentality but out of fear and hate: fear that to be an informer meant the gang would turn its wrath and bloody vengeance on its traitor; and hate, that which burned within all of them for any who would seek to control and prevent the ugly outpouring of their rage.

13

A New Beginning

Willie's mother worried about her son, terribly. She did not know whom he met when he went out or where he went. But she knew he was involved in the gangs and that was enough to frighten her.

'Whaur ye goin', William?' she would call after him. But the door would bang and he would be gone.

It was hard for Willie to speak to his mother these days. Either Spendley was there, cramping all conversation with his presence, or Willie found himself floundering against the constant, unmentionable questions he wanted to ask: why was the lodger there? The younger ones were terrified of him. Could they not manage now Willie had a proper job? (Willie had always given most of his earnings to his mother.) Why was she putting them through all this? And why was he, Willie, not able to do something about it?

As the final straw, Willie had known for some time that his mother was expecting another child – Spendley's child. The thought disgusted him. He could not even bear to look at her sometimes. Was she not ashamed? Did she not hate herself for this ultimate betrayal of their father, and of them?

But so much was left unsaid now. It was hard to find a way to start to talk again. Now Willie had found new friends and a new life outside home – and that was the way he wanted it. It was the only way he could cope.

It was after Willie had worked with Jimmy Kerr for a year and a half that he was transferred to a motor van in another district. What a relief it was to be away from that horse! He did not miss the wind and rain in his face either. Neither did he miss Jimmy's wildness although he had known a certain kindness too from his fiery driver.

Willie's new district was Blackhill. This was the roughest run on Beatties' deliveries. Here they would not just steal an odd roll or loaf as he had known before – here they would make off with a whole board! Willie had to watch his back at all times.

Although the work was easier and Willie did not have to harness the horse in the morning, still he was often late. After a late night with the Stick-It, it was hard to drag himself out of bed. On other nights he would hang about the street corners delaying going home, so he was often tired in the morning. Coming in from work at two or three o'clock in the afternoon, he would throw himself into a chair and be asleep in moments. But Willie did not care what Mr McGowan did to him – or how his mother remonstrated with him. He just did not care.

There was one morning, however, when almost everyone in Glasgow slept in. No one minded however, for the night before had seen the Victory in Europe celebrations in George Square – VE Day! The war was over! No more sirens; no more invasion threats; no more blackouts; no more bombers darkening the sky like black crows in formation, dropping their deadly sticks of bombs across the city. After so many years, the whole of Glasgow was ready for a party – and that is what it had!

It seemed to Willie that the entire population of Glasgow was packed into the city centre, with George Square itself seething with people. Roof tops, statues, open windows – every vantage point was crawling. For everyone wanted to see the Victory Parade.

Every regiment was passing through the square in full regalia, or as much of it as remained from the battlefields across the Channel. But if the uniforms were worn out, every soldier's face was revitalised, full of delight in being home.

And the watchers cheered as each battleclad section marched past. Drums pounded, bands played, flags waved and the people danced. Crammed as it was, nobody could stop themselves, it seemed, from dancing and singing and even weeping to the brisk military marches being rung out.

The highlight of the Victory Parade was the march-past of

Glasgow's own Highland Light Infantry. The undisguisable skirl of the bagpipes intimated their arrival and the cheer that rose from the crowd was deafening!

'Talk aboot the Hampden Roar' called one. But he was shouted down by the cries of 'We are the people!' from the sidelines. No football match was ever so loudly acclaimed – not even in Glasgow!

For as well as being a mighty welcome for their own boys back from war, this was a celebration of being alive together; of Glaswegians who had stuck together; of a people who were 'hard to beat' – and who had not been beaten.

The party in the city lasted all night. Not restricted to the centre, it seemed that now the curfew was over and the blackout ended, nobody wanted to leave the streets, to turn off the music or extinguish any lights. Indeed, the whole city was beaming like a torch, brighter than after any bombing attack during the worst of the Blitz.

Peace or no peace, however, the lifting of these restrictions meant that it was easier for the gangs to meet together. The local warfare in the streets continued therefore with its usual ferocity, irrespective of the greater cessation of hostilities elsewhere. No victory parades or ceasefires made any difference to the situations in which Willie and the others found themselves. Willie was as keen as ever to stay away from home and taste violence elsewhere.

Willie found that he was able to avoid being at home but he could not avoid his old friends and neighbours all the time. Meeting up with Alex Dennison and Gordon Clarke who were both still at school was very strange. There seemed nothing to say. Their worlds were too far apart.

Yet Willie felt he was seeing Mr and Mrs Clarke much too often for his liking. So hospitable had they been to him before that he was ashamed now of his avoidance of them. But it was always the same with them. They would ask, 'When'll we be seein' ye doon the Tent Hall again, William? It's bin a long time, ye know.'

It always made Willie squirm. Sometimes he would hear the message passed on to him by his mother: 'Ah wis speakin' wi' yon Mrs Clarke today, William. Ye know, she's ayeways askin' fur ye – wantin' tae know when they'll be seein' ye at the Tent Hall. Naw that wid be a guid thing tae do, wid it no'? Better than runnin' about wi' a' thae wild boys, so it wid.'

'Huh, so the holy Joes huv bin nippin yer ear, too, Mammy?' he would reply. 'Well, Ah jist jook up the back an' hide in the close if Ah seez them comin'. It's ayeways the same wi' them – canny leave a bloke alone.'

But it was different when Willie met Mrs Clarke alone one day on the stair. She was so nice, he could not tell her to 'get stuffed' and push past her as he bragged he would. She was soft spoken and gentle and her eyes spoke the kindness of her heart as she asked Willie yet again, 'Whit about it, William? It'd be right fine tae see ye there again.'

Willie shuffled his feet and looked away. Now he was really cornered. How could he get out of it?

'Well, ah, ye see...' he looked up again into Mrs Clarke's smiling face. 'Well, Ah suppose so,' he shrugged. 'Yer lot did gi' me yon Christmas Treat an' that holiday. An' ma Daddy wis ayeways there, ye know,' he admitted grudgingly. 'But,' he added quickly, even although it *was* Mrs Clarke, 'But Ah dinny want ony o' this Holy Joe, converted stuff, ye know. A load o' rubbish, so it is.' Willie stuck his chin out defiantly. He was in the razor gangs. He was no soft touch.

'You come – Saturday night,' said Mrs Clarke gently and without another word she walked off down the stairs. Willie looked after her in wonder – now why had he just promised to do that?

When Saturday night came Willie would have given anything rather than to be stepping inside the huge open doors of the Tent Hall. He had forgotten how big it was and how many people it could hold. For the hall was packed.

Willie had left his arrival till the last minute so he had to squeeze into an end seat not far from the door. He looked round at the high walls and ceilings, the balcony and the great painted texts high up on the walls. Different colours of the rainbow, they were. He remembered how he had sat on Granny Slaven's knee as a little boy, looking up at the huge coloured verses. He would stare uncomprehendingly until his neck became sore and he would settle back into the old woman's shawl. 'Is she still here?' Willie thought fleetingly.

He looked round to see if he could see Jock Troup or Peter McCrostie who had both been in charge when he and his father had been there, but he could not see them. He was not even sure that he wanted them to see him. He felt uncomfortable enough.

Willie's eye then caught the door where his father had always stood. The Tent Hall workers had been positioned at the various doors of the building to welcome those who came. He remembered watching his father's glowing face as he greeted people, his height making him stand out above the others.

Sometimes Jock Troup had called out to these men at the doors round the Hall, 'Give us your favourite verse,' and they had called back one by one. Willie recalled snippets of these verses, and they echoed round and round his head: 'every one that thirsteth...ye must be born again...the wages of sin is death...perfect love casts out fear...peace of God...shall keep your hearts and minds...hidden with Christ...in Him is no darkness at all.'

Willie shook his head to rid himself of these too vivid memories. He was surprised he could remember so much. Funny how he had not thought of all this for so long.

Willie was pulled out of his reverie by movement on the big stage at the front. The first hymn was being called out and the huge choir in their tiered seats was getting to its feet. It was about to begin.

The speaker that night was Mr Seth Sykes. He was a tram

conductor by trade who had a real gift of preaching. He was leading a series of meetings in the Tent Hall. As was the Tent Hall's custom, Seth Sykes was there to reach people with the gospel; to tell them of Jesus Christ the Saviour in direct, straightforward terms.

And this was Seth Sykes' strength. He spoke from the front just as if he were talking to a close friend on the trams. And he spoke in a way that the men and women from the Glasgow streets outside the Tent Hall doors could understand.

Seth Sykes was the author also of several hymns and choruses, many of them well known. Now he led the huge congregation in song from the front. His wife also sang and it seemed to Willie that the theme was always the same: the love of God. Again and again Seth Sykes said it and they sang it too: the love of God, the love of God.

A big screen was set up at the front and as the lights went down, great pictures appeared lit up by a lantern. They told the story of this love of God: how Jesus came into the world to find and save those who knew they had sinned; how He was made to suffer and die for this; how Jesus had died there and then for each one who would believe in Him.

Willie listened and watched intently. The love of God. What did he know about love? He knew all about hate. Yes, he knew plenty about that. But love – the love of God? He felt bewildered.

'He's sayin' it's fur emdy,' he puzzled. 'No' me. It canny be fur the likes o' me ... can it?'

His head felt like it was buzzing. The verses he remembered, the pictures on the screen, the love of God. What was it all about?

As soon as the meeting finished, Willie knew he had to find out more or he would go mad. He had to make sense of it all. As the people stood to leave he walked to where Seth Sykes was speaking to some other men in front of the stage. Taking his chance as he caught the man's eye, Willie spoke up.

Willie's brows were furrowed together and he questioned the

speaker vehemently: 'Ah canny believe it, mister. God's away up there in the clouds, ye know. He's no' interested in *me*. He's no time fur *me*.'

'Oh,' replied the speaker, 'that's whit *you* think. Look at this.' And he opened his Bible and pointed to a verse. 'Let me read this tae ye, son. Whit's yer name?'

Willie told him. Then he listened in amazement as Seth Sykes read the verse to him: 'For God so loved Willie Gilvear, that He gave Willie Gilvear His only begotten Son, that if Willie Gilvear will believe on Him, Willie Gilvear will not perish, but Willie Gilvear will have eternal life.'

Seth Sykes looked up into Willie's thunderstruck face.

'It's fur *you* the Saviour died, son.'

Willie could barely believe what he was hearing. As he and Seth Sykes spoke some more it began to sink into his head. It was amazing. For him, Willie Gilvear? What had he ever done to deserve this love? Nothing. Just the opposite, in fact.

Seth Sykes could see the turmoil that was going on inside Willie. Reaching out and gripping his shoulder, he asked him straight: 'Willie, whit will ye dae wi' Jesus, son? Will ye no' take Him home wi' ye?'

Willie hardly remembered leaving the Hall and striding home. He felt like running his steps were so light. As soon as he got into the house, he went through to the bedroom. His two brothers were in bed but not asleep. Hardly noticing them, Willie knelt down by the bed and began to pray.

'God, Ah'm sorry fur ma sins. Ah've heard tonight that the blood o' Jesus can clean me right out. Will Ye clean me? An' will Ye be ma Saviour an' ma Lord?'

Willie spoke out loud, every word clear and strong, straight from the heart. He looked up when he finished and saw his brothers' bewildered faces and he laughed. It was a happy, carefree laugh such as Kenneth and Jim had not heard from him in a long time. His huge grin looked ready to split his face in two.

They looked back to each other, tapping their heads: 'He's away in the heid. Daft. He'll be a' right the morn.' And they rolled over and left Willie to get into bed and lie there quietly, to bask in this new-found, all changing love of God.

14

Facing Up

Willie's brothers were left to wait and wait for Willie to return to 'normal'. For Willie was changed irreversibly that night. Without a shadow of a doubt, he knew that he had been plucked out of an inner world of darkness and hate and guilt. And there was no way he could go back.

As his father had done before him, Willie knew at once that he must read God's book, the Bible. It seemed natural to find out what God said about everything. So he looked in the house until he found the Bible given to his father all those years before. It was dusty and untouched. He wiped the dust off with the back of his hand and as he began to read, stumbling over the unaccustomed words, he smiled as he remembered his father's shining face as he read from his precious book.

One of the first passages that Willie found in that Bible was a promise which flowed like a river into the dry, parched places of his heart. It made him want to sing out with the wonder of it all. It read: 'I will never leave you or forsake you. I will be with you, to the end of time.' Coming from the loneliness and solitary torment he had known in the last few years, Willie now felt there was Someone close to him on whom he could rely; Someone strong enough and loving enough to take control where he was helpless. It was such a wonderful release. And as Willie tried to explain to everyone around him, 'that's a promise o' a gentleman, who's gonny keep it!'

For Willie could not stop himself from telling those around him of what had happened. His family were first. His mother seemed pleased if only so that it would tame her wild son. His brothers remained sceptical but watched him closely. Spendley chose to use it to torment him: his new nickname of 'Holy Willie' was constantly flung at him.

However, Willie knew that some of the first people to know of his change of heart must be his fellow gang members. He had to face the Stick-It and tell them what had happened. They had to know too that he was never going back. Apart from anything else, Willie knew of some of the jobs that were coming up, raids that were planned. The boys had to know that he was not just running scared and was not going to tell the police all about them.

As the night for the next meeting approached, Willie was very nervous. He had no idea how they would react. If they thought he might be an informer he knew how he would be treated: he would be turned on as if he were the enemy and left to bleed and die. He had seen it happen before now. He had seen also families of past members tormented and hurt. He had to try to explain the truth.

As Willie read more from the big Bible and spoke with others at the Tent Hall, he discovered a verse which he felt had been written just for him. So amazed was he to see it there in the Book of Proverbs that he read it over and over again: 'When a young man's ways are pleasing to the Lord, He makes even his enemies live at peace with him.' This was about him and the Stick-It! It had to be!

On the night of the meeting, Willie stepped out confidently. This was God's Word and he believed it implicitly. To make the Stick-It see sense, after all, was only a minor miracle compared with the new beginning and forgiveness of sin that God had granted him.

It was the hardest thing he had ever done however to stand in the middle of the gang and tell them what had happened. The words which meant so much to him seemed to be bounced back at him, virtually unheard. Suspicion was written on every face. Even hate was there where only days before there had been camaraderie and trust. But Willie understood that hate, borne out of frustration and ill-treatment.

So finally Willie just said, 'Look, boys, Ah'm no' coming back. Ye'll understand, Ah jist canny come back. Every'hin's different now.' He waited for the abuse, the accusations, the blows. But they did not come. Only, 'Ya stupit, daft Holy Joe, ye'll be back in a couple o' weeks!' And that was it! Willie walked away down Glen Dale barely feeling the pavement under his feet – his enemies were at peace with him. It worked! It worked!

After the elation of that experience, to return to work was much easier. Again when he explained the change that had taken place in him there was the teasing and the wariness of those who would watch and see what difference it made. But Willie's happiness was so great that he was not troubled by it all.

For immediately there was a remarkable change in Willie. Gone was the 'do-as-little-as-possible, arrive late, leave early' attitude. Now he wanted to do every job as well as he could. Sometimes he was out almost as late at the Tent Hall as he had been with the gang but he did not have the lethargy and apathy he had known before. Getting up in the mornings was not the problem it had been.

And Willie had become honest overnight it seemed. Mr McGowan, the boss, was amazed: 'Whit in all the world has happened tae Gilvear? Not only is he comin' in on time in the mornin', he's no' stealin' eny more swiss rolls! Something's happened!'

It was not long indeed before Mr McGowan sent for Willie to come to his office. Amid all the shouts from the other boys of, 'Ye've done it noo, Willie!' 'Ye'll be fur gettin' yer books,' he headed off to the office with a heavy heart. Yes he *had* been a rascal. He *had* been given all those warnings. Trust him to get the sack just when he had changed his ways.

But Mr McGowan did not give Willie his books – just the opposite, in fact. So radical was the change in Willie that no one could miss it and Mr McGowan liked what he saw. 'Ah'm makin' you, Gilvear, the prefect,' he announced. 'Ye know whit that means. Ye'll be in charge of all the van boys here in Paton Street in Dennistoun, and round in Weslyn Street. And if ye dae well, ye'll be the prefect in the Gallowgate and Milanda. It's a big job, lad. Let's see if ye can dae it."

15

New Friends

So now Willie was 'the gaffer'. He was in charge of all the van boys at Beatties. He had to see that they turned up on time, that each driver had a boy, that they did their job properly. It was a complete turn around, especially as Willie had been the one to give his own prefect the biggest headaches in time gone by.

Life outside Beatties had changed completely for Willie too. It was not long before Willie was out delivering tracts and inviting people just as he had been invited to the Tent Hall. Knocking on doors in the Gallowgate or the Gorbals or wherever he was sent was terrifying. But those who opened the door often responded to the tall, spiky haired youth who greeted them with his grinning, happy face. Just as he had been as a wee boy, playing in the back closes and stairwells, it was hard to be angry with Willie Gilvear's cheery face for long.

The leader of the youth work in the Tent Hall at that time was a man named Peter Donald. He had a good group of young people, particularly boys, and Willie made many new friends amongst the group. He and Gordon Clarke from his stair were now friendly again and together with others such as Sidney Elliot from Roystonhill, Jimmy Houston and Bert Norris, Willie spent many hours at the Hall that previously had been squandered, prowling the streets with the gang. Together they poured over the Bible, reading it, memorising it, being taught what it meant. And Willie loved it, soaking up the truths he discovered there and finding real satisfaction for the empty craving his heart had known for so long.

Willie only ever managed to take one of the gang boys along to a meeting at the Tent Hall. For most of the Stick-It, curiosity at the change in Willie was tempered by the fear of such a change occurring in them, as well as the fear of ridicule by the others. Yet one gang boy did go with Willie one night.

He sat beside Willie in the big hall as the meeting began. Nervous and edgy, he could hardly sit still. Even the atmosphere of worship in the place seemed to be actively distressing him. By the time the speaker began to give his message, the boy was shaking and sweating. Total fear was written in his darting eyes, his wringing hands, his shifting restlessness. Willie was amazed. Was this what he had been like only weeks before?

It was as if great forces were in action around the young man and he was being torn apart in the middle. He looked deathly white and Willie wondered if he would last out till it all finished. He did but only just and he scarpered as soon as the big doors opened.

Willie never heard from him again. And no others were prepared to go with Willie thereafter. Word had got out clearly that to be near Willie or the Tent Hall was dangerous – more dangerous than risking arrest, not to mention injury and death on the streets with the gangs.

It was while Willie and his friends were together in the Tent Hall that Peter Donald was approached by the people of the Glasgow Medical Mission. This was a place in Oxford Street in the Gorbals where Christian doctors in the city gave of their time to tend and help those who could not get medical treatment otherwise. Those with severe conditions like tuberculosis and cancer were treated as well as those with more minor ailments or injuries. It was a clinic which was open to all.

In addition, however, the workers of the Medical Mission sought to reach out to the people around them in the Gorbals with the Word of God, healing not only their bodies but their souls. It was in this work that Peter Donald was asked to give some people to serve.

Soon Willie and his friends were spending many hours in the Gorbals at the Mission. They led Sunday Schools, took meetings for patients and meetings for those whom they contacted by going round the doors. Some of the poorest families in Glasgow lived around the Mission Hall and Willie and his friends were able to help to extend the practical aid that they had learned to appreciate themselves in the Tent Hall. So between the two meeting places, Willie spent almost all of his free time. Indeed, they were to fill Willie's life for the next two and a half years.

There were other attractions, however, at the Medical Mission for Willie, namely one Jean Gillespie*. Jean was a patient there, a sufferer from tuberculosis. She was under the care of a Dr May Oastler who worked at the Mission. Although Jean had received treatment and was making a good recovery, Dr Oastler still kept an eye on her improvement.

Jean, however, had become one of the workers practically at the Mission. She had responded not only physically but spiritually to the aid offered there and Willie found a fellow-feeling with this girl whose life was 'hidden with Christ's' as his now was. Soon she became his first girlfriend.

While Willie had been in the gangs he had little time for girls. Some of the older ones had taken their 'queens' as they called them along to meetings sometimes, although never on a raid. But primarily the gangs had been only for the men.

Now Willie and Jean worked together and saw each other whenever possible. Neither of them had any spare money so much of their time was spent down at the Mission Hall or walking the streets nearby. Apart from anything else, it was another distraction for Willie from the ever-constant tensions at home.

Although Willie found it easier now to relinquish the rage and anger he had known before, Spendley was still a constant irritant to him. Apart from the drunken violence, the lodger took delight in mocking Willie whenever he saw him. Seeing Willie in the house seemed to bring out the worst in him and Willie thought often that it was easier for everyone, especially his mother, if Spendley saw

* Some names have been changed to maintain confidentiality.

as little of him as possible.

Willie's biggest frustration with the lodger was that he still demanded that Willie do his gambling for him. He had to pass 'the bookies' on the way to the Tent Hall and the lodger took pleasure in getting Willie to do his dirty work for him. Feeling uncomfortable and knowing he was involved in wrong-doing, Willie would creep up the bookies' close and 'pit the usual on the favourite fur the two thirty' just as he had been ordered. He felt he was letting God down, but what could he do?

Willie spoke to his mother about it to see if she could stop the lodger's demands.

'Ah dinny like it, Mammy. Ah feel Ah shouldny be daein' it, ye know. Ah've put a' that behind me. Can ye no' speak tae him?' But Willie knew it was useless. Harry Spendley had a position of tyranny in the house. It was pointless to challenge him for someone always suffered as a result – usually their mother. Willie knew too that young Jim was terrified of the lodger and when any violence took place Jim was unable to bear it. He cowered into himself or fled completely. The terror and unhappiness seemed constant for him.

Willie's mother could do nothing.

'Fur Pete's sake, William,' she railed. 'Jist dae it fur a bit o' peace.' So that was that. Willie could not put his past behind him completely even when he wanted to, and he struggled within himself with the shame he felt for what he was forced to do.

16

Called Up

Although the war was over, young men everywhere were being called to do National Service. One by one, Willie's friends were receiving their notices to enlist telling them what their futures would hold for the next few years. Sidney and Jimmy were off to the Army like nearly all the young men their age. Bert, however, was to be a 'Brill Creme Boy' in the Royal Air Force.

When the official-looking envelope arrived for Willie he carried it through to his mother in the kitchen. He stood beside her at the sink while he opened it.

'It's ma letter frae the King, Mammy. See – the fancy paper an' all. This is it.' He read the short decree carefully before looking up at her in delight. 'It's the Navy, Mammy! See.' He pointed to the words on the page. 'His Majesty the King wants me tae jine him in service in the Royal Navy.'

'Well, is that no' amazin'? she replied. 'A' yer sisters' men wur in the Navy – an' noo here's you. It must've bin thae two weeks in the Sea Cadets that swang it fur ye,' she added, laughingly. 'Ye wur ayeways dead jammy, William Gilvear.'

'Well, it's frae the King, Mammy. Whit can Ah dae but oblige him, ye know?'

Willie and his mother kept up the banter between them, not willing to admit what they both knew. Willie would be leaving behind so much with which his mother would have to cope alone. The leave-taking would be hard, they knew, but no bewailing the situation could change it. Willie had always been like his mother and each knew that this was just their way.

Before he left Glasgow, friends at the Mission put Willie in contact with a man named Robert Steven. He worked for SASRA – the Soldiers' and Airmen's Scripture Readers Association. Robert Steven invited Willie down to his office in Woodlands Road for a chat.

Mr Steven gave Willie good advice that day as well as praying with him and promising to contact other Christians if he could wherever Willie was sent. The advice he gave Willie was this: 'Whatever happens, Willie, pin your colours to the mast for Jesus. From the word go, let them know where you stand.'

Willie left the office inspired to spread the gospel wherever he went: he would give these sailors no chance of missing out on God's goodness and saving grace. He was soon to discover however that even to do what Robert Steven had advised would be a difficult enough task in itself.

The first six weeks of Willie's Navy career were to be spent at HMS Royal Arthur, a naval base at Cosham, near Bath. It was a long journey for a teenager who had never been further from Glasgow than the Ayrshire coast. Willie was nervous and excited as the train sped southwards, leaving all the known landmarks and place names behind.

Having been dealt out their navy gear on the first morning at HMS Royal Arthur, the new recruits were shown round their barracks and Mess Tent. The metal frame beds looked hard and the huge dormitories were laid out in regimental order. Their loud and forceful Gunnery Instructor assured the newcomers that this is the way it would remain.

The tour completed, the next appointment was with Phoebe, the barber. 'Old-timers' passing them who had been there for all of a week or two, rubbed their bristled heads tenderly as they delightedly warned the newcomers, 'Wait till Phoebe gets you! Hold onto your ears!'

Willie and the others filed into Phoebe's domain where they were greeted with the sound of a huge, electric razor. One after another they were pushed unceremoniously into a chair and

'Phoebe' set their brains rattling with the machine. In seconds Willie felt himself scalped and he looked up to find just the tiny blond tuft remaining across his forehead! Even the Green Ladies at home had not been so drastic when they had found the dreaded nits!

'Square bashing' began in earnest at HMS Royal Arthur. Under the fierce eye and cursing tongue of their Gunnery Instructor, Willie and the others in his squad doubled round and round the parade ground square.

'At the double!' their Instructor bawled. 'Hup! Hup! Keep it up! Head up! Back straight! You bunch of nancy boys. Just off civvy street, eh? I'll soon sort you out. Abo... ut turn ... Hup! Hup!'

What amazed Willie too was that their loud-mouthed Gunnery Instructor attended the daily church parade with them in the morning. And there he bawled out the hymns in the same raucous, deafening roar – 'Rock of Ages, cleft for me ...'.

Willie and the others did not know what had hit them. Here they were suddenly in uniform, in the Navy, sweating and puffing as they paraded and trotted through their paces. They had no intention of dying for King and country. What was going on here?

But it was their Instructor's job to get the new recruits into shape and he had them hard at work. When they were not high-stepping round the parade ground they were giving their boots and buckles the essential 'spit and polish'. The boys' arms and shoulders ached. Every boot and button must shine, every speck must be removed, every cap must fold and sit at just the right angle for the daily inspection.

Willie felt as if he had stepped into another world. Only a week before he had been a van prefect for Beatties of Glasgow. All his friends were near him there; he had seen them nearly every night. And Jean. What was she doing? Willie had a big photograph of her which he looked at often and he scored her name in ink on the inside of his belt. It made her and all the others seem a bit closer.

For Willie found that he could hardly even make himself understood. Nobody could untangle his Glasgow speech it seemed, and try as he might, he could barely make out the conglomeration of accents from all over the country that constantly assaulted his ears. His unknown tongue soon became a source of ridicule amongst the others. He was 'Jock' or 'Scottie' from then on.

Then one day, Willie incurred the wrath of the Petty Officer. It was during a fire drill and Willie was positioned at the end of the hose. The orders were flying: 'Lift hose. Point hose. Brace yourself ... and ... water!'

Willie fumbled furiously to turn on the hose. Then, all at once, a great arc of water flew out of the huge nozzle and Willie and the others lost their grip. The hose leapt out of control. And water cascaded wildly all over the watching Petty Officer.

'Gi-lvear!' came the roar and Willie knew he was in trouble. The stifled sniggers and sudden outbreak of coughing behind him made no difference.

Once he had been singled out in this way, Willie was given no respite. His name was known and he was bawled out across the parade ground for any misdemeanour, real or imagined it seemed. Soon he was heartily sick of it.

If it had not been for the foresight and connections of SASRA's Robert Steven, homesickness might have overtaken Willie altogether. But Robert Steven had contacted a young, married Christian couple in Cosham and they opened their home to Willie to come at any time. There was an evangelist there too who toured the country, Harry Matthews. Whenever Willie had time off he could travel with Harry to wherever he was going to meetings.

Through the help of these new friends, Willie was able to try to stand up and be counted as a Christian. But in the Mess Tent it was almost impossible. Even if he tried to read his Bible the questions and taunts began immediately. He could get no peace.

'Hey, what's that you're reading? A Bible? Are you desperate, mate? What're you doing that for?'

On Sunday nights, however, there was a high point to the week. All the men on the base seemed to head into Bath seeking out bars and any form of entertainment. Willie too headed into the town but not to the pubs. He had heard of a meeting which was held in Bath for the boys in the Forces. It was run by a man named Dr John Hunter who opened up a restaurant there on Sunday nights as a free cafe to the men. Once some had gathered, he or others with him would give a gospel message from the front. Dr Hunter sent all the boys he knew to be Christians to the basement where they prayed together for the outreach going on upstairs. It was there in the basement of Firs Restaurant in Bath that Willie met other Christians from HMS Royal Arthur for the first time.

17

'The South Seas'

Towards the end of Willie's first six weeks in the Navy came the time when all the new recruits were to chose which occupation or trade they wanted to pursue. They filed into a large room where various stalls were set up. Above each one were pictures and information. Willie walked round with the others. What could he do? There were pictures of a cook, a stoker, a signaller, a mechanic. Nothing really appealed to him.

Then, just ahead, Willie saw a big picture of an operating theatre. A doctor stood all gowned up over the patient, gloved hands at the ready. Willie's eyes lit up. He thought of the Green Ladies who had cared for him so often when he was little. He remembered the doctor leaning over him after he spiked his head.

'That wid be smashin',' he thought. Yet even as he imagined it, he knew to be a doctor was beyond him. As far as he knew you had to have gone to school for that!

'But if Ah canny be a doctor, Ah'll be the wan tae help the doctor.' So there and then Willie signed up to become a Sick Berth Attendant in the Royal Navy.

Willie's training to become a qualified Sick Berth Attendant (SBA) began immediately and with his square bashing behind him he was sent to Gosport on the south coast, near Portsmouth. He was to work in the Royal Naval Hospital there, in Haslar, and attend the necessary twelve week course.

To begin with, Willie and several of the others on the course were barracked at HMS Hornet, the Motor Torpedo Base. Each morning they marched up in their uniforms to the hospital, blue serge trousers and jackets with their red cross badges blazoned across their sleeve. The uniform was to be worn at all times, even

when he was off duty. Willie soon found it was common to be
accosted in the street for any and every accident or emergency
which cropped up. It was as if people thought he was some
walking medical know-all.

Willie threw himself into the work at Gosport with the relief of
having found something worthwhile and enjoyable to do. At least
the practical work was enjoyable; the studying was more like
Double-Dutch to Willie but he attended the classes faithfully and
tried to take in what he was taught.

One big advantage of being in Gosport was that Willie's sister,
Lily, was serving with the WRENs in Portsmouth, just across the
Solent in the ferry. As soon as Willie was given some time off he
headed over on the ferry to try and find her.

It was strange meeting up with Lily so far from home. Glasgow
seemed like another world when they met, decked out in their
uniforms and telling each other of this story and that from the
barracks and the hospital. They shared what news they had
although they would avoid speaking of home too much. Being so
far away they felt more helpless than ever to help their mother in
the struggles with the lodger. It was best to leave these worries
unvoiced.

But it was wonderful to hear a homely tongue. Willie still felt
like resorting to Deaf and Dumb Sign Language when the lads
could not understand him. With Lily it was lovely to be able to
speak without constantly repeating and explaining every second
word!

So Willie travelled back and forth to Portsmouth often. It
seemed that these crossings were all this sailor was going to see
of the sea. They nick-named HMS Hornet, 'HMS Never Budge'.
It seemed their lives on the ocean wave were to be spent serving
time on the Gosport Ferry!

Whenever he could, Willie attended Sunday Services in
Gosport. He quickly found a home in Middlecroft Gospel Hall
there. Several servicemen of various ranks worshipped there and

Willie again appreciated the contact with a SASRA man.

SASRA's representative in Gosport was a Mr Hitchcock. He had been a missionary in India in years past and now he put all his evangelistic zeal and undoubted energy into the Scripture Readers' work.

Once a week Mr Hitchcock had what he called 'a blackboard meeting' in his house in Gosport. The name intrigued Willie and when he went along he was delighted to find how similar were these blackboard sessions to the training classes for the boys at the Tent Hall. Mr Hitchcock fixed up a small blackboard in the lounge and with the Navy boys gathered around him, he asked for a favourite verse. 'John 3:16' would come the reply, or 'Romans 8:28', or perhaps '1 John 4:10'. The chosen verse was chalked up. This was to be their Golden Verse. Then others were added: a Silver Verse was chosen and a Bronze. Mr Hitchcock then spoke briefly on the Golden Verse. Willie found these stuck in his head from one week to another.

For Willie was desperately needing something to help him remain afloat as a Christian. In the Mess Deck amongst the men, thirty in all, it was harder than ever to stand for what he knew to be right. All the talk was of how the boys had spent each night off, drinking and dating girls. Pornographic magazines and posters were everywhere. He was mocked and derided continually for not joining in. He could not even find peace to open his Bible; praying in that antagonistic and unwholesome atmosphere often seemed out of the question.

Although Willie's home life had been anything but sheltered, in the Tent Hall he had been sheltered spiritually. Cocooned there with Christian friends and leaders whom he trusted and respected, he had felt removed from the hardships which awaited him outside its huge, wooden doors. Now Willie was thrust suddenly into this world outside, amongst the roughest characters and strongest temptations, without the chance to hide away and be revived spiritually whenever he so desired. For this reason Mr Hitchcock's house became like an oasis in an otherwise dry and unpleasant desert.

There were other Christians at the hospital in Haslar, however, and Willie met some of them through Mr Hitchcock and the Gospel Hall. One was an Irishman, Chief Petty Officer Norman Knox. He at least seemed to understand Willie's accent a little better than most so they were able to speak more easily together.

One Sunday at the Gospel Hall Willie actually overheard a Scottish voice. He dashed over and soon was deep in conversation with a Peter Munn from Greenock. Although he hardly knew what they talked about, they agreed it was 'jist smashin" to hear a voice from home.

But the Christians whom Mr Hitchcock contacted came from all walks of life and it was through one of the SASRA man's campaigns that Willie met up with Sergeant Douglas Patterson. Douglas, for all his Scottish-sounding name, was thoroughly English; a Cambridge graduate serving in the Education Corps. There could hardly be anyone less like Willie.

But Mr Hitchcock paired them up as he explained his latest plan: it was enough to put the fear of death into Willie. They were to go in groups of two on the bus to the Hillsea Army Barracks nearby and invite the soldiers there to a gospel meeting on their camp.

Willie was terrified: 'If the lads in wi' me on the Mess Deck are no' bad enough, whit will thae roughneck Army boys dae tae me?' he thought. 'We'll be kicked oot before wuv a foot across the door! Specially with Mr Swankey-voice wi' his pan-loaf accent here wi' me! Help, Lord!'

But Willie and his well-spoken companion soon found they had more common ground than they thought, partly through their faith and partly through a shared sense of humour. Willie was soon convinced that for all his plummy accent, Douglas was really a Scotsman: each time they travelled to the Barracks on the bus, Douglas never had any change for the tickets. He would produce a solitary £5 note and shake his head apologetically at Willie. Willie would laugh: 'Yer a Scot right enough, man. Ah'm goan tae check yer fiver next week an' see if that's the same wan yiv goat then!'

So the visits to the Barracks did not seem so bad. Venturing into the Nissen huts was very daunting but perhaps Willie's time going from door to door in the Gorbals for the Glasgow Medical Mission served to prepare him for this. Now, as then, people responded to his direct and friendly approach. And it was encouraging to see some of the young soldiers listening and joining them to hear Mr Hitchcock in one of the other huts as he told the story of the gospel to those gathered.

Meeting other Christians where he worked was such a rarity for Willie that he was surprised and thrilled to discover that his Ward Master Lieutenant, Douglas Barnard was a Christian man. Barnard had worked his way up through the ranks of Sick Berth Attendants to become the head of the hospital in Haslar, and both he and his faith were respected by all.

Willie had an early experience of this when one of the 'top brass', the Naval surgeon, Rear Admiral Hunt came to conduct a hospital inspection. Willie and the other trainee SBAs had been warned of what would happen if the Rear Admiral, wearing his white gloves, found the slightest grain of dust on any surface. They would be 'for the jankers' without a doubt.

It was a tribute to their Ward Master Lieutenant's standing amongst one and all that when the Rear Admiral left a ward with his gloves unmarked he turned to Barnard with the words, 'I suppose one of *your* men is in there?'

For the Ward Master Lieutenant took time to encourage his fellow Christians in the ranks and he knew them all. He urged them to rise early in the morning to pray together before beginning the day's duties at their various wards. And he always encouraged Willie in particular to be the best in all he did. Perhaps sensing Willie's struggles both in his studies and in standing up for his faith, he saw also Willie's devoted heart and longing to serve his Lord.

So Barnard went out of his way to assist him if he could. He even took Willie in his car to a Christian conference nearby. Willie was given the front seat while Mrs Barnard sat behind. He was thrust the road map and asked to navigate. Willie felt very privileged and was anxious to please, not to mention being a little over-awed. For how was his Ward Master Lieutenant to know that this was the first time that he had ever sat in a motor car in his life?

18

Second Chance

After three months at the Naval Hospital in Haslar, the time came for the SBA examinations to be sat. All the boys were dreading it, not least Willie. He felt he was coping with the practical side of the work on the wards, although from time to time he seemed to be driving his immediate superior, Leading SBA, John Hammond, up the wall. Big John was patient and soft-spoken but even he was driven to raise his voice at Willie's unconventional bed-making and bathing.

But Willie had no idea what to expect from the examination on the material from lectures. There was so much to learn. Even reading the text books took all his time. He did not know where to start when it came to learning and memorising names of bones and systems and medical procedures.

His worst fears were realised during the exam. Each paper was a torture for Willie. Even trying to understand the questions seemed impossible; answering them was a shot in the dark. The final straw came in the oral examination when he was ushered into a large room where a surgeon stood with an array of bones before him. He handed Willie a big bone from the table. 'What's that?' he was asked.

Willie knew that he was in trouble. He thought quickly: A tibia? Whaur wis that wan again? Fibula – naw, fibia, or wis it a scapula, scipia – ah, help, Ah hivny a clue! 'Eh ... A ... rib, sir?' It was a wild guess and from the doctor's startled face he knew he had blown it.

When the results came through, to Willie's great shame he had failed every examination. Each mark was worse than the last. But apart from his own feelings being dented, Willie felt he had let

down his Lord. Here he was trying to stand up and be known to
belong to Jesus Christ, to be doing his best for Him. Complete
failure did not tie in with Willie's idea of shining out as a follower
of Christ.

He sought out Douglas Barnard in his disappointment and
distress.

'Whit can Ah do? Ah jist dinny know whaur tae start. A' thae
questions an' funny words an' names.'

Poor Willie. His lack of schooling which had come about
through no fault of his own was plainly evident now. If he had been
asked what a noun or a verb was he would have thought they were
something for eating! How could he start suddenly writing essays
and learning medical phraseology.

But Barnard spoke calmly to him, encouraging him to hold on
and see if he could try again. Anything was possible with God,
he reminded Willie and he told him to lay his hurt pride and shame
at his Saviour's door.

Willie went away with a lot to think about. Perhaps God was
trying to tell him something. He knew he still had to face the Navy
board; he might even be booted out. What could he do?

Willie did the only thing he knew to do. He prayed to God and
poured out his heart.

'Lord,' he cried, 'Ah dinny even know whit they lecturers are
sayin', nivir mind studyin' it. Ah need wisdom, Lord and
understandin'. You said tae ask an' it wid be given if Ah asked
in faith. Lord, Ah'm askin'. Help!'

Willie discovered there and then a wonderful thing: when he
had been saved, it was as if he had opened up an account in the
Bank of Heaven, an account with an unexhaustible credit. If only
he asked, believing in the Giver, he would be heard and an answer
given according to God's great mercy.

When he was called before his superiors, Willie felt nervous
and unsure, but he was not afraid. He knew what would be said
probably but he knew too that his God was in control.

The onslaught began immediately. Willie's examination papers were on the desk.

'What is all this drivel, Gilvear? How in all the world did you get in here in the first place? I can see no way to bring you up to standard, Gilvear. I'm afraid you're out!'

'Oh, no, sir, dinny do that, sir. Dinny put me out!' he begged. 'Y'see, Ah've nivir hud much in the way of schoolin', ye know, sir. It wis jist the way it wis, like, sir.' And Willie proceeded to explain some of his background to the officers and all about himself.

As he spoke he caught their interest. 'This boy has something' they seemed to be thinking.

'But if ye jist gi'e me wan more chance, sir. Ah'm sure it'll be different this time. Jist wan more chance, sir.' Willie's good intentions of trying to 'talk proper' to his superiors had disappeared in his earnest, eager requests.

There was a brief silence. Glances were exchanged behind the desk. Then the verdict was given.

'Well, Gilvear. All you've told us is very enlightening. If you have come this far, perhaps there is hope for you. All right. You have one more chance. You will remain here and do the course all over again. But if you don't get it second time around – you're out. All right. Dismissed!'

Willie left the office with a light step and a huge grin. God had heard! God was in charge here. He had been given his second chance.

So Willie stayed in Gosport while all his colleagues who had passed left for their appointed postings. It was not pleasant being left behind but Willie was not worried. At least it meant he could still attend Middlecroft Gospel Hall, and see Lily from time to time too. And he meant, in God's strength, to study for all he was worth.

19

A Sincere Heart

Thus began an arduous few months for Willie. The work on the wards was as strenuous as ever although he was learning not to infuriate Big John too much these days. Lectures were more familiar, thankfully, but Willie still sweated and struggled over his text books and notes till he felt his eyes and brain glazing over. There was just so much for his untutored mind to learn.

In addition, if Willie had hoped that life on the Mess Deck with a new set of lads would be easier, he quickly found that this was not so. If anything, he was given a harder time. Writing home, particularly to Jean, he explained a little of the struggle to maintain his stand before God. It was 'pure murder', he wrote, in this battle for his mind. Constantly he was being tempted to turn away from all he knew to be right and enter instead into the pleasures his fellow sailors enjoyed and which were being thrust all too regularly before him. This spiritual struggle gave him little respite or rest.

After one particularly bad day when he was taunted by the boys, he was unable to sleep. He felt overwhelmed by the atmosphere in the place and weak in his attempts to resist it. So early in the morning Willie took himself off and went for a walk down to the sea wall at Gosport.

The sea pounded against the breakwater in steady, relentless waves. Somehow the noise and the crashing of the sea before him made it easier to think and to pray. As he paced back and forth, Willie opened his heart to his God.

'Lord, You know whit it's like fur me in there,' he prayed. 'Forgive ma mind that keeps wanderin' ontae whit thae boys are ayeways gaun on aboot. Yiv told me that "whatsoever is pure,

think on these things". But it's so hard, Lord. Help me! Show me
how tae dae it!'

As he stood still for a moment there on the sea wall, words
came to Willie which he had learned previously. The years of
instruction under Peter Donald and the other leaders in the Tent
Hall had taught him to know his Bible well. Now verses of
encouragement came into his head with great clarity: 'Let us draw
near to God with a sincere heart in full assurance of faith, having
our hearts sprinkled to cleanse us from a guilty conscience and
having our bodies washed with pure water. Let us hold unswervingly to the hope we profess, for He who promised is faithful.'

Willie mulled over these words in his mind. The sea swirled
before him in all its ferocity and wrath, but now Willie was calm
and in deep thought. He knew that on that night beside his bed
in Ballindalloch Drive, Jesus had cleansed his heart. And ever
since then, Willie had prayed that God would take away the sin
which seemed to entangle him from day to day.

He praised God now for reminding him of His faithfulness and
nearness. That was what he needed to hear. His conscience was
a battlefield of temptations and reminders of the past. He felt
bruised and worn down by the constant warfare. Yet he knew he
sincerely sought freedom from it all. He knew he desired more
than anything to cling on, to 'hold unswervingly' to his new life
and hope in Jesus Christ. In those moments on the sea wall he felt
he had drawn nearer to God than he had been able to for many
months.

The more Willie thought of it all, he longed to find some way
of acknowledging God's continuing protection of him – some
outward expression of the cleansing and renewal which were
going on inside. As he stood there, unnoticing of the November
wind and the cold spray of the sea, Willie became convinced that
he should show his love for God and obedience to Him in being
baptised.

Mr Hitchcock was delighted to hear of Willie's decision and

he set about arranging with Middlecroft Gospel Hall when his baptism could take place. Willie wrote to his friends at the Tent Hall, telling them of the forthcoming event, knowing they would be pleased to know of how God was dealing with him while he was so far away.

It was more difficult to try to explain to his own family. Even if he had been able to speak to them in person he could not know that they would understand how important this step was to him. How he longed that they could be there to see him stand up for Jesus Christ and acknowledge Him as Lord before the big congregation!

Willie was overjoyed, therefore, when on the night of his baptism, Mr Hitchcock managed to bring his sister, Lily, over from Portsmouth to the service. She had never come to church with him before. Now Willie prayed that in his actions, she might see something of the power of love which had drawn Willie irresistibly to his Saviour. The words spoken and the hymns sung that night touched Willie deeply. Mr Hitchcock spoke from Colossians chapter three: 'Set your minds on things above, not on earthly things. For you died and your life is now hidden with Christ in God.'

'Hidden with Christ': Willie thrilled to these familiar words which, in his troubles of recent months, came as a huge comfort. He was not alone. He could never be alone again. However inferior he was made to feel, when it came to examinations or when confronted with the evidences of social class and status which were all around him in the Navy, still he knew he was chosen by Christ, loved by Christ and hidden with Christ where no snare could lay hold upon him.

Willie stepped confidently into the water of the baptismal tank to make his confession of Christ. As he came up and was led out, his grin stretched from ear to ear, filling his shining face. Two young sailors stood at the edge with towels and they clapped them round his shoulders in encouragement and love. And the congregation sang the hymn, 'Blessed be the tie that binds our hearts in Christian love...'

Willie need not have felt so far away from home. He had an additional new family here on hand in Gosport.

20

Moving On

Willie's delight some months later when he actually passed his SBA examinations second time around was tempered slightly by the fact that immediately he was given his posting. Having found such a home from home at the Gospel Hall in Gosport, he was reluctant to leave. And having Lily so close had meant a lot to Willie too.

He appealed to his Ward Master Lieutenant but it was no use. Barnard merely pointed to Willie's rank and number, CMX875508. The 'C' stood for Chatham in Kent where he was to be sent. Finally and very reluctantly, with many farewells, Willie packed his kit bag, rolled up his sleeping bag and hammock and boarded the train for Chatham.

Kent, he discovered, was a beautiful place. Green fields and softly rolling hills were Willie's first view from the train windows. It hardly seemed the landscape for a sailor somehow.

The scenery, however, was largely immaterial to Willie as he was immediately rostered onto night duty at Chatham Naval Hospital. He was to work on the officer's tuberculosis ward which was a new experience for Willie. He recalled the queues of grey-faced Glasgow men, women and children at the Medical Mission in the Gorbals, all waiting to receive the busy doctor's attention.

But he knew too of cures from this dreadful illness. Had not his own Jean been a success story of the Mission doctors there? It made the nursing of the sick men a bit easier, somehow, to think of it.

Some respite was given too from the perpetual Mess Deck badgering. As Willie was working night shifts, he slept during the day so he was removed from the men. In addition, the Roman

Catholic chaplain at Chatham became friendly with Willie and he put the chapel at his disposal any time as a place where he could come and read his Bible and pray. Often as Willie sat there with his Bible before him and the candles and statues at his back, he wondered how the staunchly sectarian Glaswegians would have viewed him now. 'An' there's me, the biggest blue-nose o' the lot of o' them wance!' he grinned.

But Willie did not remain in Chatham long. He received another posting, this time to the Royal Naval Air Station, HMS Fulmer, at Lossiemouth.

It was when the postings came through that Willie often felt the loneliest. Just as he began to settle in and get to know a few of his colleagues it seemed he was moved on without any warning. It was all part of service life but a part which Willie never enjoyed.

One of the least enjoyable parts of being moved about was 'going through barracks'. This was the administrative checking that was always necessary whenever a serviceman moved from one base to another. Willie hated it. Carting his kit bag and other gear with him, he stood in queues of waiting seamen for hour after hour before being shunted from one desk to another.

After a morning of it, Willie retreated thankfully to the canteen for lunch. As he looked around for a seat, tray in hand, he heard a Scottish voice rising up from a table nearby. A Scotsman! Willie always went by the rule that, if you heard a Scotsman, you grabbed him, there and then! So Willie squeezed in at the table and struck up conversation with the seaman. Even when Willie, a Glaswegian, found that the boy was from Edinburgh, he was not deterred!

'Where are you headed?' the sailor asked.

'Lossiemouth,' replied Willie. 'At least it's in Scotland, Ah suppose.'

'You're kidding? I've just come from there,' his new friend returned.

Before long the two were deep in conversation, and Willie was delighted to discover this Scotsman was a Christian.

'I've got a home all ready for you, boy,' the sailor declared. 'Just go to Mr and Mrs Stewart in the Baptist Church in Lossiemouth and tell them I sent you.' He gave Willie their address. 'They'll take good care of you,' he promised.

Willie was delighted. Now at least he had some Christian contact to whom he could turn when he arrived in this unknown place.

In Lossiemouth, Willie was sent to work in the Station Sick Bay. It was a small hospital with ten beds for overnight patients. With him in the Sick Bay were three other SBAs. One was a Jewish boy from Giffnock and the other two were training to be doctors, SBAs Munro and Pim. Both were Scottish which was a relief for Willie. Since being in the Navy Willie had been forced to change his speech and lose some of his colourful Glasgow dialect. But it was a struggle to try to 'talk proper' constantly. At least with these Scotsmen he felt he had a better chance of being understood than he had been down south.

Part of their duties involved being on call for any emergencies either on base or at sea, as two SBAs were needed always in attendance with the ambulance men. The ambulance driver would receive the alarm and the first two out of the door went with him. They would race to the ambulance and then the plane if it was needed. Munro and Pim were small, wiry boys who could sprint fast. Willie would complain that he was 'always bin left holdin' the jaikits'!

But Willie's gangly height came into its own at football when the Navy discovered that he was an excellent goalkeeper. The years of kicking a can or ball round the gutters in the Gallowgate with stones or jumpers for goalposts paid off as Willie was soon selected to play in goal for HMS Fulmer against the RAF Lossiemouth team.

'It's always a real needle-match,' Willie was warned. 'We have to show these Brill Creme Boys a thing or two.' The rivalry between the two services was intense at this local derby. At each game Willie felt as if he was in an 'Old Firm' match at home in Glasgow, so much seemed to rest on every fixture.

Being a small group working together constantly, Willie soon became very friendly with his fellow SBAs. During breaks or on night duty there was plenty of time to get to know each other. They would while away the hours after the work was finished playing darts or some other game. Sometimes at nights the SBAs were required to provide cover with the ambulancemen. If pilots were landing from other countries they had to sit in the ambulance at the end of the long tarmac runway until the last plane was in, whenever that would be. It was a long, usually uneventful night only filled by talk and any other attempts to keep each other awake.

It was not long before his colleagues – SBAs, ambulancemen and the officers who were doctors – learned of Willie's faith and the effect it had on his life. He spoke unreservedly about it. And there was a lot that was different about Willie too for them to see: his free time was spent differently from theirs; he chose to seek out church services and made many friends amongst the Christians in Lossiemouth, including the Stewarts; Willie's attitude to work was different; all he did was for a purpose, it seemed, and that was not to please himself or any watching officer. He made neither show nor pretence about reading his Bible but they all knew it was the most important thing to him. Above all he was always scrupulously honest and straight – you always knew where you stood with Willie. So although he was teased by the others, he also received the unspoken respect of those around him.

The impact of Willie's faith was felt by them all on one occasion when the Navy's Mass Radiography Unit (MRU) Team came to HMS Fulmer to x-ray all 3500 men on the base. It was part of the SBAs' job to look after the visiting MRU Team and to assist them in any way they could.

One evening the medical and dental officers were entertaining the MRU Team in their Mess by the Sick Bay. Willie was on night duty in the ward and he could hear the sound of the party through the walls.

Unknown to Willie, however, one of the MRU Team was a practising spiritual medium and it was not long before it was suggested that they hold a seance in the Mess. Lights were lowered, they were positioned in a large circle and quiet was demanded. Then the medium began.

Meanwhile Willie was next door in the kitchen having finished his duties for the time being. As he wandered about making himself something to drink, he decided to take coffee through to the Officers' Mess which had gone very quiet. So, mugs and hot brew before him, Willie barged into the Mess with a cry of 'Coffee up, sir!' and proceeded to pass round the drinks.

It was not until the next morning that Willie became aware of the impact he had made. The officers kept coming up to him with wide grins and slapping him on the back. 'Good work, Gilvear!' they laughed. Willie was mystified. 'You've really done it this time, Gilvear!' they warned jokingly. Increasingly concerned, Willie demanded of them, 'Whit did Ah do, sir?'

It was one of the Dental Officers who explained about the seance and how Willie had ruined the whole thing.

'You're timing was uncanny,' he was told. 'Just before you came in that medium chap was about to make contact with the other side! As soon as you came in he couldn't do another thing. He couldn't do flip-all. You bust the whole thing up! We nearly wet ourselves. Best bit of the whole night. It was a riot! Good man, Gilvear! Any time you need a favour, you let me know,' and he went off, laughing again at the confusion caused the night before.

And the officer was as good as his word. Shortly afterwards he arranged for Willie to receive an unexpected flight home to Glasgow on one of the troop carriers flying down to the airport near Rosyth. Willie was not sure what he had done to receive such treatment. But he was glad that God had intervened through him even in this peculiar and very public way.

21

Home From Home

As usual, however, life on the Mess Deck was a battle for Willie. He tried to 'pin his colours to the mast' but he was given no peace. His Bible would be snatched from him or some seaman's boot would sail over his head as he tried to pray. It did not help that he could find no other Christians around him. It was easy to feel isolated and lonely as he had done before.

Nevertheless, when the opportunity came, Willie did not shrink from making life more difficult for himself for the sake of telling others about the gospel. It began one night when some sailors came in from a night of heavy drinking and began to fight in the Mess Deck. Chairs and blankets and kit went flying. But the most important 'casualty' was the Mess Deck radio which fell to the floor and smashed.

The radio was the sailors' lifeline and daily contact with the world outside their service regime. It played continually whenever the Mess Deck was occupied. It was not long before the hat went round so a replacement could be bought.

When they reached him for his donation, Willie decided to speak up. 'It's a' right fur you guys wi' yer top twenty, a' day long. Ah'm only gonnie put ma money in if Ah can huv ma programme.'

'Sure, Jock,' came the reply. 'When's your programme then?'

Willie was ready for them: 'Wednesday night, eleven o'clock, 208 Radio Luxembourg.' Only too keen to take his money, Willie's condition was accepted. 'Right Jock, you're on.' Gleefully, if a little fearfully, Willie looked forward to Wednesday night.

By eleven o'clock, Willie knew the sailors would all be in their

bunks so they would have to listen to his programme whether they
wanted to or not. So on that Wednesday and every other until he
left Lossiemouth, Willie went up and turned the radio to Radio
Luxembourg before lying back with all the others to listen. It was
'The Old Fashioned Revival Hour', broadcast from Long Beach,
California, a programme of hymns and Christian testimony. After
the singing, the speaker, Charles E Fuller, would preach the
gospel across the airwaves to those thirty sailors in their Mess
Deck on Scotland's Moray Coast.

'Ah'm away tae ma scratcher an' the Lord's daein' a' the
work!' thought Willie, grinning to himself.

After some months at Lossiemouth, the opportunity came for
one of the four SBAs to be seconded to a camp further north in
Alness for two weeks. The Admiral of the Fleet's battleship was
docked presently along the Cromarty Firth in Invergordon. The
Admiral chose to visit the sailors on land by plane and the nearest
airstrip was in Alness. Therefore an SBA had to be on hand in case
of emergencies.

Excitement was high in the Sick Bay when news of the possible
trip came out. 'It's like a holiday camp,' they heard. 'There's no
officers and the Purser's going with enough food to feed the
Western Front. And you'll have no patients. Yes, sir, this is what
I joined the Navy for!'

Willie and the other SBAs were all desperate for the trip. They
all volunteered so quickly their names had to be put in the hat and
picked at random. Willie could not believe it when his name came
out. He gave a shout and danced round the kitchen.

Laughing at his antics, the others could not be too disappointed. All Duncan Munro said was, 'We always knew you were
jammy, Gilvear. Ever since you won that bag of butteries at the
darts with your first – and last –bullseye. I've always said you
were jammy!'

Willie's popularity both amongst his colleagues and on the
base at large was undeniable and nobody begrudged him his treat.

So Willie was sent north for his two week holiday! It was fine to get away from the base for a while. The monotony of service life in peace time was a complaint of many of the men. Now Willie revelled in the freedom he was allowed. And the food was good too. Who would have thought that rationing was still being enforced?

Those two weeks, however, brought their own problems. With all the free time, the servicemen were enjoying their unexpected break also and were travelling into nearby Invergordon at every opportunity, filling the pubs and bars until closing time. Once again Willie was under pressure – to conform, to be one of the boys, to join in. Out of his usual environment, and away from his friends and his church, Willie felt more tempted to give in than perhaps ever before, even for the company and camaraderie of it all. It was harder and harder to resist.

Escaping as soon as he was off duty, Willie avoided the others leaving and set off for a walk in the opposite direction. 'Ah'll walk off these awfy feelings, mibbe, onywy,' he thought, setting off briskly.

It was early evening and the sky was still light. The road stretched ahead of him with open fields on either side. There was little traffic to break the stillness all around. But Willie would barely have noticed it anyway as his mind was elsewhere. For as he walked, he prayed. As so often before, he had no one else to turn to. He could only look up and as then his prayer was a simple plea: 'Help, Lord!' he cried, to the God who knew his situation, his struggle and weakness.

Before he knew it, Willie had walked a few miles and found himself entering a small village. 'Evanton' a sign read. Willie had not heard of it before. But the first building he noticed there was a church. Drawn as to a magnet, Willie walked up to the noticeboard. 'Free Church of Scotland', it declared.

'Nivir heard o' them,' he thought. But written there was the name and address of the minister.

'Mibbe this is the answer, Lord,' he queried and set off at once to find this minister's home. In a small village this was an easy task and soon he was knocking on this stranger's door.

'Mr MacDonald?' he asked nervously as a black-suited gentleman stood before him.

'Yes,' came the reply with a warm and welcoming smile.

Soon Willie was ensconced in the manse lounge, sharing his story and recent troubles with the minister. Quickly a rapport and friendship grew between them, Willie enjoying John MacDonald's understanding and his wise and prayerful support, and the minister was impressed by this tall, grinning serviceman with his deep appreciation of the gospel and his obvious love for the Lord. On this common ground the two chatted eagerly together.

When Mr MacDonald's three sons came home shortly, they too warmed to Willie with his quick sense of fun and willingness to chat with them. Although they were just of primary school age, Willie loved the refreshing directness and energy of Fergus, Alpin and Evan and he never spurned the opportunities of the next few days to explore with them, tramping through the forest nearby or hiking up the hills.

For Willie was quickly invited to return and spend all his free time at the MacDonalds' home. Willie accepted eagerly, especially as the next few days were to be filled with church services. Willie could hardly believe there were so many, for it was the preparatory week before communion in Mr MacDonald's church. From the Wednesday to the Monday there were meetings almost twice every day.

Willie managed to attend many of these services and he felt it was as if they were laid on solely for him. The solemn Bible teaching he received and the practical love of the Christians were just what he needed and seemed to water the dry and arid places of his heart. Combined with the kindness of the MacDonald family, it made those days in Alness more than a holiday from normal work for Willie. He had found a place of refreshing and a home where the Christian conversation and joyful family life gave encouragement and rest to his soul amidst his usual solitary stand for his Saviour on the base. He was to return many times to this haven in subsequent years.

Back in Lossiemouth, Willie was grateful for his short break as he discovered that his precious home leave had been summarily cancelled. As Munro and Pim were studying to be doctors, priority was given to their training and getting it completed. Willie, it appeared, had to take second place. He was frustrated and annoyed, all the more so because there was nothing he could do about it.

'It's no' fair!' he said to himself. 'Jist 'cause they're the wans wi' the brains!'

If he had not had the unexpected flight home previously and his recent days up in Alness, he would have felt very low. For it was not just on his own behalf. He knew how much his mother leant on him whenever he was at home. As it was he sent her nearly every penny of his Naval wages but it was not the same as being there, even periodically.

Willie, however, was soon to be given an enforced 'holiday' of a sort. During his time in Alness, Willie had eaten his fill of the best food the Navy could provide. The Purser had provided royally indeed for the few personnel there and Willie had enjoyed every morsel of it. With civilian rationing and then army canteen food having been his stable diet for as many years as he could remember, he 'got tore right into' all there was on offer, as he told his green-eyed colleagues on his return.

They had little sympathy therefore when Willie began to complain of stomach pains. 'Over-eating', 'gluttony' and 'turning your nose up at anything from a tin now', were all accusations jokingly thrust upon him by his friends.

But one night the pain became particularly bad. Willie had been with his friends, the Stewarts, in Lossiemouth for his meal. Willie was a frequent guest there, enjoying the family's warm hospitality and genuine Christian care. And as normal, the food was delicious, especially Mrs Stewart's fish soup. But Willie could not eat more than a few mouthfuls. Such uncharacteristic restraint was remarked upon, but Willie was suspicious of what this grumbling pain might be.

Back at the base that night, Willie was soon convinced he knew what was wrong. Rushing to the Sick Bay in great pain he found Munro was on duty: 'It's MacBurnie's Point! See man, it's text book stuff. Gi'e me a prod jist here, like' and Willie gesticulated to his stomach. 'Ahh! No' that hard. It's pure murder, like – but Ah'm right enough, am Ah no?'

Munro nodded slowly. 'Yes, Willie,' came the reply. 'There's no doubt. You're certainly tender over MacBurnie's Point' (an area of the abdomen). 'With the other symptoms you describe, I'd say there was no doubt. Appendicitis it is.'

22

Tables Turned

After the doctor had confirmed it, Willie was whisked by ambulance that night to the hospital in Inverness. So advanced was his condition that he was operated on there and then. Willie was in such agony by the time he arrived that he was only grateful that something was being done to take away this gnawing, blinding pain.

When he came round from the anaesthetic, however, another pain replaced the appendicitis. He gazed in ghastly wonder at the huge gash across his abdomen. As it had been an emergency, the incision had been larger than usual and Willie counted twelve big surgical clips and two stitches under the dressing. He looked away quickly as the nausea rose in his throat. It was one thing to apply dressings and treatment to wounds as part of his job; it was another to have this great hole made in his own body!

Willie soon cheered up when the visitors arrived. Two girls from the Lossiemouth Church turned up and Willie was delighted to see them.

'Two beautiful Highland princesses tae see me,' he teased them. 'Here, bring the doctor,' he called out to a passing nurse. 'He should be takin' ma pulse now!'

And Willie was soon feeling well enough to join in all the activities and banter of the ward. He was on a ward exclusively for servicemen in the hospital and some of the seamen knew each other from the Lossiemouth base. Those who did not were soon introduced as well as the few soldiers on the ward. Like Willie, several were recovering from operations and it seemed that the fitter they were the more they gave the nurses to do. After the all-male environment of the base or camp, the boys could not resist calling on the nurses for any and every excuse. Most knew how to deal with the men's cheekiness and bare-faced flattery, but great delight was taken by the men if they could raise a blush on a nurse's face.

But the fun was not all at the nurses' expense: other patients received the same treatment from the recuperating men. In particular, when a young RAF boy was admitted for a routine operation, the others on the ward determined to 'get him'. The rivalry amongst the services was always great, and the Brill Creme Boys of the RAF were often the butt of the others' jokes. Even in these circumstances, the chance to put one over the RAF was not to be missed.

Listening intently, the boys overheard a nurse explaining to the new patient behind his curtain that she would give him something which would cause him to go to the toilet, a necessary procedure before his operation. The men looked at each other sympathetically. They all knew the overwhelming and unstoppable 'need to go' brought on so suddenly by this treatment. They had all known the undignified rush along the corridor at a moments notice!

Then an Army Sergeant put the word round that he had an idea: 'We'll make it an obstacle course! The minute the nurses are out, pull all the beds and tables and chairs into the middle of the floor. Let's see how good he is at the high jump, eh!'

With muffled sniggers and stifled laughs, the fitter ones carried out the plan. And they finished not a moment too soon. With a sudden sweep of the curtain, the RAF boy leaped into view from his bed. Immediately he saw the middle of the ward cluttered with furniture his face filled with horror and he set off at a run. He dodged past chairs, clambering and stumbling over beds and round tables. The shouts from the beds on either sides were like those of punters at the races: 'Go on, boy! Gee up! Knees over the hurdles! Show him a bit of the stick!'

The whole ward was in an uproar. Great gales of laughter, shouts and bellows of mirth filled the room. Willie felt he would split himself with laughter. 'Stop!' he cried weakly, as his bed shook and tears rolled down his cheeks. Between fits and bursts of laughing, he begged unheard for mercy. 'Help, Ah'm gonny bust open! Ma stitches.' Still the RAF boy scrambled frantically up the ward. Willie held his wound and dived beneath the blankets. 'Ah canny take ony more o' this!' he hiccupped, giggling helplessly. Thankfully, under the covers Willie missed the inevitable, embarrassing outcome for the RAF boy as he finally reached the corridor – too late. It saved Willie probably a return to theatre to be re-stitched!

Having had his leave cancelled previously, Willie was grateful to receive some time at home in Glasgow while he recovered from his operation. It was never restful to be at home but at least he was there. And now no longer a mere raw teenager, he offered more protection for his mother from Spendley.

It was good also to see his old friends in the Tent Hall and the Mission. How Willie had missed knowing first-hand their support and encouragement. He begged for their continued prayers at the early morning prayer meetings. He knew this was often all that had helped him maintain his stand for Christ on the base.

For the entire period of his posting in Lossiemouth, Willie never found another Christian on the huge base. In other parts of the service the United Naval Christian Fellowship was strong with many men attending its various meetings. Yet at Lossiemouth, Willie relied entirely on the Baptist Church and Brethren Assembly in the town for Christian teaching and local support. Ironically, after he left and a new influx of men arrived, HMS Fulmer became the most lively base in the service for Christian activity and fellowship.

For Willie was on the move again. He dreaded another posting but this time he was to be sent back to Chatham in Kent. Having made many friends in the church and assembly in the town, Willie was sad to leave Lossiemouth. He would miss too his occasional visits up to Evanton to the MacDonald's home.

Lossiemouth too had given Willie his first experience as a qualified SBA and he had enjoyed the job. Although treated still as a minion and always feeling inferior in the Navy ranks and comparing himself with the greater intelligence of Munro and Pim, still he felt he knew his job and was good at it. Perhaps too the men on the Mess Deck would not miss their continuing weekly Bible bashing from Radio Luxembourg, but Willie would miss those to whom he had grown close for all the struggle Mess Deck life had been.

And there was another reason for not relishing a return to Chatham. For the Navy was sending Willie there to sit yet more exams.

23

Chatham

It was with a heavy heart that Willie passed through barracks once more and headed south for Kent. Yet how could he complain? The Navy had arranged and were paying for him to sit his State Preliminary Nursing Exams, the examinations which would enable him to work once he left the Navy after his National Service. Willie knew it was what he needed to do to continue the work he had learned to love.

The examination was in two parts, practical and written, and Willie was sent to two different hospitals nearby. In Maidstone for his practical, it was strange to be in a civilian hospital, outwith the service regime. But Willie felt he acquitted himself quite well. In the hospital in nearby Rochester for his written exam, however, it was different altogether. Willie sat in a great hall at a desk with all the other examinees. Nearly all the others were female nurses, sitting their final examinations after their hospital training. Feeling out of place and inferior to these trained nurses, Willie struggled over his question paper. So much of it was alien to him and beyond his experience. What he did know he found so hard to express. It came as no surprise when his results came through and he had passed without difficulty in the practical examination but had failed miserably in the written.

Once again Willie's superiors sent for him and he had to ask for another chance. 'Here he is again,' they jeered. 'Another chance, Gilvear?' Yet once again they relented and Willie was permitted to take the examinations all over again a few months later. The fight was beginning again. If Willie had hoped it would be easy, he was wrong. He must be strong and patient it seemed. If nothing else, he was being taught to persevere.

During those months in Chatham, Willie worshipped nearby in Gillingham. He quickly made friends and relished the fellowship of other believers there. And it was in that assembly through a miraculous incident that Willie was made aware once more of God's mercy to him and particularly to his family.

It was at that time that Willie's younger brother, Kenneth, was called up to do his National Service. Unlike Willie who had never left the mainland, Kenneth was being sent by troop ship to the war zone in Korea. On the Sunday morning after Kenneth had left, Willie was worshipping in the assembly in Gillingham when a man rose from the congregation asking if he might share with them all what had occurred the previous night.

'I was asleep in bed,' the man explained, 'when I heard a great cry. It woke me up, yet there was no one there. But I could still hear it and I knew that it came from the sea. I didn't know what was happening. Yet someone was in distress, I was sure, out there somewhere on a boat. So I got up and knelt by my bed and prayed for that boat – prayed for God's mercy that no lives would be lost.'

The man went on to explain that he had turned on his radio that morning to find out what had happened. A troop ship, it transpired, bound for South Korea had gone on fire. All the men had been forced to abandon ship. Willie listened with rising concern; surely this was Kenneth's vessel? Yes, the name was the same. What about his brother?

It was with tremendous relief that Willie heard the man's next words: '... but not one man was lost.'

'Including Kenneth!' breathed Willie and he bowed his head in heartful thanks to his sovereign Lord whose hand was so graciously and clearly upon the family of the Gilvears.

During those months in Chatham, Willie needed this encouragement and the prayers of those there in Gillingham as well as at home in Glasgow. For the studying was hard. There was no easy or quick solution. Willie had to read and reread his textbooks. He had to pore over the diagrams and learn to commit great volumes of work to memory.

The work on the wards was taxing too. Long hours on duty were not helpful when he knew he had to open up his books again at the end of a shift. And Willie felt different too from the other men whose lifestyles were so far removed from his own.

The others in his ward learned to be grateful for this, however, perhaps most markedly at Christmas. During the Officers' Inspections on the ward Willie had to bundle his colleagues unceremoniously into a cupboard and lock the door as they were all in various stages of drunkenness, having been imbibing secretly all day. Willie was left as the only sober nurse on the ward!

He may be indispensable on the wards, but after eight months back in Chatham, Willie still had to retake his examinations. During his two years in the Navy, Willie had learned much more than just his nursing skills. The years had been characterised by long periods of loneliness and isolation, even in the most crowded conditions. Failure too had followed Willie at every step. Time and again he had been humbled by being bottom of the class, left behind as his colleagues progressed, forced to beg to try again. His relief was immense, therefore, when, with demobilization only weeks away, he passed his State exams.

'Hallelujah!' he cried. 'Now wur talkin'! Ah've goat ma exams, Ah'm leavin' these Mess Decks fur good, an' Ah'm goin home.' Life had never seemed so good.

24

Civvy Street

Riding home on the train to Glasgow, Willie could hardly contain his excitement. At last he was out of uniform. This was no holiday. He had been demobbed. No longer was he going to be posted around the country, no more Mess Decks, no more Navy food, no more brief visits home, and best of all no more exams. It was as if normal life was about to start again.

Willie's mother too was overjoyed to see him. Hugging her big son as tightly as the little woman could, she cried with relief and happiness: 'Yer home, son! Oh, William, its right guid tae see ye!' Over and over again she repeated it.

Friends at the Tent Hall too were thrilled to see him again. Although many faces had changed, the love Willie remembered, and the nearness to God he experienced as soon as he entered, were just the same. Oh, it was good to be home.

In those first days at home, however, it became evident that the situation in the house had worsened. Spendley, of course, was still there and making his presence felt. It was something Willie had inured himself to. But it seemed now that Jim, Willie's youngest brother, was suffering as a result.

Jim had always been a quiet, timid boy. Spendley had terrified him always: whenever the big man's voice would rise and temper worsen, Jim would run out of the house, yelling and holding his head. He would hide away till it was all over. Now, however, the years of violence – the fear and trauma – had affected him so badly that he could barely communicate. He stayed at home all day. He seemed unable to look for work. Willie could see his mother's worry and distress.

As soon as he could, Willie went to register for nursing work.

At least once he had a job he would be giving something to the family. It may ease some of his mother's worries at least.

But a terrible shock awaited Willie at the College of Nursing. Confidently he handed over his nursing qualifications, not least the hard-won State Preliminary Nursing Certificate. But what was this – they were summarily pushed back at him.

'Whit's wrang?' asked Willie. 'See they're mine a' right – and recent too!' But still there was stony-faced response.

Willie now faced a new disaster which was to crush his hopes and ruin his plans. Because his qualifications related to English and Welsh Councils they were no use in Scotland, it seemed. All his certificates and all his Navy nursing counted as nothing – they were worthless!

Willie was horrified. No one had told him this. What could he do?

'Ah'll nivir git a joab!' he cried.

Crushingly disappointed, Willie felt angry also. What was the point of the hard work of his Navy years? Was all that mind-bending studying a waste of time? And all those exams! It just did not seem fair that it was all for nothing.

For some time Willie felt too down to think of what to do next. He was confused and not a little sorry for himself. All his home-coming seemed ruined. He was back to the bottom of the pile again. All his struggling, all the reproach and the disappointments had resulted in nothing.

Yet throughout his life what distinguished Willie was his ability to discover happiness in whatever situation. Naturally optimistic, his smile and good humour were hard to remove. On countless occasions it seemed, events had almost overcome him, dampening his spirits and quelling his sunny nature. Yet his grin soon came back – it was irrespressibly there. This was unaccountable to some. But Willie took no credit for his ability to bounce back; 'it is Christ who strengthens me' he quoted and this was his firm belief. Before long therefore, he determined to apply to study nursing, from the beginning again. For he was immensely practical and refreshingly down to earth: 'Well, onywy,' he mused, 'whit else am Ah gonny do, ye know?'

And so Willie, once more, asked if he could start again. It would involve three long years on a student nurse's pay, starting from the very bottom again.

The first hurdle was to pass an entrance exam. More exams! As Willie sat in the hall at Oakbank Glasgow Western District Hospital looking at the paper in front of him, he became very nervous. 'Write a composition of your own choice,' it read. 'A composition! They'll find me oot!' he thought – 'Ma grammar an' that.' But he began to write his essay. He chose as his theme the words of the hymn, 'Something lives in every hue, Christless eyes have never seen'. He wrote of the wonders of creation and what he knew of his Creator's love for what He had made. Willie's pen fairly flew across the page as he warmed to his task, not worrying about his spelling or syntax – just enthusiastic for his subject.

After the examination, Willie was called to see Mrs Martin, the Nursing Officer. She looked at the paper, full of mistakes, scrawled in Willie's large, shaky handwriting. How could she take this uneducated boy? And yet as she interviewed Willie and he spoke of what he had written, and of nursing and all it meant to him, it was as if she saw something in him – something beyond the rough speech and unschooled hand. Willie's grin came bursting out as she closed the interview: 'Yes,' she said, 'I'll take you in. Come back next week and you can start.'

The next three years were the hardest Willie had known. The Navy had presented its own problems but this seemed much worse. Allocated to night shift, Willie worked from 8 pm to 8 am with lectures both before and after his shift. He was working seventeen hours out of twenty four. And then he was supposed to study! Quickly he became exhausted. He lost weight and seemed to be doing nothing but nursing, nursing, nursing, day after day, night after night.

And there was something else to face up to now that Willie was home. Jean! The initial euphoria at being back in Glasgow and amongst his friends had soon worn off now that he was working so hard. He had to face facts. It was all getting too close to the wedding ring stage for his comfort. He did not know how but he would have to finish it. And so he tried to explain.

'Ah think wull huv tae finish, ye know, Jean. Ah mean, it's no gaun onywhere. An' wi' me back as a student again, well, Ah'm gettin' peanuts, Jean ... It's jist nae on ... Ah'm sorry, ye know ... really sorry.' But no reasoning or excuses made any difference and Willie left finally, hearing her crying as he walked down the street.

25

Oakbank

The Glasgow Western District Hospital, where Willie was sent as a Student Nurse, known as Oakbank, was situated on Garscube Road. 'Gaspipe Road' as it was nicknamed was a desperately needy area near Possilpark, a huge housing estate. 'Wur nursin' a' the weans fae the Possil',' moaned the nurses and the hospital was put to good use certainly with every type of ailment. Casualties from various domestic fracas often ended up in the wards too, most regularly from the Tower Ballroom. This unusual dance hall was a tall building up by the Round Toll on Garscube Road itself. So wild was it that if there was trouble, the bouncers would tip the undesirables out of the top windows of the Tower rather than the door, so they ended up in Oakbank – if they were lucky!

But because of its unsavoury neighbourhood, nursing at Oakbank was rarely dull. Sometimes the visitors were more trouble than the patients. On one occasion when Willie was on a male medical ward the son of a very sick patient came to see his father. Unfortunately the visitor was extremely drunk as well as being extremely large, and he was shouting and staggering around the ward.

Willie called for the porter to remove the man but was dismayed to see Charlie, the smallest porter in Oakbank appear.

'Whit's a' this,' piped up Charlie, the size of tuppence next to the huge, swaying visitor. The porter made a grab for the man's shoulder. As Charlie could only reach the other's elbow, it was not very effective and before Charlie could do any more, he was picked right up off the floor. The drunken son carried Charlie to the lift, dumped him inside and pressed the button! The porter was gone and Willie had to learn quickly to deal with problems on his own!

But it was the staff more than the patients that gave Willie and the others their fun. Life on night duty would have been long and dreary without some relief and one of Willie's fellow students often provided it. Fancying himself as a bit of an artist, this male nurse disappeared one night during his meal break. He was off to paint the Round Toll on Garscube Road, he said. The police found him much later, paints in hand, sitting in the dark on the road. As Willie fetched him from the police station, the painter agreed with Willie that perhaps he was not cut out for nursing after all.

There were few male nurses, however, at that time and Willie was always outnumbered by the female nurses. On one occasion a young female student replaced Willie at night when he was on a male surgical ward. Unknown to Willie, she had never been on a male ward before and Willie went off unsuspecting for his meal.

He arrived back to find chaos in the ward. Several men were shouting out and jumping about on the beds like hens on a hot girdle. 'Nurse, whaur's that lassie gaun? We sent her fur a slipper an' she's no comin' back.'

Willie quickly found the 'slippers', the men's slang for their urine bottles and distributed them to the grateful patients. He then went off in search of his relief nurse. Where had she gone? Finally Willie found her in the linen cupboard, snowed under by scores of slippers which she was painstakingly sorting out into pairs – and these for men that were not even allowed out of bed!

But the student nurses were all in awe of the Sisters who wielded great power and whose word was to be obeyed by one and all. Each ward was ruled to varying degrees by a rod of iron and everything from the wheels on the beds to the corners of the sheets had to be regimentally straight and correct. Nurses might think this would be relaxed in the busy Outpatients Department where Willie spent some months, but he soon found this to be untrue, to his cost.

Once a week the Outpatients Department was taken over for Ante-Natal Clinics. Midwives swarmed everywhere and the Outpatients Department had to be moved for the afternoon to the small gatehouse at the entrance to the hospital. It was a weekly ordeal which Sister demanded was carried out with precision and much preparation – or there was trouble. Therefore before the clinic, Willie and the others would make up dressings, cut up gauze and put it all in a clean pillowcase. Along with various other equipment and paraphernalia, this was carried up to the gatehouse.

One wet afternoon, however, Willie discovered to his horror that he had forgotten the pillowcase of dressings. Everything else was in readiness but no pillowcase! What could he do? As a male nurse, Willie was not allowed into the Ante-Natal clinic. Yet if he valued his life he needed the dressings! It was a simple decision and grabbing a raincoat, Willie ran down through the rain to the department. He slipped in and grabbed the pillowcase, tucking it under his raincoat to keep it dry. But he had been spotted and noting his enormous 'bump', the midwives began pulling Willie in to get weighted like an expectant mum!

'Ah wis shoutin', "Help",' he recounted to the others back at the gatehouse when he finally escaped, 'but they wur withoot mercy: weighed, measured, the works! Ach, ma face wis red, white an' blue, so it wis!'

All too often, however, Willie's face was pale and drawn with tiredness and the effort to study. Trying to open his books at home was impossible. Kenneth was back from National Service and working on the steam trains as a fireman. Like Willie, he worked shifts so the bedroom was never free. Even when he could sleep, Willie often had to share the bed with his two brothers just as they had done as little boys.

After eighteen months of the lack of sleep, the hard work and the pressure to keep up with the lectures and written work, Willie decided enough was enough.

'Ah've hud it, Mam,' he explained. 'Ah'm knockin' ma pan in fur nothin here! Mibbe it wisny fur me onywy. Ah'm off tae jine the Polis!'

'The Polis!' she exclaimed. 'Yer jokin', William. You!?', thinking of his previous run-ins with the police as a gang boy. 'They'll chase ye fur yer life!'

'It canny be that bad, surely?' grinned her son.

'Well, ye can but try,' she agreed, grudgingly, but without much hope.

Willie's own hopes were raised, however, when he attended his interview. It was with Chief Constable Robertson, a Christian man who approved of Willie's faith and commitment.

'Oh, a Tent Hall boy,' he enthused and it was quite relaxed thereafter. Willie left the interview encouraged that at least he was being given a chance; someone seemed keen on him.

Next was the medical examination with the Police Doctor, Dr Imrie. Even in the Navy, Willie had never been so thoroughly checked, tested, poked and prodded. Dr Imrie went through Willie like a dose of salts! But he seemed pleased with the results.

'No problem here, son. Only the exam to go then,' he added as Willie left.

But that was where Willie's problems began. The entrance examination was held in a little office in Oxford Street and almost at once Willie knew he would never make the grade. Once more his lack of schooling let him down as he struggled through the paper. It was no surprise when the letter arrived to tell him he had failed.

Disappointed, Willie tried to console himself: 'Ach, well, imagine that – nearly a polis. It's as weel Ah nivir waited fur them tae look up ma record, eh Mammy? They'd huv said, "Whaur huv ye bin, Gilvear? Wuv bin lookin' fur ye fur years!" an' clapped me up there an' then.'

It was all part of learning practically what God said in the Bible: 'Lean not on your own understanding' ('Well, Ah've tried that

an' it disny work!' he thought) 'but in all your ways acknowledge
Him and He will make your paths straight.' The 'straight path'
seemed to head right back to Oakbank and so Willie had to
knuckle down to work again. There was no easy way out. The
work on the wards was tiring and always eventful, the lectures
were complex and needed all his concentration, the obstacles to
studying remained formidable, and every day the final exams
came closer and closer.

A nurse's 'finals' are the most important day in his or her life.
This is only equalled by the arrival of the results and Willie, like
all the others, sat at home waiting. Each day he could hardly bear
to check the mail, sweating and shaking as he searched for the one
letter he wanted. For he knew what to look for: if he received a
small envelope he would have passed. He did not even have to
look inside, for if he failed he would receive a large envelope with
a form inside with which to re-apply.

Finally the day arrived and Willie ran to meet the 'postie'
before he had even reached the door. Fearfully, he grabbed the
letters. But immediately he knew: there was the big brown
envelope addressed to *Mr W. Gilvear* from the Royal College of
Nursing. Inside was the truth in black and white. He had passed
in his practical exam but failed in his written.

As Willie slumped onto a chair in the kitchen, a deep darkness
seemed to descend upon him. He felt so ashamed. How could
he face everyone? He had really let the side down. Tears filled his
eyes as he saw all his high hopes being stripped away from him.
After all the effort, all the struggle – three, long, dreary years of
it – Willie felt cheated and completely dejected.

And in his mind he could hear a voice speaking: 'Yer a stupit
ass, Gilvear! Ye forget yer jist a dirty, rotten gang man – Who d'ye
think ye are, Gilvear!'

It was all too easy to agree and Willie felt lower than ever. Of
all his previous failed exams and tests, this was the worst. This
was the most sought-after, this had taken the hardest work and

the longest time. But now all that was gone. What was he worth anyway? He felt like waving the white flag and giving up.

Yet even as he sat there with hot tears soaking his face he knew he was forgetting something. Even at his lowest, he knew that Jesus, his Saviour was with him. He must cling on to that.

'Get behind me, Satan,' he declared out loud, knowing clearly it had been the devil who had whispered those evil words to him at his lowest point. Now other words came to him from God's Word, assuring him not of failure but victory. 'The one who is in you is greater than the one who is in the world,' he remembered. There and then, Willie determined not to surrender. He would not lie down. He was receiving strength from outside himself. Nothing was too hard for the Lord. How then could he give in?

26

Robroyston

Having begged for another chance to sit his exams, Willie was given six months for more study before the November resits. Matron had relented to his appeals for a second chance.

'All right,' she had agreed, 'when the exam comes up again, Gilvear, you can go back and resit the whole thing all over again.'

He felt like yelling, 'Whit d' ye think Ah am? A glutton fur punishment, or whit?' But he kept his face straight and answered meekly, 'Thank you very much, Matron,' and walked out.

Willie knew this was his last chance. He had to give one final push or it would all be over. He enlisted all his Tent Hall and Mission friends to pray for him and they did so faithfully, week by week. Willie could not change his home environment or start to grow brains. But he could appeal to the Lord of the whole universe to take over when it all seemed impossible.

Some weeks before the exams, Willie received even more encouragement from Dr May Oastler with whom he had worked at the Glasgow Medical Mission as a teenager. She understood his struggle at home to find a chance to study, so she booked him into the YMCA until the exams were over.

'Now you'll get some peace, Willie,' she said, in her polite way. 'You get your head down and pass those exams.'

Willie was quite overcome that someone should do this for him. He felt he must pass to show his gratitude if nothing else. He even dosed himself with build-me-up tonics to keep up his strength as the day approached.

The exam came and went like any other. But this time the results were quite different. Willie had passed! He clutched the little envelope in a vice-like grip as if it might float away from him if he let go. And he leapt and danced round the kitchen. Whooping with delight, he dashed out to tell as many of his friends as he could find.

'Registered General Nurse – Scotland, that's me', he thought. 'Willie Gilvear, RGN.' He repeated it over and over again, hardly believing it was really true. 'Thank you, Jesus. Thank you, Jesus,' he beamed. Willie's big boyish grin could not be shifted now. Just as it had as a little boy, his smile seemed to take over his whole face. It was not hard for all who knew him to join in and share his happiness.

The celebrations over, Willie began work at Robroyston Sanatorium in Glasgow where the tuberculosis sufferers of the city were housed and treated. To everyone's amazement he also began another course – for a British Tuberculosis Association Certificate.

'Huv ye no' hud enough studyin' fur a whiley, like?' his friends begged. But this was different. Both with the Glasgow Medical Mission and in the Navy, Willie had nursed TB patients and seen the devastating, often fatal consequences of the disease. Now at Robroyston Willie discovered that these patients, without hope and in great distress, sometimes hardly able to breathe even, were being given a lifeline. By way of surgery and antibiotics many walked out of the sanatorium completely cured. It was the most satisfying nursing he had ever done.

During his training and at Robroyston, Willie received much fellowship and support from the Nurses Christian Fellowship. Working shifts wreaked havoc with attending church services. Although Willie was still involved with the free breakfasts and lunches and as many other Tent Hall services as he could, it was impossible to be there always. Often he had to rely on the NCF meetings and later, in Robroyston, the chapel services for worship and to receive fellowship and teaching.

It was known amongst Willie's colleagues where his alle-

giances lay and as it was disapproved of to approach patients
over religious beliefs, Willie talked more of his faith to the other
nurses instead. Several came to meetings with Willie and showed
an interest. And it did not mean that they thought any less of
him certainly as the following lines show, excerpts from a witty
poem presented to Willie with a host of signatures as he left one
ward in Robroyston bound for another:

> Our hearts were heavy
> The air full of sighs
> As the prize of our Staff
> Was torn from our sides.
>
> Oor Will's in 20,
> Oor Will's not here,
> We miss him Ah! plenty
> His fun and good cheer.
>
> Ah! Willie, dear Willie, farewell and adieu.
> All oor good wishes follow you.
> If you do for the boys what you did for us
> They'll be home in a jiffy on an 11A bus.

And that affection and esteem was recognised by those in
authority at Robroyston too. Not long after Willie had left
Robroyston, a letter came from the matron there. It was asking
him to go to the annual prizegiving.

'Whit? Me?' exclaimed Willie. 'There's some mistake, ye
know? Ma name's hardly bin on a *pass* list far less a *prize* list.'

Willie said as much to the tutor he met as he arrived on the
day of the prizegiving. But he was told merely to get his white
coat on and hurry to the hall.

Sitting there, surrounded by the other nurses and their families and friends, Willie felt quite alone. He was certain still he

was a fraud and was going to look very stupid when he left empty-handed. And as prizes were awarded by a grand lady on the stage, the feeling grew. One by one the prizes all disappeared: the midwifery prizes, the prizes for work in theatre and in the sanatorium.

'See!' thought Willie to himself, 'there ye are, a mistake.'

But still standing on the table was a large silver trophy. It was the David Elder Challenge Trophy, for the best all-round nurse of the year. Even as Willie began to prepare himself to leave, the voice from the front began:

'In all the years that this committee has sat, never have we come to a unanimous decision as to the recipient of this trophy – until this year. And never has this trophy been awarded to a male nurse – until this year. However, it gives me great pleasure (and I am sure this will be a popular choice) to present this trophy to the Best All Round Nurse, William Gilvear.'

Willie only heard the thunderous applause through dulled ears. He was sitting, rooted to the spot with shock. Those nearby nudged him to his feet, while he mouthed the words, 'Yer jokin'? Are ye sure?' He walked to the stage in a dream and his hand was pumped up and down by all the dignitaries. But Willie's eyes were glued to the silver cup. Yes, it had to be true. There, permanently engraved, never to be removed, disputed or denied, was his name: William Gilvear.

27

Another Calling

Willie enjoyed the TB nursing so much that he made no plans to leave. He had in his mind an idea eventually to do district nursing in the Highlands and Islands but he was in no hurry. Meanwhile there was plenty to do here in Glasgow.

Soon all his spare time was taken up with preparations for a Christian campaign which was to take place in the city. Billy Graham, the young American evangelist, was coming to the Kelvin Hall and people from hundreds of churches, assemblies and meetings were training as counsellors, Willie included. At Springburn Parish Church, Willie was learning with all the others how to lead to Christ those who would respond after Billy Graham spoke. Willie learned the numerous memory verses as he travelled back and forth to work on the bus. Yet he wondered to himself what all these counsellors would do – would they need quite so many?

The weeks that followed were to change many lives in Glasgow and all over Scotland. It was an amazing, exciting time. Every night Willie could he attended the meetings. Each night the great lights lit up the words of Glasgow's motto: 'Let Glasgow flourish by the preaching of the Word'; each night the hall echoed and rang to the glorious voices of the huge choir, peopled by church folk from all over the city; each night 15,000 people gathered to hear Billy Graham speak.

And every night the American preacher declared God's Word faithfully. 'God's Word's says this and the Bible says this,' Billy Graham repeated, so it was not one man's voice that was heard: it was the voice of God reaching out to tired, rebellious, disbelieving, sceptical, hungry hearts.

Willie never ceased to be amazed at the response as people poured forward in their hundreds, even thousands to find out how to be changed, how their lives could be turned around. With a silent prayer, Willie stepped into the fray and soon knew the delight of leading others to know and love his own Saviour and Lord. His joy was never greater than when a Santoi gang member, an old adversary and deadly enemy, came over to Willie at the end of a meeting and threw his arms around him. It was a truly blessed time. At work Willie was involved in saving bodies; here in this campaign, he was seeing God saving souls.

Willie's holidays that year were taken up touring round the various venues in Scotland: Hampden and Ibrox in Glasgow, Tynecastle in Edinburgh and Pittodrie in Aberdeen. Up in Aberdeen Willie was worried that his broad West Coast accent would be a problem.

'They'll niver un'erstan' a word Ah'm saying', ye know. Ah mean, who's counsellin' who here? Ah'm gonnie be a right waste o' space.'

However, Willie was paired up with a young University student from Edinburgh and they managed perfectly well without having to worry about deciphering the Aberdonians' doric.

Back in Glasgow, a special meeting was held for all the young men who had helped during the campaign. Sandyford Henderson Memorial Church of Scotland was filled to capacity solely with men. As Willie sat in his pew he thought how amazing it looked, how peculiar – just suits and ties and short hair for as far as he could see.

But this meeting was arranged for a specific reason. Mr Lorne Sanney, one of Billy Graham's team, was to address the gathering. And he chose for his text Ezekiel 22:30: 'I looked for a man among them who would build up the wall and stand before me in the gap ... but I found none.'

The preacher spoke of the lands overseas where missionaries worked and how there were so many women missionaries but so few men. Where were they all? Why weren't they responding to God's call?

As he spoke Willie began to feel very uncomfortable. This was hard to hear. He listened with growing unease. A voice was making the speaker's words ring in his ears: 'I looked for a man ... a man among them ... where are the men ... will you stand in the gap?'

Willie had never considered missionary work before. It had never entered his head as something for him to do. Suddenly he was being confronted by a challenge which seemed to be reaching deep inside him. Trying to deny its impact, Willie prayed silently: 'Lord, You winne want fur men tonight. This church is packed. See them a'.'

But still something was stirring his heart and refusing to go away. Lorne Sanney continued but Willie hardly heard him as he wrestled back and forth with this feeling. He felt as if he were under a huge spotlight, singling him out so there was no escape from the brightness of its glare.

'Yer nivir callin' me, Lord? Whit can Ah do? – with ma background, ma education? Look at a' these wans here, Lord – Whit can Ah do? An' there's ma mammy, a widow, she needs me, she really does, Lord.' He was tying himself in knots and even as the meeting ended he left the church just hoping the thoughts and restlessness would go away.

During the next few days Willie could get no peace. He thought of little else. He tried to ignore it but the voice inside would not give up. He thought of the men in the Bible who had prevaricated and stalled with God's call: Jeremiah, Moses. All their excuses had come to nothing too.

He remembered too a missionary meeting he had attended at the Medical Mission. A man named William Johnstone from the Unevangelised Fields Mission had spoken of his work in Belgian Congo and he had shown a film of lots of missionary work. It had showed the Amazon with boats and barges sailing up and down the river. It had all captured Willie's imagination and was recalled now.

Finally Willie decided that he would go and see what it was all about. Choosing the Unevangelised Fields Mission as it was the only Missionary Society of which he had heard, he headed into their offices in Glasgow. 'If they want me then they can huv me,' he thought. But Willie's plans of being sent on the next boat out of the Clyde were scuttled at the first step.

'If you want to be a missionary, son,' he was told, 'you'll have to go back to school.'

School! That horrible word! Willie was ready to turn tail and run at the very thought. But this was Bible School so Willie trekked over to Bothwell Street and walked into the Bible Training Institute there. As he sat in the office hearing about all the courses Willie did not know what to think. But he jumped up when the subject of fees came up. Fees? How much? £160 a term? This was money Willie had never had. Even now, working full time at Robroyston, he gave nearly all his money to his mother. There was nothing left over for these sort of sums.

Before he made it to the door, however, Willie was called back and told of the grant system. As an ex-pupil from the West of Scotland he was entitled to a sum of money from the education authority for further study. With the address of the office in his pocket, Willie set off again. What was this wild goose chase? Surely he had tried? Was that not enough?

Worse was to come at the Education Offices, however. When Willie enquired about a grant a great search began. As Willie waited he became more and more embarrassed for it seemed that not only did they not have his school records, they could not even find his name. He had never been at school long enough, it seemed, to be registered even as a pupil!

Having been summarily kicked out, Willie felt humiliated, but yet relieved. So he had been shown to be no use? Well, he

would just get back to normal and get on with his life. With a
silent, 'I told you so, Lord', that is what he tried to do.

Willie, however, may have given up but God had not and it
was not long before Willie attended a local missionary conference. There he was challenged finally to offer himself for service, 'a living sacrifice' (Romans 12:1), whatever the obstacles,
leaving his God to unravel and deal with the problems in his
way. As soon as the conference was over, Willie went into work
and handed in his notice. With fear and trembling he applied to
the Bible Training Institute to study there for two years and was
quickly accepted to begin in a few weeks time.

28

An Unlikely Angel

There was, of course, the problem of money: £160 which Willie did not have. The days drew closer to enrolment at the Bible Training Institute and Willie had no idea of what to do. To his family and his old colleagues, even Tent Hall friends, he knew he seemed a bit crazy – giving up his job, with no money and no prospect of getting any. Yet Willie knew he had been commanded to trust God for everything.

In time past he had trusted God's Word to the letter and it had proved right, against all the odds. He had been in crises situations before, such as when he had returned to face his old gang with only some Bible verses to protect him. Now he clung onto some words he had read in the book of Philippians in the Bible: 'My God shall supply all your needs, according to His riches in Christ Jesus.'

'Well, riches are whit Ah'm needin', Lord,' Willie prayed. 'It's a big need, like, an' Ah'm needin' it quick, ye know.' It was hard not to be concerned.

Willie's step of faith was to be tested to the limit yet wonderfully vindicated. Two days before term began Willie received a letter through the post. In the envelope, with no note or signature, was £160.

Glasgow's Bible Training Institute stood like a big, grim castle on Bothwell Street. Five stories high it housed, fed and taught the various students and was to be Willie's home for the next two years. Even with his fees in his pocket, Willie felt nervous and out of place as he climbed the steps the evening before term began and carried his small case through the door.

He was directed to a small room on the third floor which he

found quite easily. But there seemed to be so many other students rushing around. And they all seemed to know where they were going and what to do. Willie retreated into his room to sit tight and wait for the morning. It was a lonely beginning.

The next morning he found the Dining Room for breakfast by following the crowd. As he entered he was met by a sea of faces. There were one hundred and sixty students in the college and just by looking at them Willie could tell they were different from himself. It was just as well on that first day that he did not know that six of his own classmates were graduates from Cambridge University or he may have turned round and walked out there and then.

He took a seat, however, at a small table with five other students. To break the ice, Matron announced from the front that they should introduce themselves to their neighbour where they sat. But Willie's neighbour was a Lancashire girl to whom the name 'Gilvear' was too unfamiliar.

'Gabriel, did you say?' she queried, to a shout of laughter from the whole table. And when one of the lecturers, Rev. Geoffrey Grogan, mentioned the angel Gabriel shortly afterwards during Morning Worship as they sat at their tables, several laughing eyes fixed on Willie. From that moment his new nickname 'Gabriel' was formed and it firmly stuck.

Willie was encouraged further when the first lecture began. It was given by the Principal, Rev. Andrew MacBeath, a small man whom Willie was pleased to hear had been a missionary in Belgian Congo. This was the country which had first captured Willie's imagination when William Johnstone had first spoken of the work in this country while visiting the Mission.

Mr MacBeath seemed to know that Willie and many others were nervous and apprehensive for he spoke about two of the minor prophets in the Old Testament, Hosea and Amos. They were more worried than most about the task ahead, he said, yet God had strengthened and encouraged them.

And so the classes began. As he found his way around and met some of his fellow students, Willie felt more relaxed. Yet, even within this Christian environment he felt inferior to many of his more educated classmates. The studies were unfamiliar and his lack of knowledge made him uncomfortable once again. It was strange too that he had a room of his own after years of living in a crowded, noisy house or an equally crowded and noisy Mess Deck. The solitude and the struggles to study continued to put Willie ill at ease.

The first to recognise Willie's difficulties with the work was Mr William Livingston from Largs, who lectured in English. On entering the college, all the students had sat an examination to test their abilities. Willie had looked at the questions glumly: 'Write a poem,' he read. 'A poem?' Willie had never even *read* a poem! He stumbled through as best he could but he handed in his paper despondently.

Mr Livingston shook his head over that examination paper. Finally he looked up at Willie beside him in amazement: 'Where have you been all your life, son? Now – there's a lot of catching up to be done here.' And he looked again at the paper. There were huge gaps, clearly, in this boy's education. How was he supposed to research, analyse and scrutinize Biblical texts when he had no notion of how to write in sentences even, far less write essays and dissertations.

'Yes,' decided Mr Livingston, 'you'll come to me every morning at eight o'clock, nice and early, and we'll do some learning on nouns and verbs, spelling and such like.' He looked up enthusiastically into Willie's uncomprehending and doleful face.

'Yes, sir,' replied Willie flatly. And so began the early morning English sessions, each one generating more homework to do. Willie tried to be grateful, jogging his tired brain round grammar and punctuation morning after morning. Yet his workload was increased hugely on top of everything else. It seemed that nothing came easily, even if he was doing it for the Lord.

Willie continued to receive these extra classes for the whole of his two years at BTI. They benefited his work certainly although he was dogged initially by low marks.

And there was another change. Ever since his time in the Navy, Willie's speech had become less dialectal and more understandable to those from outside Glasgow. It was a change he was forced to make. Now in BTI with a mix of students again, his wonderfully colourful speech, his vibrant phraseology and rich language, formed and enriched as it was from the experiences of Glasgow life, were being diluted gradually and lamentably replaced.

Indeed this was part of his training under the attentive eyes of Rev. T. Hall Bissett. He lectured on Public Speaking and was a particular favourite with the students. Mr Bissett's own clear and precise diction was often interjected with bursts of impromptu mimicry of colloquial speech.

'Now I do not wish to hear any of you,' announced Mr Bissett in his own rich, round voice, 'verbalising your questions as I heard in my own parish this very morning, the lady of the house calling upstairs to her husband, encouraging him to rise: "Yup yit? Yup yit? Ah'm up, Ah'm up!"'

Willie was torn to bits regularly by Mr Bissett over his pronunciation. Listening to Willie read, Mr Bissett looked heartbroken, an expression of abject misery on his face, a fact not missed by Willie's classmates. Yet if it was necessary to change the way he spoke it seemed a small price to pay. Willie was there to learn to communicate the gospel and if this was necessary then he was ready for it.

The work of the Institute however was not academic entirely and the students were involved in various activities throughout the city. Many were sent out to the poorest areas, Drumchapel, Easterhouse and the Gorbals to give aid and assistance, to knock on doors, to tell people of the relevance of God in their situations. Occasionally students became involved in an outreach in the city such as the city-wide campaign led by Dr. D. P. Thomson and Rev. Tom Allan that year. Students were sent out, two by two, visiting pubs and bars, contacting prostitutes, reaching out to specific groups like the 5,000 office cleaners across the city and other night workers. It was a huge venture with Willie co-ordinating the BTI involvement. This was more like the work he was used to, not endless book reading and brain straining.

However, Willie was brought to earth with a bang when Mr MacBeath, the principal, accosted him in the corridor one day.

'Gabriel!' (Mr MacBeath had used Willie's nickname from that first day, even using it to call him to pray before the whole college.) 'Gabriel, are you forgetting you've an exam tomorrow, on the book of Romans, boy? That's your priority here, not all this running to and fro.'

Thoroughly rebuked, Willie raced to his room and poured over his books. He of all people could not neglect his studies. How could he have been so carried away? And for the principal to tear a strip off him...!

When Willie arrived in the classroom the next morning he had studied all night. He felt dazed and eyesore and indeed had no recollection afterwards of anything he had written. However his mark that day was the best of his whole period in college, so he felt vindicated in some way for all he had done.

29

The Wee Man

Andrew MacBeath, the Principal of BTI, had the job at that time of being motivator, reprover, encourager, teacher and friend to his students, all at the one time. It was a job description few would have relished, yet one which Mr MacBeath fulfilled extremely well and many students including Willie gained much from him. For he was devoted to his students knowing each one by name (or nickname!) and fully aware of their situations. Often when the day's activities were over he would remain at the college, spending much of his leisure time with these young men and women. For although he was strict in the classroom, demanding high standards from them, he was a warm-hearted, generous man whose gregarious nature drew people closely to him.

Willie, in particular, held 'the wee man' as he was known in high regard. He loved his lectures which seemed to flow from his heart. What they lacked in formal structure they made up for in spontaneous biblical insight and relevance to Willie's and others' situations. And his prayers – he prayed so beautifully it was as if he were reciting poetry.

Perhaps Mr MacBeath responded to Willie's keen and bright face, his open eagerness to learn, or perhaps he appreciated Willie's struggles thus far. But 'the wee man' seemed to know always how to relate to his lanky, enthusiastic pupil. Whether it was with a word of encouragement or understanding or rebuke, he nudged Willie through those first hard, discouraging months. For marks were low, the environment was alien, and there was news from home with which to contend also. Fresh in his mind was the knowledge that another lodger, Mr Whinning, who also rented a room with his wife in Ballindalloch Drive, had taken Spendley out into the back court and beaten the living daylights out of him, a punishment for attacking Willie's mother. Willie did not know whether to be pleased or not. It might cure Spendley for a while but it might not: broken teeth and bruised faces combined with the inevitable police sirens and overnight imprisonment might inflame the drunken bully more.

Willie's presence had that effect certainly. Although he continued to go home as often as he could, sometimes taking a college friend with him, it made matters worse usually, by incurring Spendley's wrath. Willie was grateful for the kindness of Mr and Mrs Mitchell, friends from the Tent Hall, who opened their home in Oatlands across the city to him every Sunday. There he could have his lunch and a well-earned rest.

Yet Mr MacBeath had a special regard for those students who were preparing to go overseas to work. Having been in Belgian Congo and then South Africa as well as Canada for a spell, he was a missionary at heart as well as an academic. For Willie, in particular, with his growing burden for the Congo and its people there was much encouragement and support.

That is not to say the Principal was not strict. Rules were rigidly kept and the workload was heavy. He believed, however, in making the students their own taskmasters rather than brow beating them. One morning he informed the class of the next section of work:

'During the next three weeks I will be lecturing on the prophet Jeremiah,' he said. 'I want you all to read right through the book during that time.' The class soon learned to take note of what Mr MacBeath said for three weeks later, to the day, each was presented with a piece of paper.

'Today is examination day,' he announced to his students' horror. 'Write the answer to this one question – "Have you read through the Book of Jeremiah in the past three weeks?"'

No one moved. After a long, pregnant moment, he continued stonily, 'Now fold the paper and put it in your pocket? Your conscience is your examiner.' What Mr MacBeath said was taken very seriously.

In that first term Mr MacBeath and the whole college had an extra problem with which to deal, quite apart from studies and student life. It was the 'Asian 'flu' which hit the whole of Glasgow: a particularly virulent bug, it struck down great numbers across the city. The city's fever hospital, Ruchill Hospital, was full to overflowing and news kept coming in of more and more deaths from the epidemic.

The college was not exempt and the 'flu raced round the students like a prairie fire. One after another they fell prey to it and had to be nursed in their rooms; there was no way to send them home or elsewhere.

Willie and a few other nurses among the students assisted Dr Robertson and Matron as best they could, but more and more became sick. Finally with two thirds of the college ill and the rest affected to some extent, only the doctor, Mrs Thompson the Matron, and Willie were free from the illness.

'Let's go off round the "wards",' Dr Robertson would say as they moved from room to room, treating their patients. It was exhausting work with so many to treat and nurse. With those recovering Willie was able to cheer them up with his ready smile and banter: 'Who'd have thought you'd have your own resident angel taking care of you,' he laughed.

Yet there was grief and sadness too when one student, a girl from Leicester, died from the illness like so many across the city.

Somehow through all this Willie began to settle in and find his place within the college. As life returned to normal and lectures and work restarted he felt he was more at home. With the encouragement of Mr MacBeath, Mr Livingston, Mr Grogan and others he started to feel that perhaps, just perhaps, he could do this after all.

The friendliness and camaraderie Willie found amongst his student friends was important, although sometimes it was hard to be grateful to them. When he heard the resident skiffle band serenading him below his window, 'Hand me down your silver trumpet, Gabriel' he felt like throwing a bucket of water over them, not being thankful! But there was lots of laughter and fun, perhaps more so because of the seriousness of their studies, and Willie was never far away from the centre of it.

One night Willie and three friends found themselves struggling to keep straight faces when they went out to speak to a men's gathering in the city. An old men's club in Larkhall had invited them. Willie and his pals assumed they were some church group, expecting them to lead a Christian meeting as was quite a common occurrence.

However, when the chairman of the club stood up and indicating Willie said, 'The Chairman of the Concert Party will now take over,' they knew someone had made a mix-up somewhere. Gallantly they went ahead with a few quick adjustments and impromptu songs to the amazement and barefaced incredulity of their seated listeners. Never had a concert party been so tuneless or delivered a Bible bashing as well. On the way home the boys laughed till tears ran down their cheeks.

'Aw, stop, I'm splitting my sides here,' one gasped.

'And did you see their faces when Gabriel started to sing? Ship Ahoy!' they warbled, mimicking Willie's unmusical effort.

'Ship Ahoy?' added Willie. 'I nearly drowned!'

And so the months passed. Exams came and went, most of them unpleasantly and unsuccessfully. But Willie knew he could cling on.

One of his favourite verses from the Bible was, 'nothing is impossible with God'. Throughout his studies, he continued to prove this to be true. On a human level it seemed impossible that Willie would ever complete his course and receive his Diploma no matter how capable he was at communicating the truth of God's Word verbally to anyone he met.

As the course progressed many doubted whether Willie's low marks could ever be converted into an acceptable pass. For however popular he was in the college, as President in his second year or as the number one goalkeeper of the BTI football team, it was examinations which counted in the final analysis. Could Willie ever pass?

So shocked were Willie's classmates when after two years he received his Diploma, they took it upon themselves to frame it for him. He held it to him like something precious which might be snatched away: living proof, he declared with his happy grin, that with God all things are possible.

30

Things Impossible

The next day, Willie ran lightly up the steps of the Unevangelised Fields Mission office. He had done what had been asked
of him, he thought to himself. It had taken two long years but he
had made it. He had persevered through all the studying, the
extra tuition, the endless homework. And he had passed: the
Diploma was his. As he sat in the corridor waiting to be seen,
he felt sure his boat down the Clyde to Africa could be only
days away. He felt a shiver of excitement run through him as he
thought of it all.

Never had so wide a grin been so quickly wiped off a face
when Willie went in for his appointment with the UFM director.
For another disappointment, another delay was to thwart his
plans. And these obstacles seemed impossible to overcome.

Back home in Ballindalloch Drive, Willie tried to explain to
his mother.

'So they say I've to go to Paris next,' said Willie, dismally.

'Paris! As in France?' exclaimed his mother, looking up from
the sink where she stood. 'Whitivir next, boy?'

'Aye, and then Antwerp.'

'An' where's that then, Mr Know-it-all, Holy Joe?' came
Spendley's gruff voice from behind the newspaper.

'Belgium,' continued Willie, trying to keep the annoyance
out of his voice. 'I've to learn French and then take a Diploma
in Tropical Medicine.'

'Ha,' jeered Spendley, dismissively.

'An' dae they speak this French then, out in whaurivir it is
yer goin' tae?' His mother was doing her best to understand.

'Well, sometimes – some of them do,' explained Willie, lamely.

How could he make all this sound necessary and sensible when he did not believe it himself?

'Not so happy with all this Bible rubbish now then, eh?' jibed Spendley. 'Where's your "Jesus loves me" now? And what are all your goody-goody friends saying to it? "Oh, William, you're so clever?"' As he mocked, Spendley's voice rose menacingly.

Willie watched his mother's hunched back at the sink. They could all feel Spendley's anger. Jim sat huddled in the corner, wide-eyed and trying to look the other way, to remain unnoticed. Very deliberately, their mother was lifting the plates one by one out of the sink.

Staring at her Willie knew he could say nothing. It had all been said before. Nothing would ever change. If his mother had been alone they could have chatted about it together. She would perhaps not understand the situation but she would understand his need to do it. They could have had a good laugh about it probably. She could always cheer him up.

But there had been very little humour in this house for a long time. With a carefully silent sigh, Willie left the room.

As he heard Spendley's harsh laugh behind him, Willie smiled ruefully at how his friends had reacted: one and all they had shown on their faces utter disbelief that he could ever do such a thing. Mr Livingston had put it bluntly: 'How's this boy going to get French? He hasn't even got English yet!'

But it had to be done. As Willie attended the Tent Hall prayer meeting, the Friday Night Power House, he asked for their help.

'I know you've been praying me through so much already. And I'm really relying on you now. Here's me off to France and I can hardly say "Bonjour"! So, please, remember me.'

Willie knew these friends did not make empty promises: he would be remembered.

Nevertheless, it was with great trepidation that Willie set out for France and the Alliance Francaise school in Paris. He was to study there with intensive French classes until he had mastered the language – 'or until I die of old age, whichever comes first', grinned Willie to himself.

A further shock awaited Willie once classes began. The teacher began to lecture in French! He had been assured that the tuition would be in English. But he soon discovered that he was the only British student there. All the others were German, Dutch, Spanish and such like, so the lectures were in French. How was he ever going to learn? He filed out of the first lecture in a daze: he had not understood a single word!

But Willie's friends were praying for him. God had not forgotten him and on the first Sunday Willie found a church to attend. As he sat in the pew, unable to understand any of the prayers or hymns or whatever was said, he was spotted by an elderly lady. Even as Willie was pouring out his problem to God, silently crying out for help, someone beside him spoke – in English! Overjoyed, Willie could have hugged the man. But he had a message from the lady: 'Send that boy to me,' she was saying. 'I want to help him.'

And so began the most bizarre French classes ever. Willie spoke no French and 'Madame' spoke no English but he would sit in her home and together they would pour over her French Bible. Madame would read one verse and Willie would try to repeat it, time and time again.

'Non, non.' She would shake her head and point to one word after another.

Sometimes she taught him hymns and songs. Before long they were even praying together. For soon Willie had clear and living proof that God answers prayer: within the nine months of the course in the school in Paris, he was not merely speaking in French, he was preaching it in church on Sundays.

The success of the time in Paris encouraged Willie when he set off across Europe to Belgium. Paris had been a beautiful city although he had had little enough time to sight-see. But he had lived abroad and survived it. It was no longer all so alien to him.

And he felt quite confident that he could communicate at least in Antwerp, unlike his enforced silence on arriving in France.

In addition, the year-long course at the Prince Leopold School of Medicine was on Tropical Diseases. At least it was related to his nursing background, he felt. However, waiting for Willie in Antwerp was one of the biggest obstacles he had ever faced, perhaps the hardest mountain of his whole life to climb. Would he ever make it? Was he really bound for Belgian Congo? And why did it have to be all so hard?

When Willie arrived in Antwerp, the first surprise was that the people of the region did not speak French. In the shops and on the streets Willie heard a different language – Flemish – which made no sense to him. In dismay, he resorted to English but to the Belgians this seemed worse even than attempting French. Instant dislike was written on their faces as soon as he opened his mouth. Whatever was he to do? And if he could not practise his French, might he not start to forget it?

This initial worry was soon overshadowed by what Willie discovered at his first lecture at the Prince Leopold School. To attain his Diploma he would have to pass nine subjects, in French. Previous missionaries from Britain had sat only two subjects, having studied the others elsewhere. But Willie was to do them all. To make matters worse, Willie's classmates were all doctors – forty medical officers in the Belgian Army!

'What am I doing here?' Willie cried to himself. 'Who's got me into this? I'm going to look like a fool! I'm the one who couldn't even pass an exam in English – far less nine in French!' But there was no way out. He was here in Antwerp to study for a year and he needed his Diploma at the end of it.

Lonely and afraid, Willie despaired of ever coping with the work. Here he was offered no help. He had been left to find his own accommodation even and had wandered the unknown streets, unable to ask even for help. Finally he had come upon some student apartments and found a room. But he felt very alone.

Day after day the lectures went on. Willie worried more than studied, watching the intent, intelligent faces of his classmates and feeling more and more inferior. He dreaded tests and exams, weeping in his room at night with the struggle to learn. Soon he began to lose weight and his heart was sore with the isolation of it all.

In addition, the little news that he did receive from home was informing him of trouble in Belgium Congo. Here in Antwerp he discovered that Belgian nationals were being encouraged to return home. What was happening? Would he be allowed to go to Africa even after all these years of work and preparation? Why was God letting all this happen?

On three occasions Willie tried to run away. Leaving the city behind he would head for the suburbs, the countryside, anywhere outside the four walls of his classroom or of his room. But he had nowhere to go, no money and no contacts in the country. He had nowhere to turn. And so he would make his weary way back to his room.

There was no great breakthrough. There was no intervention which turned his situation around. Right to the end of his course, to the final lecture, the final exam, Willie struggled. Hour upon hour he learned all the tropical diseases, all their symptoms, all their causes, all their treatments, all the bugs, flies and insect carriers of disease. Then, after all his classmates had closed their books and gone to bed, Willie translated all his learning into French.

Sometimes the students who shared his apartment block helped him to study. Of various nationalities themselves, they appreciated Willie's struggles and would sit with him while he recited his learnt work.

Yet although Willie was grateful, he was still alone. During those months Willie's prayers were increasingly desperate and his only means of receiving help. For there was very little contact with other Christians and even if it had been available, Willie had time for little other than study. So he had to rely solely on his direct link to God.

It was with real fear of the shame of failing and of having proved his unworthiness of God's call that Willie waited for the results of his exams. The whole class was summoned into the Assembly Hall to hear the results read out from the front. Willie felt weak at the knees with the tension and anxiety of it all. These were increased hugely when it was announced that ten of his classmates, doctors in the Belgian Army, had failed. It was surprising then that Willie did not collapse in shock when 'William Gilvear – Pass' was read out!

He had done it! It had required every ounce of his energy and stamina. It had involved real heart-searching and doubt over his call to missionary work. It had brought him face to face with his sovereign God in a more direct and demanding way than ever before. Yet he had been assured by his Lord that 'those who honour Me I will honour' and as Willie accepted his Diploma and set sail for Scotland, he felt he had been honoured indeed.

31

Marking Time

As Willie had feared there were real problems in Belgian Congo and UFM were refusing to send anyone into the situation temporarily. There had been much unrest in previous months with guerrilla warfare and anti-white feeling. In their struggle for independence the Congolese rebels under their leader, Patrice Lumumba, were becoming increasingly violent and in July of that year, 1960, Belgium beat a hasty and relieved retreat out of the country. Thus the new Democratic Republic of Congo was formed.

There was no peaceful take-over, however, for within a few months Patrice Lumumba who had become Prime Minister of the new Republic was murdered and a bitter struggle for power ensued with a series of unsuccessful leaders. With rival factions roaming the country, armed and prepared to fight, it was a situation too volatile to consider entering. Few missionaries chose to come home but no new missionaries were being sent.

With this further delay on his return from Belgium, Willie felt very low. Everything was so uncertain he did not know if he would ever get to Africa. There were encouraging words from his friends which he wanted to believe but he could not help wondering if they were true. Had it perhaps not just been a waste of time? Had he really heard God speaking to him in that church in Glasgow? Had God really been interested in his battle with the studies for the past few years of preparation? Had he just been gullible and jumped at the first opportunity? Or had his choice of Congo perhaps been misled?

With all these jumbled thoughts and doubts, Willie found himself in Keswick in the Lake District that summer with a

houseparty of UFM workers. The annual Christian Keswick
Convention was taking place and he had been invited to attend.
But it was with a heavy heart that Willie surveyed the months
ahead.

God, however, had not forgotten Willie and during that week
he bumped into his old friend from Tent Hall days, the Superintendent, John Moore. Never able to hide his feelings for long,
soon Willie was pouring out to his friend the questions he could
not ignore and the uncertainty with which it was so hard to
cope.

The two walked slowly up the hills above Keswick together.
And as they walked an idea began to form in John's mind.
Finally they reached a tiny chapel set up in the fell where they
stopped and went inside. It was deserted. They sat down and
the two friends prayed together. Somehow it seemed much easier
for Willie when he was not alone.

Then John revealed his plan. Willie would come back to
Glasgow for a time to assist him in the Tent Hall, taking over
some of his Superintendent duties.

Willie was incredulous. 'You're jokin', John? I can't do that!'
Immediately he was full of excuses. But as he realised his friend
was serious Willie thought hard. He had no other offers and at
least he would know what he was taking on. And he would be
among friends. Finally he agreed with some relief. Perhaps there
was a plan to all this after all.

His relief was short-lived however, for when having just
arrived at his new job, John announced he was going away on
holiday! Willie was thrown in immediately at the deep end. This
was not what he had envisaged at all. But his natural optimism
and ability to cope soon took over and before long he was
quite familiar with his new duties.

As assistant he was responsible for organising the various
meetings run by the Hall. He would arrange for speakers to
come, lead the meetings, provide the singers, order food for

the free meals and ensure that these all ran smoothly, work with
the caretakers and look after the halls and building. On top of
this he had to deal with any problems, as well as visiting the
sick or bereaved.

Much of it was new and frightening, yet it was much more to
Willie's liking than years of study and exams had been. And the
leadership and organisation and having to cope with whatever
was presented to him were great training for the mission field.

John Moore had another scheme for Willie's preparation for
going overseas too. He suggested that Willie set off travelling
round the country. He would visit wherever people would come
and listen and he would tell them all about the Tent Hall and
what it did.

'And of course you can tell them about yourself too,' John
explained. 'That way, when the green light comes and you do
go off to Congo, you'll have people from all over Scotland
praying for you.'

It seemed a great idea at the time but as Willie stood waiting
on train and bus stations the length and breadth of the country,
he was not so sure. Oh, to have a car! But he did not even have
a bike! And there was so much to carry. He had a suitcase of
his own clothes to last him the whole trip, a case of Bibles
which he could distribute, and a great bag of 'loaves' – bread-
shaped containers which he left with those he visited as collecting boxes for donations to the Tent Hall. When he arrived at
people's houses he looked as if he was coming for a week or a
fortnight!

But this trip was well worth the effort with a real interest
shown both in the Tent Hall and in Willie's situation. Soon support was coming in for the work in Glasgow and Willie was
assured of prayers for himself too. With his friendly manner
and his ease of speaking of spiritual matters as readily as he
spoke of everyday life, he became endeared to many.

Some time after this trip things began to change at the Tent

Hall as John Moore moved away and a new Superintendent was installed, Rev. Stanley Collins. With life again uncertain, Willie was thankful, if a little surprised, when an invitation came from Mr MacBeath: 'Could he return to the BTI, this time as a member of staff?'

For the first time in his life, Willie was referred to as Mr Gilvear! 'I feel like Lord Muck,' he laughed. He even had his own office. From here he was to co-ordinate the student out-reach activities of the college. Recalling his own 'Concert Party' experiences, Willie was not sure that he was particularly quali-fied for the job!

But as it transpired he was perfect. This part of his training at BTI had always been his favourite and what he felt most suited to – working amongst the people of Glasgow, presenting the gospel to them, providing opportunities for them to come to know Christ. In addition, he had been a student so recently himself, he felt quite at home with his 'pupils'.

Not long after his return to the college, Mr MacBeath called Willie to his room late one afternoon. Knowing that the Princi-pal had been unwell throughout the day, Willie thought he might be needing his nursing skills and rushed over to help. However Mr McBeath's request was quite different.

'I've an engagement tonight, Gabriel,' Mr MacBeath an-nounced, 'and it looks as if I'm not going to manage to go.'

Willie was all concern: 'No. You don't look like you're bound for anywhere but bed just now, Mr MacBeath,' he agreed.

'So,' continued the wee man, 'I would like you to go in my place.'

'Me!' exclaimed Willie. 'Mr MacBeath, please don't ask me. There are many things in this world that I can't do – and standing in for you is definitely one of them!'

But his boss would hear none of it. 'Now, Gabriel, there's a car coming for me at six o'clock but it'll be you in it instead of me.' And he firmly ignored any more protests.

Knowing no more than this, Willie boarded the car which arrived and was whisked off to the Coatbridge Baptist Church on the outskirts of Glasgow. Getting involved in conversation in the car, he had no time to ask his companion about the meeting. But when they pulled up in the car park, Willie saw cars and people everywhere. There were full buses too, one from Edinburgh and one from Glasgow. It was worse when they got inside. An enormous amount of food was set out in the hall and the church itself was packed. Willie began to feel very apprehensive.

'What exactly is happening tonight?' he managed to ask eventually and a programme was thrust towards him. Willie read it with mounting panic.

'Valedictory Service for Dr Victor Smith ... leaving for Ethiopia ... Main Address by Rev. Andrew MacBeath, MA, BD.'

Willie leapt up and was almost out of the door before the minister caught him and dragged him back into the church, Willie complaining and remonstrating all the while.

But there was no escape. Willie – 'Oor Willie frae the Gallowgate', as so many of his friends had dubbed him – Willie, with no missionary experience and just out of college, had to get up as the main speaker and address these hundreds of people, utterly unprepared and with them expecting to hear the eloquent and learned Principal of the Bible Training Institute – lecturer, experienced pastor and missionary of the church. Shaking and sweating, Willie stood up to speak.

Later that night, Willie lay on his bed and thanked God for His provision. As he had looked at all those good people his mind had been blank. He felt the word, 'PANIC' must be tattooed across his forehead for all to see! Yet he had suddenly recalled and related a story he had heard of King George V, how he had encouraged the troops in the trenches during the war just before they went over the top to fight. He had praised them for their willingness to fight for their country and for himself and assured them that it was as if he were beside each one of them, fighting with them. With the High King of Heaven truly standing with each one of us as we head into the fray, Willie had said, how much greater should be our courage and determination to give our all for Him. It was a message which Willie took to his own heart as much as did his listeners that night.

It was not long, however, before Willie was attending his own Valedictory Service, held in the Tent Hall. UFM had announced that he would be leaving in the next month and Willie was only too eager to be off.

On the night of the service the back room of the Tent Hall which was used normally for these occasions was not big enough to hold all the people who arrived from all over the Central Belt of Scotland and beyond. Not long after they had started they all had to get up and move through to the main hall. And still they kept coming. Willie was thrilled to see so many familiar faces from his past there to wish him well and to encourage him on his way: friends from the Tent Hall, from the Glasgow Medical Mission, from the BTI, from the Nurses' and Naval Christian Fellowships and many more.

And Willie was especially pleased to see at the front the snowy-white head he remembered from many years before. It was George I. Stewart, the Child Evangelist who had provided his Fresh Air Fortnight in the big house at Shandon as a little boy. As the evening went on Mr Stewart took part, singing and then joining the others who spoke, assuring Willie of their continued support as he left for Congo and the work there.

Once the night was over the days quickly rushed past with farewells to be made, medicines to be sought, shopping to be done, and materials to collect for going abroad. On a recent shopping expedition Willie had bought a special gift for his mother. Rarely in her life had she ever received anything new and it was seldom that Willie ever had any extra money of his own to spend. However, after saving carefully, Willie took her to an exclusive drapers in Glasgow and there he bought her a beautiful fur coat. Tears rolled down both their faces as she stroked the gentle fabric and wrapped it round her tiny frame. Seldom had Willie seen such joy in her tired eyes.

She wore the coat when she came to wave him off at the station. It would be a painful goodbye as Willie had been her mainstay in the troubled years behind them. And Willie felt a terrible wrench at leaving her to cope alone. Both of them tried to stay cheerful as they walked into the station, together with his sister Cathy who had come to support their mother and to see him off.

But on the platform was a full reception party: friends from the Tent Hall, the BTI and elsewhere. There were so many Willie had trouble seeing who all was there.

And before the train chuffed in, his student friends burst into song – in French! 'Saisir mes mains crantive et conduis moi' – 'Hold my trembling hands and guide me.'

Having boarded the train, Willie looked out for the last time to wave. There was his mother, small and frail and yet the survivor of so much, standing with her arm looped through Cathy's. And there were his young friends, so lively and encouraging. There too were old friends who knew just how far he had travelled in his pursuit of this call to work in Congo. What would be waiting for him there? And what all, he wondered, was he leaving behind?

32

Unwelcome Introductions

Of all the things Willie might have expected on arriving in Congo, he did not anticipate trouble. But that is what he walked straight into on his very first day. Having been met at Stanleyville airport by the UFM Field Leader, Al Larson and his wife, Willie was taken to their home. That night, just as he was beginning to relax from the long journey and get accustomed to the suffocating heat, the house was surrounded suddenly by a band of young Congolese soldiers. They were shouting and shrieking, brandishing clubs and spears as well as heavy-duty army guns. Many were dressed scantily in leaves and greenery, looking alarmingly to Willie like wild, jungle warriors.

The shouting was deafening, and all in a language Willie could not understand. They went outside to investigate. What was going on? What sort of reception committee was this? Al Larson was trying to speak to the men. He looked very worried. Willie turned to ask what was going on. The answer took his breath away.

'You are being arrested,' he was told, 'on suspicion of being a Belgian spy!'

If he had not been so scared he would have laughed. A spy! Now he had heard everything! But it was indeed true. These ragged, desperate looking men were demanding that Willie come to their camp where he would be beaten severely for his supposed crime!

Finally, Mr Larson managed to persuade the soldiers to let Willie stay with them that night although they demanded that a six-man guard remain with him. It was a long and terrifying night and the next morning he was unceremoniously marched off to their camp.

He found himself imprisoned in a make-shift cell. Staring in at him were his captors, these ragged men, most without uniforms or even shoes but who evidently had the authority to incarcerate whom they chose. These, he learned, were rebel soldiers, faithful to the memory of their dead leader, Patrice Lumumba, and bitterly opposed to the current administration. They were known as the 'Simbas' – the Swahili word for 'lion'. Certainly their ferocity and wildness lived up to their name, Willie thought.

All Willie's papers were confiscated and he could see them exclaiming loudly at the Belgian stamps on his passport and his Belgian certificates. Anything Belgian it seemed was despised and hated since the earlier rebellion. Even the name of the city was changed.

'No Stanleyville – Kisangani,' the Simbas shouted into his face.

There was such hysteria and violence that Willie was deeply worried. He was interrogated but he could neither understand nor explain anything. 'Scotch Broth in the jungle tonight' he told himself, as he recalled all the tales of cannibalism that he had heard from Central Africa. As night came his worries grew, yet he was so very tired. But how could he sleep? He would be pawed over and gaped at all night.

Even as he worried, however, Willie recalled verses he had learnt years before. So vivid were the words in his mind that it could have been written on the wall of his cell: 'He that keepeth Israel shall neither slumber nor sleep.'

There was someone else not sleeping, then. Surely his God was watching over him now and He was seeing what was happening. He would watch over Willie while he took some rest. So despite his circumstances, his captors, his imprisonment, the discomfort, the heat and the strangeness and uncertainty of it all, Willie curled up where he was and slept.

Finally, it took two official attempts to free him. First of all, the Commander of the United Nations Forces currently in Congo turned up to appeal for his release. But he was summarily ignored. The Patrice Lumumba soldiers holding Willie despised the UN Forces which were trying to keep the peace in the volatile political situation but whom they saw as interfering.

However, when verbal appeals were exhausted and Willie was beginning to despair himself, a whole truckload of UN soldiers, waving their UN flag descended on the rebels' camp. Finally outnumbered and outgunned, the Simba soldiers had to give way and Willie was borne off by his UN Ethiopian deliverers. And so he arrived back with the Larsons at the UFM Headquarters in Kisangani to everyone's intense relief. But what a beginning!

But this was the first hurdle of many before Willie was ever to reach his own station of Bongondza in the North East province. His papers having been returned, he proudly presented his qualifications to the UFM staff. Now surely he could set off into the Congo he had come to find. But no – there was another problem.

'We're sorry you had no warning of this in Britain, but with all the unrest the authorities here won't accept any Belgian certificates. "Belgium" is a bad word here now. So,' (Willie could almost sense what was coming next) 'you'll have to do some hospital work here and sit a government exam, before you go. Otherwise there will be no nursing for you.'

Willie could hardly believe it. 'It's twelve years since I started out to be a nurse, you know,' he sighed. 'I could have been a master surgeon at this rate!'

But there was no way out. He began work at the government hospital in Kisangani so he could sit this latest examination.

If it had not been for the missionaries at Kilometre 8 (the unimaginative title given to the mission headquarters just that distance from the city centre), Willie would have felt he was seeing nothing of Congo. The government hospital looked straight out onto the airport. He did not feel as if he had come very far! If he had not been so busy, he might have wondered what he was doing here. But the hospital was full and there was plenty to occupy his mind.

One of Willie's main jobs was to conduct the medical examinations on the scores of young Congolese men who were lining up to leave the country. For several years in Congo there had been a steady stream of departures of the most able and committed youths bound for further education in the communist regimes of the USSR and China. Having been highly trained these Simbas returned to lead and promote the growing rebel Communist party in Congo. Various administrations had sought to contain this growing powerbase, but with little success and anti-capitalist, anti-white rhetoric and reprisals were set to increase.

So Willie watched these boys leave the hospital and set off for the airport. They, like him, would be leaving families and friends behind, learning a new language, experiencing a new culture. But with what a different end in view. Political rebellion at any cost was their goal, whereas Willie had a more spiritual renewal in mind.

Because of the growing unrest in the region, the government down in the south in Kinshasa were concerned, and not long after Willie began work in the Kisangani hospital, a large contingent of UN peacekeeping soldiers descended on the city. They arrived unannounced in huge troop-carrying planes which swooped into the airport.

Immediately the hospital was thrown into confusion! Willie was working in the children's ward at the time and everyone stopped what they were doing. They stood transfixed by the windows. Then suddenly everyone broke into a run. Willie gazed round in amazement. There was shouting and screaming. And everyone was pouring out of the hospital gates. They were all running away! Patients, nurses, doctors, relatives – they were all running for their lives!

Even worse, when Willie arrived outside himself, he found the government soldiers who were patients lined up, fully armed, ready to fight. Running past Willie was the hospital secretary.

Willie grabbed him, shouting, 'Stop these people!'

But the man looked at Willie as if he were crazy: 'Oh no! Look at all these soldiers coming to kill us. Run! Run!'

As the last patients were straggling out of the hospital clutching their possessions and trailing drips and bandages, the UN commander appeared in a jeep with a handful of his men. Willie could hear the line of soldiers beside him cocking their rifles ready to fire.

'Can you speak English?' the Commander asked of Willie who was the only staff member to be seen. 'Tell these soldiers that we come as friends. We are here to help them. What would they like us to do?'

So Willie stepped into the line of fire of the Congolese soldiers' guns and tried in the little Lingala that he had picked up in his few weeks in Kisangani to explain the situation. He felt like a referee – he had the United Nations army on his left and the Republican Army of Congo on his right. And he was stuck there in the middle of them!

Slowly the guns were lowered and to Willie's intense relief, hands were gingerly shaken. It was an easy job then to guide the soldiers back to their beds and let the UN Commander lead his troops into the city. However it was more difficult to retrieve the escaped patients: it took six weeks for them all to come back.

33

New Names

In those first weeks, Willie had the opportunity to get to know his American host and hostess at Kilometre 8, Rev Al Larson and his wife, Jean. Al Larson was the Field Director for UFM and had the task of linking all the mission stations scattered over the North East of Congo. This had been a troubled area for a long time, during the political upheavals of recent times and prior to these, and the region maintained a strong pro-Communist presence. As much of the tension and growing unrest was focused here it was a difficult job, especially as communications and transport in such a wide-spread rural area were limited.

At one time or another, all UFM missionaries had stayed at Kilometre 8, whether as a stopover when shopping in Kisangani for supplies, or using the hostel there for a holiday and recuperation. Willie, like others before him, enjoyed the happy, open atmosphere of the home created by the Larsons and was able to ask constant questions about Congo from his well-informed host.

There was so much to which he had to get accustomed: simple things like the strength-sapping weather, particularly in the city; the language; the new hospital environment; the suspicion of the authorities; and his new position as a missionary. Willie had always been used to standing out as a Christian but here he felt so conspicuous. Every step he took was watched.

One thing which was one of the hardest to get used to was the change of his name. Although his mother for some reason had always called him William, for as long as he could remember, he had been known as Willie: 'oor Willie frae the Gallowgate' as he jokingly referred to himself. Throughout his life he had assumed

a few nick-names, such as 'Gil' when he ran with the gangs and
'Gabriel' as a student at BTI. And in the Navy he become
accustomed to answering to anything! But he always thought of
himself as Willie.

But here in Congo there were missionaries from many countries. UFM itself was cosmopolitan with several workers from
America as well as Australia, Canada, Ireland and Germany. To
them Willie's name was very Scottish and unfamiliar. So from the
outset he became known to his colleagues simply as 'Bill'.
Whoever started it, the name stuck and he was to be known as
Bill Gilvear for the rest of his life. This was hard enough to become
accustomed to but when the Congolese began calling him 'Bwana
William', he thought he would become completely confused!

Having passed the government exam in the hospital in Kisangani
much to his amazement, 'Bill's' next appointment was with Mr
Herbert Jenkinson for some language training. 'Kinso', as he was
affectionately known to the Congolese, had been in the country
since 1920 and had been one of the pioneer missionaries there.

The mission field which Bill was entering was very different
from the one which Kinso had encountered all those years ago.
Kinso had been one of the first to venture into the interior with the
Christian message and it was he who had built from scratch the
very mission station for which Bill was bound, Bongondza. It had
been built on virgin land, hewn out of the forest and he had
supervised its development as more and more buildings were
added till it became known as a hospital and centre for the spread
of the gospel.

So Bill began language learning again with Kinso and his wife,
Alice. In the Government hospital he had begun to pick up some
Lingala. This, he discovered was the official language, used by
the authorities and the police. To communicate with the Congolese on a day to day level however he had to learn another
language, Bangala. As if it was not all confusing enough!

'It's a bit like in Scotland,' he told Kinso as he began to

understand the differences. 'In Edinburgh you get all the posh nobs speaking one way. And then through in Glasgow you get everyone talking in slang – the way the ordinary folks speak.' So he tried to learn his Bangala 'slang'.

Yet the confusion did not stop here. The official language of Congo was French, with all education and government work conducted in this language. And yet half of the people of Congo had another language as their first, Swahili! Bill began to wonder if he was coming or going! When he heard that in Bongondza the people would more than likely speak in another language altogether – their tribal language, Baboa – Bill thought enough was enough. He would muddle through somehow as best he could.

But whatever the language problems might be, Kinso's style of teaching suited Bill certainly. He was not one to sit poreing over books. Rather he took Bill to meet the Congolese and involved him in whatever project he happened to be working on. So Bill found himself in Banjwadi, north of Kisangani, doing jobs like cementing the church floor. With no building experience and hardly any means of communicating, Bill felt he was worse than useless. However, his happy nature and willingness to learn quickly endeared him to his Congolese co-builders and they forgave his messy lack of expertise as well as his many linguistic blunders.

But although Bill claimed to have made a fool of himself too many times to care how he sounded, it was another matter when it came to speaking about his faith. In France he had preached in French after a short time, but here it seemed different.

'It's too soon,' he explained or made other excuses: 'I want them to be able to understand me. It would be terrible to make a bad mistake.'

But in Banjwadi were two Congolese evangelists – older men named Badi and Jacques. They befriended Bill and sought to encourage him.

'We will teach you to give your testimony in Bangala, Bwana

William,' said Badi. 'Then you will be able to begin.' Having primed him in this, yet still seeing his fear, they persuaded him to put this little Bangala he had to good use.

'Bwana William, come with us. We will show you how to start. Come.'

So Bill was led to a dug-out canoe and was soon being paddled downstream. All around was the heavy vegetation of the jungle and the water was very murky. Bill did not want to speculate as to what might be below the surface. He kept his arms inside the boat and watched out for low hanging branches. Who knew what they might hold?

But they soon arrived at a tiny riverside village. Having pulled the canoe from the water they already had an audience. It seemed very natural then to explain why they were there and to tell the villagers the Christian message. And so Bill was able to speak for the first time for Christ to the people he had waited all these years to meet and to reach for his Saviour.

But Bill was itching to get into the interior and begin work in earnest. To his delight, Kinso felt that he was learning quickly and within three months Bill had sat and passed the necessary government exam (in Lingala!). Kinso announced that Bill would be as well on his own station, settling in with the people there.

Bill's excitement grew as the day drew closer. In Banjwadi he had been helping in the large dispensary there so he had been of some use, at least. But he could not feel that he had arrived properly in Congo until he reached the place where he would make his home – Bongondza, 140 miles north-east of Kisangani.

34

Bongondza

The UFM station at Bongondza was built on a large tract of land, several acres in area. It edged onto the dense Ituri forest, the largest of the equatorial forests in Congo which occupied most of the north and north-east of the country. In contrast to the dark and virtually impenetrable tropical forest, Bongondza was a bright spot of great activity and a magnet for those who were sick or wanting education in the vast 60,000 square miles it served. To Bill's western experience of city hospital work, the fact that the doctor and the hospital here served some 500,000 people seemed inconceivable.

The doctor at the station was Ian Sharpe, a young English surgeon who had been in Congo for five years with his wife Audrey. She worked beside him as the theatre Sister, as well as caring for their three young children. Already Bill had heard that Ian was an expert surgeon and that his meticulous skills meant that the medical work in Bongondza was always busy.

All that he had heard about his future home buzzed around Bill's head as he bounced and jolted along the forests in Al Larson's car towards Bongondza. There was such an intense feeling of relief, of achievement and of excitement at this new move he was about to make, he hardly felt the bumpy ride.

They turned off the rutted roads eventually and drove into a wide, spacious compound, covered with huts and larger buildings. They stopped outside the first house on the right of the entrance and Hector MacMillan came down the steps of his house to greet them.

Hector MacMillan was the Station Leader at Bongondza. He was a small man, stocky with bright penetrating eyes which smiled out behind his glasses. He greeted Bill enthusiastically on his arrival: 'It's great to have you here, Bill. We've been looking forward to this day,' he exclaimed.

'Not as much as I have!' Bill returned, feelingly.

'And a Scotsman too! Hear that Iona,' he turned to his wife. Although Hector himself was Canadian and Iona an American, Bill was soon to learn that they had Scottish connections and, like many North Americans, were keen on anything or anyone Scottish. It was a good start.

Before long the MacMillans had gathered the other missionaries: Ian and Audrey Sharpe and their three children and Violet Walker who worked at the station too. Together they had a meal and quickly Bill felt at ease. As the evening progressed they prayed and talked together, Bill telling them something of himself and hearing lots about the work in Bongondza in which they were all involved.

In the morning Bill was shown round. There was a disarming number of buildings and there seemed to be people everywhere trying to get a look at him. Faithfully Bill shook hands and frantically tried to remember names.

The hospital itself was made up of several buildings, set at the far end of the compound. At the front was a large veranda which served as a huge, overcrowded outpatients department, with treatment areas at one side and microscopes for specimen analysis at the other. Beyond this were the other departments and Bill was soon being led proudly round the various sections: the theatre, the pharmacy, the doctor's consulting room, the male and female wards at the back and the treatment room between.

Behind the hospital was a large area of cleared ground and the sight which met Bill's eyes here was a strange one. All sorts of little shacks and temporary shelters were erected there. And there seemed to be scores of people milling about. Children were everywhere, playing and watching and sitting by their mothers. Fires were lit outside each shack or leaf shelter and the smoke curled up and out towards the forest beyond.

'These are the relatives,' Ian explained, who was showing Bill the hospital work. 'They are here to feed those who come as in-patients. Now don't be bamboozled into treating any of them,' he added with a grin. 'They'll develop an ailment as soon as look at you and they're supposed to be the healthy ones, so let's go on!'

Beyond the main hospital buildings and to the right was another cluster of huts and shacks. Here was the isolation unit where the infectious diseases were treated, such as the tuberculosis patients. In particular, Bongondza had a large leper population. Not only were they cared for and able to live with their own families on the Mission station, but Ian Sharpe was able through surgery to treat and improve their otherwise neglected situations.

A few hundred yards from the hospital and down one of the numerous paths which intersected the central area of the station stood the Maternity Hospital. Here Congolese midwives were trained and a new UFM missionary from Ireland was expected before long to assist with this work. Bill was only relieved that this was something with which he would not have too much to do!

Apart from the hospital complex at Bongondza there were several other buildings including a Primary School which taught pupils of all ages. This doubled as a Bible School at night where Congolese pastors, evangelists and church workers could be trained. There was also a large church, houses to accommodate the school pupils, and a number of other houses where the various missionaries and Congolese teachers and evangelists lived.

Bill was shown his new home and soon settled in. It was built in the African style, round and made of mud and wattle and with a thatched roof. He had to bend to get through the door but once inside it proved to be spacious enough. Just at the entrance was the kitchen with a small sitting room behind. His bedroom and bathroom were at the back. There were windows cut in the walls and some basic furniture. He placed his few belongings where he could but it did not take long. His only decoration was his treasured Diploma in Tropical Medicine which he hung lovingly on the wall. The rest was bare.

If Bill had not been heartwarmed enough by the delight and joy shown by both missionaries and Congolese on his arrival, more was to come for on the first Sunday a service of welcome and thanksgiving was held in his honour. Called to the front Bill felt very self-conscious as he stood facing the huge congregation, for the church was big and every seat was taken. Then suddenly everyone seemed to be flooding towards him. They got up out of their seats and descended on him, each one carrying gifts: flowers were placed on him and fruit and vegetables were thrust into his hands and scattered at his feet; produce of all sorts – bananas, coconuts, plantain, dishes of oil and baskets of grain – were piled onto him where he stood. Laden knee-deep in these gifts, Bill was quite overcome and could only beam out his irrepressible grin to the congregation as they streamed back and forth with their offerings to him.

Masini Phillipe, the Zairian pastor, spoke for a long time after this while Bill sweated it out in the heat. As he spoke in Baboa, the local tribe language, Bill did not know what was being said but from the smiles it seemed to be complimentary, so Bill just smiled back, getting hotter and more embarrassed by the minute.

Above the platform where he stood was a text, in huge letters. It had been painted by Alice Kinso years before and it read, 'Be still and know that I am God.' Bill focused on those words while he stood before them.

Finally it was indicated that Bill should say something. Stammering and unsure, he managed a few words which he hoped were of thanks, trying to express his appreciation of his welcome and the deep sense of humility he increasingly felt in the company of these gracious and loving people. For although he could understand little of what was being said and the exuberance and excitability of the worshippers was unfamiliar to him, he could recognise their joy and their generosity out of their own poverty which was so similar to that of the worshippers and workers in his own fellowship back in Glasgow's Tent Hall. If he needed any confirmation that he was in the right place and in God's will, this was it: he felt like he was coming home.

35

Ready For Anything

And so Bill began work. It started early in Bongondza with the first clinic at the hospital for station staff at 7 am. So many people lived on the station, with about two hundred pupils in the school alone, that the first hour was taken up regularly in this way and it was after eight o'clock that the growing number of other patients began to be seen.

There was always a great crowd gathered on the veranda where the Outpatients' Clinic was held. More queued and took their places on the surrounding ground and a vast array of ailments and illnesses were waiting attention. Bill could see that many of the people must have travelled long distances to reach the hospital and many of the more minor problems like ulcers and wounds were aggravated by the travel and delay.

In addition, Bill soon learnt to recognise those who had sought treatment from their witchdoctors first: limbs were scored across with knives, and wounds were encrusted with various grasses and muddy ointments, hair was braided with charms, and fetishes were worn round their necks. Invariably these patients required extra treatment due to the infection and aggravation to their wounds and the time wasted in seeking help.

But before any work started the Station Evangelist, a Congolese preacher named Patrice Likali conducted a short service on the veranda. The physical needs of the patients were secondary always to their spiritual needs and every morning he would address the gathering and they were compelled to listen as he presented the message of the gospel. Sometimes it was the first time they had heard of Jesus and as Patrice talked with them afterwards or visited the patients in the wards many responded

178

to the message of freedom and forgiveness that was preached. It was a thrilling way to begin the day.

Bill soon fitted into the routine of the work. There was so much to learn with new diseases to recognise and treat and, of course, the language to conquer. But although it was a struggle to make himself understood in any language – Lingala, Bangala, French or English! – this was a problem Bill had encountered almost all his life even in his own country, so it did not worry him! He just wanted to get on with it and get the job done. And there was a lot of variety. He and the others took turns in the different departments, distributing drugs in the pharmacy, examining samples under the microscope, theatre work and even dental work! Bill had attended a brief two week class for missionary nurses on dentistry before leaving for Congo which was enough merely to show him one end of a drill from another! Here his equipment consisted of a pair of pliers and a lot of prayer!

There was always prayer in the theatre too. Before each patient was anaesthetised Ian would pray in whichever language would be understood, asking for God's direction and healing. It seemed an incredible record but Bill was told that Ian Sharpe had never lost a patient in theatre. Yet seeing his skill and brilliance, aligned to his faith, Bill could believe it easily.

Ian's wife, Audrey was the theatre sister and it was a domain she ruled with an iron hand. Her thin face would be set in concentration throughout with only her dark, curly hair and quick, darting eyes behind her glasses, visible above her surgical mask. Bill learnt very quickly to be ready always with his instruments and to have all his sutures and dressings meticulously prepared, for Audrey's eyes missed nothing and she would tear a strip off him as soon as look at him, colleague and friend notwithstanding.

Often on the veranda during a clinic, Bill was assigned to the microscope work. Samples were not sent to a laboratory for testing: it all had to be carried out on site. The blood samples regularly showed the particular disorder or infection which was involved and Bill became adept at identifying the various worms and bacteria which wiggled distinctively under his magnified gaze. The patients were intrigued by this procedure and often pressed as close as they dared to catch a glimpse of how this 'magical' art was performed. But Bill was always keen to learn new skills – and Ian was a constant and excellent teacher – and if it took some of the burden from the doctor, then the more Bill could do himself the better.

In addition to the various jobs to which he was assigned, there was the daily work in the wards. Ward rounds and treatment took up most of the day, with a steady influx of patients, and Bill thrived on caring for them. This, he considered, was an easy way to be a missionary – everyone was so appreciative of all that the hospital was doing for them, it was a joy to serve them. From the very first, Bill threw himself into the work wholeheartedly. He suffered no homesickness and found those with whom he worked so friendly that he never felt lonely.

He was helped also by advice he had received at the beginning. In his initial weeks in Banjwadi, Kinso had suggested he do two things: keep a daily diary so that he had plenty to tell when he went home on furlough, and write a letter home every night. This ensured he was always in contact with those back home, people were able to pray informedly for him and he would receive lots of letters back. Bill followed these instructions daily and both received many letters and never felt the isolation which he knew many had been known to suffer.

Bill's easy and cheerful manner too played a major part in his acceptance by the Africans. He felt a real kinship with them. By nature they seemed to be straightforward people: people who would speak their minds and be 'upfront' about any situation, very much like Bill knew Glaswegians would do. And they seemed to have his countrymen's knack of assessing someone with great accuracy. They may watch you guardedly for half an hour but if you passed their 'test' you became a friend for life.

Similarly, they showed emotion readily, often volatile and excitable and always ready to laugh. Sometimes apart from the language, Bill felt if he closed his eyes (and if it was cold, and wet maybe, with a touch of smog in the air!) he could be back in Gallowgate in Glasgow's East End.

Once, at the Outpatients Clinic, out of pure mischief to see his patient's shocked reaction, Bill offered a patient a look at his own blood through the microscope. The man suffered from filarious, an infestation of tiny worms which circulate in the sufferer's system and Bill watched to see how his excitable patient would react. With one look at the wriggling hoards the patient leapt back in horror and gave a terrific scream. He ran to and fro on the veranda, his arms waving and wailing at the top of his voice: 'I've animals in me – animals in my blood!' Bill knew he would be shocked but he had not counted on this degree of alarm! The other patients were being trampled underfoot! This was more of a reaction than a Scotsman would have made certainly.

Deep friendships were soon forged too with the other missionaries, particularly with the Sharpes. Respect for their skills in the hospital soon increased into love for themselves and Bill was a regular visitor at their house. This provided a happier home environment than Bill had ever known in his own home and he loved to be with them. Although he was shorter than Bill, Ian and he were teased by the Africans that they must be related, for although they were both young they bore the 'same tribal marks' – a balding head! Bill responded that no, he merely had a wide parting but yes, they were brothers in the Lord!

And there was a true brotherhood there. Sometimes they ate together, just chatted or talked about medical cases. Sometimes Ian entertained them on his treasured organ. He was exceptionally skilled and it was a joy to listen to him play. For all his busy days at the hospital and being on call twenty four hours a day, Ian had time for everyone and nothing seemed too much trouble. His children doted on him and Bill could see the devotion he inspired in his colleagues and patients alike. 'A man of gold' Bill thought of him as, and it was a view shared by many.

Bill knew too that he took his work extremely seriously. Even after particularly late nights, Bill discovered that Ian would put in up to two extra hours study of medical journals and textbooks to keep himself up to date with the latest findings and procedures. And this was put to good use. On one occasion when the operating theatre was out of use during some repairs, an emergency obstetric case cropped up. The patient required a caesarean section but this was impossible without the use of the theatre. But Ian remembered a description of an operation which he had read in a British Medical Journal one night. It was extremely delicate but could be done under local anaesthetic. Although he had never seen it done, this was the only way to save the mother and the baby; so Ian performed the symphysiotomy there and then in the Maternity unit. And mother and baby survived.

It was to Ian and Audrey that Bill turned when he took his first bout of illness in Congo. Sickness can descend very quickly in the heat and humidity of that climate and Bill took unwell suddenly. Whatever the bug causing his illness, he was incapacitated and remained with the Sharpes for some time regaining his strength. He experienced then the care and love Audrey poured out on her patients. And he appreciated her energy and capacity to work. It made him quite breathless just to watch her!

Ian and Audrey had three young children too, Jillian, Alison and Andrew. Soon he was referred to by them as 'Uncle' Willie and they loved his visits with their riotous games and endless fun. They were too young to be away at school, indeed Andrew was only three years old. Bill was amazed by his understanding of the different languages in their part of the Congo. Although so young he was able to speak in three languages – French, Langala and Swahili – and he seemed to know instinctively which language to use for whoever he met. Bill wished it was a skill he could possess himself. It became a regular event for the three children to come to tea with him on Fridays in his hut. There they would play hide and seek or tag or any other game they chose: 'Uncle' Willie would be sure to join in.

With the MacMillans too Bill soon became friendly. Iona was very caring and had her hands full, especially when her six sons were home from school. Apart from that she taught in the Bible School in the evenings as well as leading the Congolese choir there. So there was always plenty to do.

Bill had never found rising early a problem and in Bongondza he got up each morning at six o'clock to have a time with the Lord before work began. Yet however early he was up he discovered that he was never up earlier that Hector. Every morning Hector would begin the day with a period of devotional time, alone with his Lord. Bill soon learnt that during this time he sought from God words of encouragement for his family and others who worked with him. It was a regular occurrence for Hector to come up to Bill or another member of the staff and give him a verse for that day which he had received from the Lord that morning. He was 'fur ben wi' the Maister' as they might have described him in the Tent Hall.

As Station Leader, Hector had many responsibilities, not least the oversight of work in Bongondza and the witness there. He was an ordained minister but his work was largely administrative, dealing with the maintenance of the station and the care of the workers there.

It was his wonderful practical skills which endeared him so closely to the Congolese. For Hector was the type of man who seemed able to turn his hand to any job, no matter how difficult. His motto was 'Ready For Anything'.

'You must earn these letters after your name on the Mission Field,' he would tell Bill. 'Forget diplomas and degrees, son. You must be Bill Gilvear, RFA – Ready For Anything!' And Hector certainly was that!

He had a large workshop which was built between his house

and Bill's which was always full of Africans whom he taught in woodwork and any mechanical and electrical work. He was always teaching how to fix machinery, mend cars, erect or repair buildings, lay plumbing – anything he happened to be doing at the time.

As a teacher, Hector was endlessly patient and Bill never knew him to be angry with anyone – even when mistakes were made. And if he was doing something elsewhere there was always a list of jobs to do on the wall of the workshop so no-one need ever be idle. He was the type of man every Mission Field should have and he proved himself indispensable over and over again.

It was a red letter – a red tam-tam – day in Bongondza when Hector set up his projector. From time to time Hector would put on a cinefilm show, powering his projector with a car battery. The word would go out all around. The drums could be heard carrying the message far afield and into the forest that this treat was to be shown at the Mission Station. And they would come pouring out of nowhere it seemed.

Once Hector had his assembled audience, he would begin. The films showed African scenes which were familiar to all and the 'oohs' and 'aahs' and peals of laughter showed the enjoyment they all felt. Hector always gave the Christian story too by film and as he spoke he never missed a chance to tell his happy listeners of his Saviour and Jesus' love for them. Ready For Anything also meant being ready to share his faith at a moment's notice and to all who would listen.

36

African Bonds

If Bill's days were busy, so were his evenings with duties at the hospital whatever the time of day or night as well as Bible Studies and services to attend. One night a week the missionaries met at the Sharpes' for discussion and prayer and another night at the MacMillans'. On another night there was a church prayer meeting which was led by the Congolese men.

In addition, Bill ran the 'Flambeaux' movement in Bongondza for the boys, along with a Congolese teacher, M'bongo Samuel, the son of the Pastor, Masini Phillipe. 'Flambeaux' was a youth organisation, similar to the Boys' Brigade or Scouts, which sought to teach the boys the truth of the Bible as well as let them learn new skills and have fun into the bargain. Groups such as these existed on several Mission stations and had been the means of teaching many young boys about Christ and of training them up in the faith.

In conjunction with the 'Flambeaux' there was also the 'Lumiere' group for girls and this was run by the new midwife at Bongondza, Ruby Gray. She was from Dromara in Northern Ireland and, like Bill, Ruby had experienced difficulty in being allowed to go to Congo. Now that she was there she revelled in it, entering into all the activities wholeheartedly. In the hospital, soon she was training new midwives to work with her and she was unstinting in her sharing of her faith with her patients on the wards. Initially she had lived with Violet Walker, but since Violet's departure for another station, Ruby lived alone in a house like Bill's down by the Maternity Unit.

Bill loved the work with the boys in 'Flambeaux' as he had always got on well with youngsters and enjoyed their company.

And he became very friendly too with his co-leader, M'bongo. There were of a similar age and M'bongo showed great hospitality, inviting Bill to his home to be with his wife and family. And as they worked together and prepared for the meetings with the boys, Bill discovered how upright and conscientious M'bongo was in all he did. To some, M'bongo appeared stubborn and unyielding. Yet with Bill this was never the case. He may not act on Bill's suggestions straight away, but having thought the issues through he would come back with agreement or other possible solutions. He was a deep thinker and Bill respected that in him. And so their friendship grew with mutual appreciation and love.

Another Congolese man with whom Bill became close friends was Sioli Gilbert, the other male nurse. Bill and Sioli worked together on the wards and around the hospital. If many of the Congolese were exuberant and outgoing by nature, Sioli was the reverse. He was extremely shy and got on with his work quietly and unobtrusively. Bill soon discovered that Sioli was an excellent nurse although he was still very young. However he needed encouragement as he always underestimated his capabilities and was genuinely humble about all he did. So Bill encouraged Sioli whenever he could and was rewarded with a loyal and devoted friendship and a happy working relationship where they nursed together as equals in the wards.

It was because of his deep personal involvement in the lives of those around him that Bill felt it all the more deeply if something occurred to upset these relationships. Nothing made him so low as when he felt he had done something to offend and one night Bill sat in his hut greatly upset. Earlier in the day he had arranged for two boys from the nearby village to come and do some odd jobs in his garden. Having agreed a price Bill had left them to it. On his return at the end of the day he found that the two boys had reneged on the deal and were demanding more money. Tired and frustrated, Bill had 'lost the head' and shouted at them, something he never allowed himself to do.

Sitting alone in his house that night he felt more and more ashamed. Even although he may have been justified in his anger, Bill felt he had let down his Lord. The only thing he could do was go and apologise. So he left the house at once and walked out of the compound and down the road to the boys' village. There, in front of the other villagers and the boys' families, Bill said he was sorry for his behaviour and asked them to forgive him.

Later Masini Phillipe heard of the trouble and he approached Bill. Bill was very embarrassed and began to apologise to the Head Pastor. But Masini stopped him.

'You have done something of which we are proud, Bwana William,' he said. 'Nobody in the village can believe that a white missionary has gone to apologise to two bad boys. In that one act you have done more than many sermons could to show the love and forgiveness of God.'

Perhaps it was this attitude of Bill's which endeared him to the Africans so much. He never considered himself better than them in any way. Instead he was continually impressed by the graciousness and patience of so many of his Congolese colleagues. And never did Bill consider himself to be in a position of authority over any of the national workers. His natural humility and personal diffidence would have made this alien to him. Instead dignified men like M'bongo or the hard-working Patrice Likali or quiet Sioli recognised in him one who would be a true friend, one who wanted to know them for who they were and not just as those who could be used in the pursuit of a greater cause.

Unfortunately this was not always the case and while Bill was there another young male missionary worked with Bill in the hospital. Although his credentials seemed right it soon became obvious that, unlike Bill, he seemed set on claiming a position of authority over his black co-workers and had no respect for their opinions or ways of working. Instead of trying to learn their ways he seemed bent on enforcing his own.

To Bill, who had spent months building strong bonds of

friendship on the station, this was very distressing: he felt he should support his fellow-missionary on the field, yet he was appalled by the way he referred to the Congolese and showed such disrespect for them. Bill felt torn both ways. Time and again he found himself talking his colleague out of trouble or explaining away his actions to the justly irate Africans. Bill even took the problem to Hector but it was hard to see what could be done.

However it was not long before the church in Bongondza under the pastorship of Masini Phillipe discovered what was going on and took the matter into its own hands. After only a short troublesome stay, Bill's colleague was sent home in disgrace.

But Bill too faced criticism. In seeking to defend him, Bill had jeopardised his own witness it seemed. He had almost let himself be dragged into the mess the other man had created. It was difficult to understand what he could have done differently but it impressed on Bill the responsibility he had to be thoroughly upright and uncompromising in all that he did.

It had been stressed to all missionaries in Congo that since Independence in particular in 1960, they were there only at the invitation of the national church. This meant that not only did the church have authority over their actions, but they were to act always as servants of the Congolese and not in a role of mastery over them. During the harsh decades of colonialism and centuries of slavery, Congo and its African neighbours had had enough of white rule and its selfish authority. Although this might not be the attitude of those in direct contact with the missionaries, it was an attitude which underpinned so much of the continuing unrest in the country.

For since 1960 there remained a strong nationalist undercurrent in the North East Province where Bongondza lay. Although this rarely impinged on their work, there was a growing awareness of the sporadic terrorist activities and of the affinity many Congolese felt with their nationalistic cause. As the terrorism was predominantly against whites and their 'collaborators', tensions rose throughout 1963 and missionaries were encouraged to contact each other more frequently by radio and to take care in their dealings with any unknown visitors. Travel became more awkward and many hesitated before setting off to Kisangani or elsewhere. Out on the road a lone car was much more susceptible to ambush or theft.

However, these threats seemed to come and go and did not impeach upon the work in Bongondza. It was an accepted part of life that political upheavals occurred, that crimes like looting and pilfering were common, that the rebel group named the Simbas who often carried out the crimes were troublesome and increasingly agitated, and that some Congolese viewed the whites in the country as intruders, even exploiters. So often had they heard all this that it seemed like old news.

Certainly Bill did not encounter any such animosity, even from those in authority. It became a bit of a long-running joke on the station that Bill was friendly with the local chief. Nobody knew how it had begun really but the Chief of the Baboa tribe, who had oversight over all his people in the area and who lived in relative luxury in Kole, ten miles away, picked Bill out as a friend and confidant. Bill was even made guest of honour at a Baboan tribal gathering. When Bill managed a few words in Baboa as he left the celebrations, his preferment was secured!

Known as 'Big John', the Chief kept a protective eye on his favourite missionary thereafter and although he never professed personally to believe what Bill and the others were teaching and living out in Bongondza, he put no obstacles in the way of the evangelisation of his people.

As Bill travelled around the surrounding villages with the medical work, he came across Big John regularly and if the Chief found him walking anywhere – for Bill had no transport – he would arrange for a car or truck to give him a lift. Once Big John heard that Bill was stranded several miles away, having missed one of the few buses which travelled the rough roads. Immediately, he

sent word across the jungle by tom-tom telling Hector to pick up
Bill in his truck!

Hector arrived with a wry grin on his face: 'What do you think
this is?' he teased. 'A taxi service?'

He only laughed at Bill's embarrassed pleas of, 'It wasn't me,
it was the Chief!'

From time to time the medical staff at Bongondza ventured
into the more distant regions of their district, taking medical
equipment and medicines. They were accompanied by an evangelist who would preach to the people also and they were often
gone for days at a time. Whenever Ian left on safari like this, Bill
would panic. What would they do without their doctor? What
would he do in an emergency?

Ian tried to train Bill as far as possible in various emergency
techniques before he left but it was still nerve-racking. On Ian's
first trip away since Bill's arrival, hardly had he left when a man
was carried into the hospital writhing in pain and in deep distress.
Even as Bill examined him he seemed to be slipping into
unconsciousness. Bill's brain was buzzing with all the possibili-
ties. 'Why now?' he thought and he prayed fervently as he
worked. Soon he diagnosed the problem – a strangulated hernia.
Many of the men spent their days in the forest hewing down the
enormous trees with only hand-held machetes: hernias were an
occupational hazard.

Quickly Bill carried out Ian's precise yet simple instructions:
'raise the bed end on blocks, ice pack on rupture, jag of
morphine'. It seemed too little, yet in this case and in every other
like it thereafter, it did the trick. Next morning the patient was
bright and cheerful – Bill could only breathe a sigh of relief and
a grateful prayer.

It was not long, however, before an opportunity came for Bill
to go on safari himself. Since his arrival in Bongondza, he had
wanted to venture into the dense forest which encircled them and
reach out to the tribes who lived in its mysterious and hidden

reaches. In particular he wanted to find the Bambotis, or pygmies, as they are otherwise known. Seldom had any missionary sought to find them, yet Bill knew that their needs were just the same as the rest of the people whom he came across every day. So, permission having been granted and a guide found, Bill gathered all the medical supplies he would be able to carry and prepared to set off on his expedition.

Bill's guide was a man named Ndimo Gaspar. He was a Congolese trader who not only dealt with the Bambotis but also knew their language. As Ndimo and Bill took those first steps into the Ituri Forest, Bill felt fear as well as excitement. It was so dark and densely forested that within ten yards of entering Bill felt quite disorientated and without his guide could be lost for life. He could barely see in front of him: there was no glimpse of sky or sun. The heat was intense too. Damp and steaming, Bill's shirt was quickly soaked with sweat.

From time to time as they trekked, Ndimo would point out some of the jungle animals to Bill. Panthers and leopards roamed the forest and sometimes in an occasional clearing they would spot mighty elephants or lofty giraffes. The trees too were full of animal and bird life: chimpanzees and baboons could be heard chattering and shrieking high above them; multi-coloured parrots and beautiful sunbirds sometimes burst into view. Bill gazed in wonderment and awe at all he saw. The rivers too he knew were full of life: pelicans and flamingos were there as well as the more threatening crocodiles and hippos. Those, he felt, he could happily keep at a distance.

Eventually, after several days of walking fifteen to twenty miles a day, they reached the Bamboti villages and Bill presented himself to the Chief. Bill felt like a giant next to this tiny man who only came up to his waist. And everything was of Lilliputian dimensions: when he was invited into his hut, Bill had to crawl on hands and knees and crouch uncomfortably inside. While Ndimo spoke on his behalf Bill watched the Chief's face. Unlike the

black-skinned Africans in Bongondza and the rest of Congo, the
Bambotis had pale, golden skin. The children and many of the
adults had never seen a white man before and ran away at the sight
of Bill. Yet many came creeping back, intrigued and inquisitive
as Bill was granted permission and set to work with his medical
kit. Kneeling on the ground Bill looked up from treating one man's
ulcerated leg to be confronted by a crowd of smiling brown faces,
peering down trying to examine what he was doing.

While Bill was there he saw many sick, as each day more and
more appeared out of the darkness of the forest. And as he did
more for them, the Bambotis responded, and asked Bill about
himself and the work he was doing. When he asked if he could
tell them about his faith large numbers gathered. Bill took his Bible
and spoke from the verse which so many years before had
grabbed his attention and turned his life on its head: 'For God so
loved the world that He gave His only Son that whoever believes
on Him will not die but have everlasting life.'

During his time there the Bambotis showed Bill their villages
and their hunting lands and gardens. The tribe were well known
for their hunting abilities and Bill was intrigued as to how such tiny
people could trap elephants and other great jungle animals. He
soon found that they were masters of ingenuity and trickery. They
showed Bill how they erected trip-wires and suspended enormous spears above in the trees which pierced the fallen animal.
Once the animal was caught they would spread the word through
the forest on the tam-tams and men from villages miles away
would come with their machetes and carve their joints which
would keep them fed for months. Proudly too the chief displayed
the enormous ivory tusks which were his prize from the kill.

But the Bambotis were horticulturists too, it seemed and Bill
was led to an enormous clearing which was planted with thousands of peanut plants. Awed by its vastness, Bill tried to convey
to the Chief through his interpreter that the field was as big as
Ibrox, the ground of his football team back in Glasgow! But

judging from the blank stares this was one thing which was perhaps just untranslatable!

They told Bill instead how they were often raided by baboons who would sweep down in numbers and decimate the peanut crop. ('Ah!' thought Bill, 'monkey nuts, of course.') To prevent this a woman would sit in the centre of the field as a guard and if the baboons approached she would cry out the 'baboon signal' and the men would encircle the baboons with nets, enticing them in by imitating the baboons distress call. When they were all in, the men would descend with spears and the raid was over.

Bill marvelled at the diversity of their lives despite their separation from all other men, so isolated here in the forest. He felt very humbled at how little he knew of them and their self-sufficient lifestyle. But he was saddened too by the sight of the magic shrines and charms which seemed to hold them in such fear. As he left he longed to do more and wondered when he might ever be able to return.

As Bill trekked through the forest other settlements and villages were reached, and time and again he was surrounded by a dark, dense atmosphere of evil. It felt like a tangible, deadly force which sent a chill through his body. Never was it stronger than when he met witchdoctors. Even to look at them was frightening: they wore head-dresses of animals skins and skulls and their bodies were adorned in sharp leopards' teeth and strips of skins. Fetishes in the shape of pieces of skins, bones and feathers were tied to limbs and hands and feet.

Yet it was the fearful look in their eyes which was most frightening. There was a blankness and darkness there which seemed to exude evil. If he had not felt the power of it himself Bill could never have believed it. Then, even if he was invited to speak, he could see nothing was getting through. It was like a dark cloud had descended, and faces remained blank and untouched. It was little wonder, he thought, that the people lived in such dread of these men.

37

Out Of The Jaws Of The Lion

It seemed that the witchdoctors were enjoying an increasingly active role in Congo due to their use by the left-wing Simba movement. Some of the would-be generals of these rebels consulted their witchdoctors about terrorist attacks and also enlisted their help in terrorising whole communities of young men to join their cause. Black magic too was involved as the Simbas wore animal skin fetishes to ward off death and in particular were told that these would protect them from the guns of the National Army – 'their bullets would be turned to water', they were assured if the charms were worn.

To those who had lived through the past years of Congo's rapid and far-reaching turn to Christianity it appeared that their country was reverting back to the superstition and terror of the old ways. Masini Phillipe's own father (and M'bongo's grandfather) had been a forest-dwelling Chief whose life had centred round the magic and cruelty as well as the cannibalism of the pagan life. That had all seemed part of the past, yet with the rhetoric and propaganda of the Simbas it seemed it was being revived. To hear the Simbas proclaim that they would feast on the meat of their white enemies brought back to many the fear and darkness which had been until recently a part of their daily family lives.

Yet life went on as normal in Bongondza. The waiting list for surgery was as long as ever with Ian operating as much as he could. And the cases were seldom straightforward. Only recently Bill had assisted Ian as he removed an enormous cyst from a women's abdomen: it weighed no less than forty-five pounds!

Also a large scale vaccination programme was initiated. It took up much of their time with an endeavour to prevent the ravages caused in particular by smallpox. It was a huge undertaking, not to mention a noisy one with hundreds of screaming babies and children protesting violently against the injections. But on top of all the usual work it made the hospital very busy.

In addition, Bongondza was due to hold the UFM Conference for all the missionaries that year, 1964. This meant that the station would play host to those from all over the North-East Province, representing almost a dozen stations and about fifty missionaries and their families. Where to house everyone was a huge headache in itself.

But the annual conferences were always greatly enjoyed by everyone. It was the only time that they could gather together as a group and hear how the work was going in other areas. There was always lots of teaching and encouragement, lots of singing and lots of eating, as well as a chance to let their hair down a bit and enjoy each other's company.

There was talk of the rebels causing a problem with so much travelling involved and some were concerned about gathering all together in one place. Yet none felt troubled enough that they would feel they must stay away.

When it came at the end of June the conference was a great success. While the conference was going on, Bill became friendly with the McAllister family who worked south of Kisangani in Ponthierville. They were an Irish couple who with their three children enlivened any gathering and Bill loved their enthusiasm and fun. As Bill was due some time off, he readily agreed when the McAllisters invited him down to Ponthierville after the conference was over.

It was while he was in Ponthierville that the news came from home. Al Larson sent an urgent radio message to Bill. A telegram had just arrived for him. His mother was gravely ill: he must return home at once.

There was no time to return to Bongondza. Bob McAllister offered to take him up to Kisangani to get a flight home. So they bundled a few things in the Land Rover and set off.

Getting a plane out of Africa at the best of times was always a slow and tortuous process As Bill presented himself at the airport, he knew it could be difficult. And when he enquired about a flight to Glasgow, they looked at him as if he was asking to go to the moon! But a flight to Kinshasa was offered and that was a start so Bill said some hurried goodbyes to his hosts and those at Kilometre 8, and set off.

It was only then that Bill could start to think about his mother. For some time now he had been worried about her as she had stopped replying to his letters. Although Bill wrote to the others in the family, none had maintained contact, so he had received no information at all. Now it seemed that she was dying. He did not know if he would be in time to see her.

Bill's mind filled with images of her: his mother in her apron at the sink, her sleeves rolled up past her elbows; or coming in from work at Beatties, tired and drawn; her quick laugh at some neighbour's chat; or sitting by the fire, darning or listening to the radio with Bill and his brothers and sisters, sitting around at her feet; then the small, darkly-dressed figure at the time of his father's death; the bruised and battered face after Spendley's violence; and the dear, anxious face as his train pulled away taking him off to Africa.

She had had a lot with which to contend in her life. As a child she had been brought up in a violent home with a drunken father. When she had 'given' her eldest daughter, Ellen, to her mother to help her and protect her from Bill's grandfather, it had almost broken her heart, seeing her daughter returning to the home in which she had been so frightened and threatened herself.

The years with Bill's father now seemed like a merciful interlude in her life. Money had always been tight yet, especially when Kenneth Gilvear became involved in the Tent Hall, it became so unimportant somehow, and Bill's memories of those days were of times gathered as a family, his mother and father united in their care and love for their children and all learning together of God's love for them.

But the dark years with Spendley followed, along with the family's disintegration. Now they hardly talked to each other. His mother's cries of despair to her daughters, Bill knew, had gone unanswered. He could hardly bear to think of the stark and blank face of his mother when she returned from delivering Spendley's baby, her arms empty: the baby boy had been given away.

Sitting alone on the plane, Bill wept for her: for her loneliness and despair, her fight to survive and her pain.

His tears too were for her spiritual decline. Bill knew she was what some called a backslider: she had stopped reading the Bible, stopped praying, stopped all contact with Christian things. Where was she now, now that it seemed her life was nearly over? There and then, somewhere over central Africa, Bill prayed for her as perhaps he had never done before. 'Cast your cares on me, for I care for you', his Lord promised, so Bill poured out his worries to God.

'Lord, in case I don't get back in time for my mother, will you send someone to her. Let them tell her that although her love for you may have changed, your love for her will never change.' And even as he mouthed these words, Bill's heart washed over with a supernatural peace and he sat back in his airline seat, the dark cloud of anxiety gone.

At Kinshasa, Bill was given a flight home in circumstances little short of miraculous. Having waited all day, hoping for a cancellation on the night-time flight and pleading his case with the airport staff, Bill was told that there were no empty seats. As he began to argue in his best Gallowgate French that he must get home somehow, and quickly, the pilot of the plane came up to collect his papers. Overhearing Bill, he interrupted him, and signalled him through to the plane; he would get Bill on his flight.

Before he had time to think, Bill found himself sitting not only on the plane, but in a spacious first class compartment which he

would have all to himself! He even had his own personal air
hostess – and all on an economy ticket! It appeared that at the very
last minute an Ambassador had cancelled his flight out of
Kinshasa, so Bill – an ambassador of the King of Kings, he smiled
to himself – was given his seat. And he was home in twenty-four
hours.

Yet he was still too late. To Bill's dismay and grief he found
that his mother had died a week before: even the funeral was over.

Bill did not know what to do. He visited his family but there
was little they could tell him. She had died in the Infirmary. She
had been unwell for some time.

Spendley, Bill discovered, had died the year before. Now his
youngest brother, Jim was married and living in the Dennistoun
house. The others in the family urged Bill to turn them out and live
there himself, but Bill refused. So now he did not even have a roof
over his head.

As he walked down to the UFM offices in St Vincent Street,
he was feeling very dejected and very alone. He had not seen his
mother. He did not know how she had died. He could not even
attend her funeral. And now he was homeless too. He had no idea
what to do.

But as he walked along a familiar voice called out his name.
It was a nursing friend named Betsy Fraser. She was the
missionary secretary of the Nurses Christian Fellowship which
had meant so much to Bill during his Glasgow days working in
hospital. When Betsy heard of Bill's troubles she invited him up
to her office nearby. There she told him of a meeting she had had
with Bill's mother some time before. To his amazement, Betsy
said that she had felt that she was being told to seek out Bill's
mother. She had visited her and read the Bible with her from the
book of Hosea and they had prayed together. Betsy told Bill that
they had discussed her backsliding and her need for God. With
her hand on Bill's shoulder, Betsy was able to assure him with all
certainty: 'You need have no fears, son. Your mother was ready.'

Later Bill spoke at a meeting of the NCF and afterwards two nurses came up to him. Out of all the nine hundred nurses in the Glasgow Royal Infirmary, one of these girls had been the staff nurse on Lily Gilvear's ward and the other had been the very nurse who had sat with her holding her hand as she had died. 'I watched her pass into the presence of the King of Kings,' she told a weeping Bill. He could hardly believe God's mercy. Here God had provided his servants as substitutes for himself to be with his mother when he could not. And God had drawn her back to Himself when it had all seemed so hopeless. God had asked a lot of him and Bill had given his life, his career, his family. Yet in return he had been given much more.

Soon after this Bill was offered somewhere to stay with an older Christian lady in Glasgow. Mrs Briggs offered him a room in her house and this became his home. For there seemed no likelihood of Bill's return to Congo: as soon as he was back in Scotland, word began to filter through of trouble in Congo. Suddenly it was headline news.

Rebellion had broken out. Kisangani was overrun. The North-East Province was under attack. Bloody reprisals against whites and those who had 'collaborated' with them were carried out. The Simbas were disposing of all who came in their way. All whites were under house arrest, or imprisoned. Words like 'torture' and 'massacre' filled the news reports.

Bill could not believe his ears! This was the country he had left only days before. What about the loved ones he had left behind? Where were they? Were they in trouble? Were they suffering? Were they even still alive?

Desperate for news, Bill flooded the UFM London Offices with telephone calls, begging for information. At first it was sketchy and unsubstantiated: the country was at war and it was hard to get any accurate news. But eventually he heard that those at Bongondza were imprisoned elsewhere, possibly Banalia, and that the station itself had been destroyed. Many had not survived the Simbas' onslaught. Other stations had suffered the same fate.

Some missionaries were safe although effectively held hostage in Kilometre 8, including the McAllisters who had been unable to return to Ponthierville after taking Bill to catch his plane. Almost as soon as they had left Ponthierville to drive to Kisangani with Bill the Simbas had descended on the station and it had been destroyed, the people killed or imprisoned. It seemed that the timing of his mother's death had done something: it had taken both Bill himself and the McAllisters out of the path of the massacring Simbas; she had saved their lives.

And still there was no certainty about those from Bongondza. The rumours abounded. The MacMillans were in Kisangani with their boys at the UFM house, but what of the Sharpes and Ruby Gray? Where had they been taken? And what of those Africans left behind?

Bill was dazed and shocked. It just did not make sense. He could not understand what was going on. As the days and weeks dragged on without news he felt so useless. With every hour he wondered what his friends might be doing, and where the children might be. Were they all in jail? Did they have food? To hear some of the reports of the barbarism and viciousness of the Simbas' conquests, he sometimes wished that they may all be dead already and out of the suffering.

Finally, throughout November it seemed that the international community was about to intervene and lightening raids were orchestrated by UN Forces. Quickly they flushed the Simbas northwards. It seemed the rebels were in retreat.

But just as the news began to improve, Bill's fragile hopes were dashed. First, in their final hours in Kisangani, the rebels descended on Kilometre 8. Hector was shot and killed.

Then, in their frantic flight, the rebels had ordered the massacre of remaining hostages held at various sites in the north. Banalia was one of those sites. When the rescuing forces arrived in Banalia in early December they made a gruesome discovery.

Down by the river they found some clothes and various personal effects of Ian and Audrey and the children, of Ruby Gray, and of three other UFM missionaries, Mary Baker, Dennis and Nora Parry and two of their children. Without doubt all had been butchered there at the ferry landing point and their bodies thrown into the crocodile-infested river.

On hearing the news, Bill was inconsolable. For so long he had waited, had hoped, had prayed. And this was the result. In Bongondza he had considered the missionaries to be his family: Hector who had shown him so much and achieved so much for the Lord; Ruby who had been out in Congo for only two years and had shown how capable she was; and Ian and Audrey – Bill could hardly bear to think of them – his dear brother and sister who had opened their hearts and their home to him. Never had he had closer and dearer friends. And the children – Jillian, Alison, Andrew. His heart could hold no more and the pain of it all was breaking him apart.

There seemed nobody to whom Bill could turn in his distress. Friends in Glasgow tried to help but there seemed no-one who could be with him in his sorrow and grief. He felt shattered and broken and there was no-one to help.

And all the time he was praying. 'Why, Lord? Why Hector? Why leave Iona alone and six boys fatherless? And why Ian – who was a much better man than me, a man who was so able, who did nothing but good? Lord, why not me?'

Time and again, Bill demanded of God reasons for the massacre and why he had been saved. He could not fathom it himself and would gladly have changed places with any of them. Especially as a bachelor with no family ties and no-one to leave behind, why was he the only one left? It left him angry and distressed. Why? Why? He seemed to be raging into a silent, empty void.

The anger and questioning left him exhausted. And they seemed so pointless. He could not understand. And yet if he was left behind, if he had been spared, was there a reason for this? It was a question he was afraid almost to ask. But the only answer he received repeatedly was a simple yet frightening one: God must still have things for him to do.

38

Padre

Bill's first responsibilities in those terrible days were to the families of those who had been killed and to UFM to represent them at the various memorial services which were to be held. Several different missionary societies had worked in Congo, yet none had suffered as many deaths and seen so many martyred as UFM. When the rebellion broke out, sixty-seven UFM missionaries and their children had been trapped in the country: of those, nineteen were killed.

The hardest part for Bill was meeting the parents. He travelled to Ireland to be with Mr and Mrs Gray. But when it came to talking with them and comforting them there was little he could do. Ruby's mother was inconsolable and Bill just wept with them in their grief.

One of the largest memorial services was held in London and it was also the occasion of UFM's Jubilee. Bill went south to speak as a witness to those martyred and when he arrived he was shocked to discover that the main preacher was a Rev. Sharpe: Ian's own father was to give the main address.

From Bill's first meeting with the Sharpes they took him to their hearts and at last Bill felt there was someone with whom he could share his grief, someone who could help him to deal with the guilt he felt at still being alive and the distress and confusion he could not escape. Soon the Sharpes had insisted that he call them 'Mum' and 'Dad'. It filled a void probably for all of them at that time, and he spent many happy hours with them at their home.

At the memorial service Bill was amazed at Ian's father's composure and victorious message. He spoke from the Book of

Hebrews in the Bible about the things which 'cannot be shaken' and the things which 'remain' even after disaster and death: God's Word, our faith and the church. Bill knew he was next to speak and he felt as weak as water. He could hardly stand so drained and full of emotion did he feel. Yet if this elderly man who had loved his family so much, who had doted on his grandchildren, could speak with such assurance of faith, Bill was strengthened to do the same. A verse came into his mind: 'as your days so shall your strength be' and he stood up to speak. He spoke of those of whom 'the world was not worthy' (Hebrews 11:38) and then Dad Sharpe called on Bill to sing with him. Terrified and so aware of his lack of singing ability, Bill shook where he stood in front of the huge London congregation. But they sang of Jesus' return – of 'some golden daybreak' and they could all sense the presence of God there in that place.

Almost as soon as news of the massacres had broken, Bill was begging the UFM leaders in London to let him return. Every news bulletin told of the devastation in the area and Bill could only imagine the desperate situation of the Congolese people, especially those dear to him. He pleaded with Headquarters time and time again but the answer was always 'no'. It was too dangerous, the Simbas were still active and controlled large areas in the north and east in particular. There was no access to the area and no travel within it.

Finally, after months of his appeals, the London office summoned him with a proposal. There was a joint missionary endeavour being arranged to send aid and supplies to Congo and someone was needed to lead it: was Bill interested? He did not have to be asked twice and in September 1965, just over a year since he had left Congo in such different circumstances, he returned as the Congo Protestant Relief Officer for the whole of the North- East Province.

Based in Kisangani, Bill saw first-hand the devastation that had been brought upon the city. Although the buildings and houses were damaged and many riddled with bullet holes and damaged by grenades, it was the personal destruction that was so distressing. More than two thousand Congolese had been murdered in Kisangani alone by the Simbas, usually in front of the large monument to their early leader, Patrice Lumumba. Many had been civic leaders and any whom the rebels considered to have collaborated with the white imperialists. Tales abounded of the terrible tortures inflicted there: men dismembered while still alive; others whose hearts and organs were eaten by their killers. Even after heavy rains and many months the steps of the monument remained stained with blood.

But the murderous rampage out in the countryside had been even worse, they were told. Bill was given a five ton truck by the charity Oxfam and he began delivering supplies all over the northeast. He carried food and medicines and clothing predominantly which had been donated abroad. These were sent by river, up from Kinshasa. Having collected it, Bill and his driver, Nestor, would distribute it where they could.

But the roads were in a terrible condition. No maintenance had been done during the rebellion and they were heavily rutted and disintegrating in places. Tree roots and vines were reclaiming them into the encroaching forest. On top of this, various groups of armed Simbas were hiding in the forest, even in places which where supposedly safe and they would lie in wait for passing vehicles to ambush them. A large truck – with a white man in the cab – was a prize indeed. Because of this the Relief Agency demanded that Bill be accompanied by an armed escort. This was made up of mercenaries from various countries who had aided in the UN liberation at the end of '64 and who remained in the country, completing the task. They had a new name for Bill – 'Padre'. It was the source of some amusement to Bill, especially having been brought up as a Protestant in a sectarian city like Glasgow!

Although he had been warned of the destruction the Simbas

had inflicted, Bill was unprepared for the degree of human suffering that he met when he arrived finally at the outlying stations. Everyone was reduced to utter poverty as all possessions, money, food and even their clothes had been taken. These survivors had nothing, hundreds were ill, all were malnourished with the tell-tale bloated stomachs and spindle legs, even their strong black hair was whitened and discoloured through lack of food and illness. Many had been forced to resort to wearing clothes from the forest: men in beaten-bark loin cloths, the women in grass skirts. Many more were naked.

And disease was rampant. There were skin infections, eye disorders, tuberculosis, malaria and weeping sores. Many suffered from old wounds caused by the beatings and torture inflicted by the rebels. As Bill watched in horror he saw that his supplies were like a drop in the ocean compared with their needs. The hungry, the sick, the homeless, the refugees were coming not just in their hundreds but in their thousands. Yet he knew he must do what he could do: to become overwhelmed by the great need would be worse than useless, so he worked tirelessly, giving out the food and clothing, seeking out those whose need for medicine was the greatest and treating those whom he was able to help.

As Bill did so the tales of those months of terror unfolded. Many had stories of amazing release from the hands of those who were only too ready to take their lives. He met those who had been left for dead but who had received help from others nearby. There were some who had endured months of imprisonment in filthy conditions for no recognisable crime. They had endured beatings, lashings, rape and the cruellest torture.

And those who had escaped capture had lived from hand to mouth in rough shacks in the dense forest. Slowly starving, they had endured the constant threat of seizure as any betrayal of their whereabouts or discovery by the marauding, uncontrolled bands of rebels would mean probable death. It was a crippling state of fear in which to survive.

Bill was aware too that these were only the survivors. If their suffering was great, how much more had been that of those who had not lived through it all, who had been beaten beyond what they could stand, for whom torture had gone too far, who had been subjected to the machete before the gun as an additional agony, who had starved painfully in their shacks in the depths of the forest?

For someone who had not gone through it and had been able to enjoy the good things of home in recent months, Bill could only weep with these courageous people for whom there was no reprieve and for whom there was no other home. He was deeply humbled time and again by the forgiveness extended by these Christian men and women to their persecutors and often to their betrayers, whose lives had been up-ended because of their faith and because of their association with the missionaries. Outside of Christ there was no way of believing such remarkable love.

When Bill arrived in Bodela, the former station of the Parrys who had died in Banalia, he encountered just this kind of love. Driving in with his relief supplies for the first time, he found the whole of the compound had been razed to the ground. Nothing remained and it was deserted. All the people who remained were in hiding in the forest. Slowly, however, after hours and even days, word was passed somehow that help had arrived and those who survived appeared. And when they came, Bill saw the same sickening sight: they were dressed in rags, they were sick, they were in acute distress and in need of food and medical care. Yet Bill could only gaze transfixed at their faces: they just glowed with love and thankfulness. And there was no great rush to the lorry to claim their share. To Bill's amazement, one and all bowed down as a group.

'We just want to bow down and thank the Lord,' they said and after that they raised their voices in a Lingala hymn. It was incredible to watch. The mercenaries with Bill were almost open-mouthed with shock.

'Padre, what are they doing?' the soldiers demanded. 'We have never seen anything like this before!'

'How can you still rejoice?' asked Bill. 'Why are you happy? Your missionary has died, his wife, his two children have been murdered, you have lost your homes, everything is burned, you have nothing?'

'We will tell you,' one of the church leaders replied, and he told Bill their secret. Before his arrest, Dennis Parry had called the church together and had warned them of what was to come to them. He had likened it to the bloodshed and martyrdom of the Scottish Reformation when many Christians were tortured and killed for their faith. And he had encouraged them to remember to 'be steadfast, unmoveable, always abounding in the work of the Lord, for as much as you know that your labour is not in vain in the Lord' (1 Corinthians 15:58, AV). 'Bwana William,' he added, 'We are looking only to Jesus. We have written these words in our hearts and we believe them.'

Bill was anxious to reach his own station as soon as possible after his return but Bongondza was still in the tight grip of the Simba forces. Many in the area had given their support to the rebels' nationalistic cause and although this had all gone wrong, there were many who maintained their allegiance to it. It was unsafe therefore to approach the area.

Bill, however, had plenty to do with the constant collection, storage and distribution of supplies. He worked for many missionary organisations including the Worldwide Evangelisation Crusade. One of their doctors, Helen Roseveare, had returned to Congo some months after Bill and she was one of the few doctors working in the huge North-East area, serving some two and a half million Congolese, all of whom seemed to be in desperate need.

Yet when Bill visited her station in Nebobongo, he found this small woman undaunted by the challenge of it. Instead she was a woman of indomitable spirit and energy, putting strong men to shame with her determination to provide the very best care she could for her beloved Africans. While he was there, Dr Roseveare showed Bill round the site with its various projects. She deplored the lack of resources – no nurses, no teachers, few beds or blankets, little equipment, no blackboards or chalk for their school, and, of course, barely enough food to survive. Yet she was not one to do nothing about it and would not lie down under the overwhelming demands on her and the tremendous odds against her success. And this was a woman who had gone through the rebellion, on whom the Congolese had inflicted much suffering, great pain and extreme distress.

When Bill arrived at the station of Banjwadi where he had spent those early weeks of language training, it was underlined to Bill the evil which the Simbas had been determined to perpetrate throughout the country. It seemed they were intoxicated by the desire for blood. For there he met his old friends, Badi and Jacques, the two wise and kindly evangelists who had encouraged and helped Bill so much in his early difficulties. Both men had been cruelly tortured. The Simbas had come looking for the two men to be chaplains in their rebel army. Thinking that this might offer an opportunity to share their faith in God with the rebels, both Badi and Jacques had gone, each taken to different parts of the province. Yet immediately both were instructed to pray in the name of Patrice Lumumba before the soldiers.

'Not Lumumba – Jesus,' each had demanded.

For this refusal they were tortured. Jacques had tried to read the Bible to the soldiers with whom he had been placed, but it was thrown in his face and both his hands were slashed with a knife. Then they beat him across his back till he could hardly speak or move. Yet when he refused still to comply, Jacques was tied to a tree and a poisoned arrow was thrust into his side. These were the poisonous weapons used by the Bambotis and were unstoppable killers. So the Simbas left him to his rapid, inevitable death.

Yet as soon as he became conscious, Jacques prayed. He had worked for God in Congo for more than twenty years. Now he asked for healing, promising the Lord another twenty years if he was spared. Then with all his strength, Jacques took the arrow and pulled it from his side. He knew he should be dead already, yet the poison never took its deadly effect.

Elsewhere, Badi was suffering for the same refusal to deny his God. When he would not pray in Lumumba's name they put him in the 'command', a torture whereby the hands and feet are tied together, arching the back, and then he was beaten. When he was released, Badi still refused and the Simba captain became irate. He shouted at Badi, 'Do you not hear me?' and pulling out his knife he cut off Badi's right ear.

With blood running down his face, the evangelist still stood firm. Then the captain ordered his men to tie Badi to a chair, hand and foot. Under the chair they built a fire and thrust Badi in it.

'I felt like the three friends of Daniel,' related Badi to Bill. 'I was in the fire but I did not feel the pain I should have done. Instead I felt a power and a presence there beside me. I was not alone.'

Finally, Badi was saved when the Simbas ran away and a young boy from the Banjwadi church who had been hiding across the river came and rescued him, putting out the fire and bathing his wounds.

Bill looked down at his two dear friends with tears in his eyes. There were Jacques scored hands and the great scar in his side from the arrow; there was Badi's mutilated ear and his horribly scarred feet. And then he looked at the smiles on their faces.

'We have been counted worthy to share in our Lord's sufferings,' they said.

'And in heaven you will have scars in common with our Lord Jesus to prove it,' added Bill.

39

Reunions

The more Bill visited the stations of the North-East, the more eager he became to return to Bongondza. Yet it seemed it was to remain closed. Rebel fighting continued to go on and although Bill was often only a few miles from the fighting and the enemy lines, he could go no further. Journeys remained treacherous with road-blocks and ambushes common.

Sometimes the only way through these roadblocks was to smash their way through for to stop meant immediate death. The first time this happened, Bill's driver, Nestor, was given no choice. As they drove up the bumpy roads north of Kisangani, a manned roadblock came into view. Suddenly Nestor faced Bill with a look of panic: 'The brakes, Bwana William. I have no brakes!'

Frantically the driver pumped the pedals but to no avail: they were gaining speed. And then the barrage of bullets began. Hidden by the thick vegetation on the side of the road, the Simbas were raining bullets down on them. Nestor and Bill ducked as the truck careered onwards. Gunfire – shots – the rat-tat-tat-tat of auto-matic weapons – filled the air. The doors, the windscreen, the roof – all were torn open by the flying bullets. The makeshift barrier of wood and wire and tree trunks came rushing up. The truck would not stop. They would not stop even if they could. Crash! And with a shuddering jolt they were through! They did not stop – indeed could not – until they reached the next station down the road.

Some months after his return, Bill was able to reach the town of Kole, ten miles distant from Bongondza. Although there were refugees and needy people everywhere, Bill's main reason for going to Kole was that he had heard that his friend, M'bongo, and

his father, Masini Philippe, were both there. Having endured long
and repeated imprisonment, both had retreated into the forest,
finally coming out to this liberated town.

Bill's reunion with both these men was highly emotional, full
of grief as well as joy. Bill had not expected to see either of them
alive again and certainly they had never anticipated seeing another
missionary in the whole of Congo, far less Bill from their own
station. Bill and M'bongo could only hug each other and hold one
another as tears poured down their faces.

M'bongo had received terrible treatment at the hands of the
Simbas. Imprisoned time and again he had been sentenced to
death twice, yet had somehow been freed. On his body he bore
the brutal marks of repeated beatings and torture: his back was
so deeply bruised from kickings, whippings and various assaults
that it would never heal; one of his eyes was so badly damaged
from beatings about the head that his sight was badly affected.
And he was very thin after months in hiding, moving constantly
to avoid capture. Similarly, Masini had suffered. Indeed father
and son had been held together on more than one occasion and
had witnessed each other's torture.

But it was what they told him of Banalia and their days there
that sickened Bill the most. Masini had insisted on being taken with
the missionaries into prison there although he was later freed. But
M'bongo who was detained there too had remained imprisoned.
They told him of the tension of those days: the Simbas blood-
thirsty and vengeful, trigger-happy and looking for reasons to
shed blood. Alone in his cell, M'bongo had seen the missionaries
filing past to their deaths at the riverbank. Ian Sharpe had even
been hauled out of their hospital where he had been trying to save
the life of a young Simba. And then M'bongo had heard the distant
shots. Finally, M'bongo had been taken to die at the same spot
as the missionaries, the day after their deaths. As he had stood
at the ferry point, all the other prisoners standing in the row with
him were shot or speared to death, their bodies thrown into the

river: only M'bongo remained. Uncannily, at the last moment, the Simba captain refused to kill him and he was sent away, the only one to survive the huge Banalia massacre.

Yet M'bongo could not be relieved, for standing waiting to die, he had seen the ghastly sight of the discarded bodies of his beloved missionaries and their children, lying by the side of the river only feet away from him. Filled with horror, he had stumbled away in shock from the scene. He had been given his freedom so miraculously, yet with such bitter visions before his eyes that he could scarcely make his escape.

If Bill had wondered why he had escaped death in Congo, M'bongo had greater reason, so dramatic was his reprieve. Yet Bill was so humbled by M'bongo's reaction and by that of his father. M'bongo had already decided to leave teaching and train as a pastor like his father. Masini himself showed the ultimate graciousness, forgiving the man who had betrayed him to the Simbas and stirred up so much unrest in their area. Even at risk to himself, Masini had refused to signal this man out to the authorities when his treachery was exposed. Never had Bill known such a powerful outworking of God's message of forgiveness and love.

Bill wished that he could be so merciful, yet when he came to visit Banalia himself it was so hard to be forgiving. It was so much easier to let his old gang-boy nature rear up and think of revenge: 'if only I could get my hands on those who did this!' Yet this was not God's way, he knew, and when it transpired that the Simbas who had carried out the Banalia atrocities were imprisoned there, Bill knew God was speaking to him. He must go to these men and tell them, show them that God's way was different and was available to them.

It was something which was so hard. Bill battled within himself and begged God for strength and sincerity in speaking to these men. For it required God's grace to forgive these men: on his own, Bill knew he would much rather see them killed too.

So Bill went into the prison and confronted these men. There were sixty of them and they eyed Bill suspiciously. Looking into their hardened, fierce faces, Bill felt terribly scared. These men were vicious, they were killers, he was their enemy, they hated him and all he stood for, what was he doing here? They knew too that Bill was aware that they were the ones who had killed his friends and colleagues. He was in a position of power over them and they were terrified of what he could do. The atmosphere was heavily charged with animosity and fear.

Yet Bill was amazed to feel that he was filled to overflowing with love for these men, so much so that there was no room for hate, no room for revenge. Instead, he told them of Jesus, of God's punishment, of forgiveness and cleansing for all they had done.

Leaving some booklets with them Bill gave them one last opportunity. 'Listen,' he demanded. 'Don't turn to Jesus now because you are frightened of me or of what will happen to you. If you really mean business with God, then ask the prison officer and he will let you come and speak with me. I will be waiting for you.' And with that he left them. Never had Bill felt so certain of God's ability to override his own natural instincts and carry him through what was a harrowing experience.

The following day, Bill led a memorial service down at the ferry landing point where the massacres had taken place. It was a desperately difficult time and Bill did not know how he would be able to say a word. Indeed the Congolese pastor who should have spoken became too choked with emotion to say anything. Yet again, Bill felt as if someone else was keeping him going. He could only believe that God was keeping His promise that He would be his strength in time of need. He remembered too Hector's advice to be 'Ready For Anything' and he always carried his Bible and hymnbook with him wherever he went, so he took them out of his pocket now and carried on.

As he concluded the service, Bill prayed fervently: 'Lord, give us one soul here for each one who died here – all eleven, Lord, including the children. Let there be eleven who turn to you out of the horror of what has happened here.'

That night as he sat on the verandah of the house where he was staying, Bill received some visitors. It was some of the Simbas from the prison. They had not slept. They had taken to heart what Bill had said in the jail with them.

'Our consciences have been bothering us,' they said. 'We want to get right with God. Show us how Jesus can forgive us, Bwana William.'

Until late into the night, Bill spoke with these hard-hearted men and he saw before his eyes their faces, their hearts and lives being changed. If he had not seen it himself he would scarcely have believed it: there were eleven Simbas who sought God and received forgiveness that night – one for each of those killed, just as Bill had asked.

It was not until March of the following year that Bill was able to reach Bongondza as the Simbas retreated from the area. Bill, in his urgency to be there, was the first civilian to venture in and as usual he was heavily escorted. The mercenaries fired their guns into the air as they entered to frighten off any lingering rebels. Yet they seemed to have frightened everyone away for when Bill stepped out of the truck there was no-one to be seen.

The whole compound was quiet and deserted. He began to wander round in the eerie stillness. There was the MacMillans' house. It was an empty shell: everything had been taken. Windows were smashed, walls were pock-marked with bulletholes. The workshop next door was smashed to pieces. Bill could see the remains of the workbenches and the place on the wall where Hector had kept his tools and list of tasks to be done.

Next to this should have been Bill's house. But there was nothing there at all. Nothing remained: it had been burned to the ground. When he had left for Ponthierville he had taken only clothes and toiletries. Now he brushed his feet through the charred remains of what represented more than two years of his life.

The other houses, although most remained standing, had fared little better. In Ruby Gray's the only thing that remained – the only thing not considered to be of value, perhaps – was a plaque which was on the wall. It read, 'I will not fear. I will only trust in the Lord.'

And the hospital was empty. Every bit of equipment, every bed, every blanket had been stolen. Bill wandered through the dusty, desolate rooms, trying to recall their busyness, almost seeing before him the scores of patients, the bustle of activity in the wards, the verandah swarming with people, the little theatre with Ian and Audrey stooping over a patient, their heads together.

Finally Bill came to the church. It had always seemed large and imposing, a central focus for the community there. Now it stood empty, devoid of any of the seating, the paint flaking. Yet high on the wall was the text just as Alice Kinso had painted it so many years ago: 'Peace, be still and know that I am God.'

Bill felt he had found Congo on his return not unlike how it must have been when the Kinsos arrived first in 1920. The people were ragged and frightened to leave the jungle. Starvation was everywhere. Old tribal superstitions and enmities had been reawakened. Everywhere Bill went there was fear and the evil which had swept through the country had destroyed so much. Could it ever be washed away and a fresh start made? This big, empty church seemed to typify how alien Christian things seemed to be in this setting.

As if to shake this melancholy from him and to break free from the deadly silence of the place, Bill reached for the church bell and began to ring it vigorously. If the gunshots had chased away anyone who remained at Bongondza, surely this would bring them back. And he pulled and pulled.

He did not have to wait long and the first figure to appear was a familiar one. It was Patrice Likali, the hospital evangelist. He and his wife embraced Bill incredulously.

'We feel like the disciples seeing Jesus after his resurrection,'

Patrice exclaimed. 'Never did we expect to see a white face again and now we have you here, Bwana William!'

Witnessing such joy in the face of their great distress was so humbling yet more was to come. Patrice was particularly over-joyed to see Bill because he had something for him.

'You have something for me?' Bill could not believe it. He had just been hearing how Patrice had lost everything – the little shop with which he had supported himself and his family, the few chickens he kept and his goats, even the clothes from his back and the house where he lived. Everything had been taken away. Yet he had something for Bill?

Patrice led Bill into the forest and under a great tree he began to dig. From a foot or two under the soil, he pulled out a package. It was wrapped in two large banana leaves and looked as if it had been there for a long time. But when Patrice opened the makeshift parcel, its content was entirely intact: it was Bill's Diploma in Tropical Medicine which he had gained at such cost to himself in Belgium. It had hung on Bill's wall in his hut and this dear man had risked his life to snatch it away from the thieving and destroying Simbas and he had saved it for Bill should he ever return.

So moved was Bill that he could barely thank him. He could hardly look at this gift, thinking of all that so many had lost and so many had given up. Yet if there had been one thing which he would have wanted to save it was this precious Diploma and he could only weep at the love shown to him in the saving of it in this way.

Soon the word was sent out into the forest by tom-tom-drum that Bill had returned and scores of people came pouring out of their jungle refuges to see him. The sight of deprivation was as great as ever, if not more so, for these people had been in hiding for so long. Many familiar faces were missing and Bill heard how many had been taken away, had been killed, had not survived the traumas of the incarceration in the forest. Quickly, Bill set about distributing the supplies from the truck and examining those who needed medical aid.

Yet the welcome he received was overwhelming. Over one thousand of the Baboa tribe of that area were gathered there before him and Bill was moved to see how much his return meant to them. Seeing their shining faces, many wet with tears, many clasping and clinging to his hands as if to keep him there always, made all the trauma of the months since his return worthwhile.

40

Time in God's Hands

On top of the terrible sights of destruction and deprivation, and the constant work pressure to collect and distribute the aid as speedily as possible, Bill was in danger often. He travelled hundreds of miles by plane, truck and jeep on behalf of the several charities he represented, yet the war raged still in many places. It was the middle of 1966 and rebel ambushes and regionally-based revolts were common. The enemy lines were moving erratically and there was news continually of more deaths. It was soon after Bill's return visit to Bongondza that a new offensive was launched in the north-east. Kisangani was a main focus for this fighting and all the missionaries who like Bill were based in Kisangani were gathered together into one of the central hotels for their safety.

As gunfire and explosions filled the city night, Bill sought his bed in his top floor room. There would be no peace tonight but he thought he might as well try to sleep. Yet as he climbed into his bed, Bill felt compelled to move his bed nearer to the side of the room for safety. He did not understand it but obeyed the strange impulse. Less than a minute later as he lay down, a flurry of shots came crashing through his window! They struck the wall at the exact spot where his head would have been had he not moved his bed! Bill was left breathless. Had his life been spared again? Why was he being so carefully protected? Almost falling out of bed with shock, he knelt by his bed and poured out his wonder and thanks to God.

Within two days it was deemed wise to evacuate south to the capital, Kinshasa, away from the fighting. For three months, the north was gripped by uprisings and reprisals and Bill was forced to stay away. He spent his time serving the refugees in the Kivu

Province where many were returning to their villages for the first time in two years. The appalling deprivation was a mirror of that in the north: daily Bill saw children and adults dying from malnutrition, anaemia and disease. It was a sickening sight and the magnitude of the problem was disheartening. This was a situation that would not go away quickly: it would take years to recover from all that had been suffered.

On his return to Kisangani, Bill received more terrible news. 'Big John', the chief of the Baboas who had shown such kindness and care to Bill had been captured by the Simbas. Accusing him of treason they had killed him, forcing him to drink petrol and setting him alight. The horror of it was unbearable. Bill felt surrounded by the forces of darkness on every side.

Yet even in these desperate times it seemed that what remained of the Congolese church wanted to reach out to their countrymen in whatever way they could. It was as if an urgency had overtaken everyone to know and speak about God's Word. Even nation-wide campaigns were organised amongst all the disarray and disorder of the conflict. And the need was so great that many were turning to faith in Jesus who might otherwise have been uninterested. In Congo there was no-one who had not felt suffering in some form and many were looking for answers. It seemed unbelievable that blessing should come out of such terrible catastrophe, yet time and again Bill was asked to lead baptismal services of new believers and saw for himself how lives were being genuinely changed. In Banalia itself the church was growing daily. The eleven Simbas had been released from prison there so great was the change in them, and they were showing that they were new men entirely after that initial step of faith.

Bill needed to cling onto these signs of hope as he continued with the painful task of aid work. Gradually more and more people had been venturing out of the forest till they began to appear in their thousands and the refugee crisis was heightening. The days were too short for Bill to cover their basic needs. Emotionally and physically exhausted, he could not allow himself the luxury of a break when he knew the needs were so great. People's lives depended on the help and aid that he could bring. He requested help repeatedly but it seemed that there was no-one who could join him. So he had to continue alone.

News such as the release of his friend Siole Gilbert with whom he had nursed continued to encourage him although the relief was always tempered with grief at the suffering endured. Siole's brief note conveyed these mixed feelings too, expressed with his usual reserve:

'By the grace of God our Father the National Army delivered me up from the hands of our enemy on the 5th March along with my three children who at the time of writing are ill and in need of care. Thanks be to God, Yours, Siole.'

Soon, however, Bill was forced to abandon the aid work. In July 1967 the fighting worsened again and a white missionary was killed in Kisangani. Fearful of a repeat of the massacres of 1964, the Congolese church insisted that Bill and his colleagues evacuate and return to their own countries. And so Bill found himself back suddenly in Scotland again.

It felt very strange to be abruptly upended in this way and thrust out of the situation in which he had been so absorbed and in which he had been working so hard. For some weeks Bill felt disorientated and could get little relief from the worry for those left behind. The news reports were not encouraging. The fighting was intensifying. So many factions were now involved that if two groups were battling it out in one area, another was taking its chance to terrorise and kill opposing supporters elsewhere. Bill could only imagine the devastation that might meet him should he ever be able to return again.

For this was a real concern. How long would missionaries be able to enter these war-torn situations. Who was being put at risk by their presence? Did God really mean him to be going back and forth like this, unable to stay the course in the most severe and therefore the most needy times? It was hard to see what could be God's plan. Did God ever change His mind? Was Bill sure that he was doing with his life exactly what God wanted?

The stress of the last two years, both physical and emotional, accentuated all these concerns in his mind. In addition, soon after his return, Bill's 'second mother', Mrs Briggs, died. Sitting at her bedside as she slipped away in hospital, Bill felt very lonely. She had been his benefactress and friend, as well as the one to provide a roof over his head and a base when he was at home. Although other dear friends, the Campbells from Uddingston, came forward to offer him somewhere to live, Bill continued to miss her very much.

It was with a weary heart that Bill began the deputation work for the missionary society, visiting various church groups and supporters and telling of the recent work. However, this itself encouraged him: to see people interested to hear about Congo and her troubles, willing to pray for Bill's friends, and moved to give to those who had been impoverished by the war and turmoil of the past years. Before long he was extremely busy, often speaking at various meetings four or five times a week. The travelling was tiring as Bill was given venues across the length and breadth of the United Kingdom – most of which without a car!

Yet Bill discovered unexpectedly that he had a real talent for public speaking. His audiences became gripped, particularly when he related past events. People were moved when he spoke. Audiences responded to Bill's sincerity and his straightforward speech – as well as his sense of humour! And God saw fit to use this new-found ability, especially amongst young people. Bill saw many come to trust Jesus Christ when he spoke. He saw others challenged to commit themselves more fully than before to God. Some pledged to enter Bible School. Others determined to train as missionaries. Humble as ever concerning his abilities, Bill was thrilled to think that Congo and other countries might be populated by missionaries who were responding on hearing about the work and sacrifice of people like Ian and Audrey, like Hector and the others, and would thereby be filling their shoes.

Well-known as a missionary who had come through the troubles in Congo, friends saw Bill's life as exemplifying much of what Christian living was about. One of Bill's group of friends in the Tent Hall, Margaret Tennant, was a worker with the Bible Club Movement. This was an organisation which sought to tell young people in particular about Jesus Christ and its motto was very direct: it read, 'God says it, Jesus did it, I believe it, that settles it.' While Bill was speaking to a group of young folk on holiday with the Bible Club, Margaret could not help thinking as she listened how applicable this was to Bill himself. He took God at his Word and acted upon it. Questions could be answered, problems could be solved, means could be sought, at a later date.

As no opportunity arose for Bill to return to Africa after a busy year of deputation work, he was granted permission to return to some extra nursing training. Much of the work in Congo was centred on the children and this would be increased unfortunately by the continued fighting, so Bill applied and was accepted to work for a one-year post-graduate course in a Glasgow children's hospital where he would see a wide variety of work.

The months passed quickly with Bill relishing the chance to learn new procedures and skills which he could envisage using back in Congo. For UFM were permitting him to plan his return finally and Bill had informed the Congolese church of his arrival in Kisangani in October. It was now two years since he had been made to leave in such haste and he was eager to return, whatever he might find.

As the examinations approached, Bill became nervous as he recalled his past failures in putting pen to paper. In Congo they were planning meetings for his return. They all expected him there. He could not bear if he were to fail and disappoint everyone, not least himself. So, to calm himself and get away from the rush and bustle of the hospital and the nursing home, Bill took his car which he had bought some months before and set out for a long, relaxing drive into the west.

It was autumn and the glorious rich colours of the trees framed the banks of Loch Long as he drove the twisting road to Arrochar and Garelochhead which winds round that stretch of water. Driving was a pleasure with so many vibrant scenes around every corner. Happy and relaxed, Bill breathed in the refreshing air and felt he could shake off some of the grey city drabness in this beautiful countryside.

But suddenly the car began to slip! The corner was sharp! Bill had hit some wet, fallen leaves. He wrestled with the wheel! But it was no use. He was across the road and heading for a steep drop! And the water of the loch was below.

He felt himself flung to the edge. Bill closed his eyes and thought, 'This is it! Sudden death – sudden glory!' And a terrific 'bang' echoed into the air.

41

Happiness From Harm

If Bill had expected to see heavenly angels in front of his eyes when he opened them, he was in for a shock for all he could see was mangled metal, his own blood and the moving water perilously close below. Looking around he found his glasses – amazingly intact – and saw what had happened. Above him, a huge tree stump had checked his fall, as well as smashing in the whole side of the car. And as he could tell from the excruciating pain, his arm had taken the force of it. Shocked and light-headed, he gazed down in horror. His right arm was in pieces! It had two elbows instead of one!

Gulping in air to steady himself, he tried to focus away from the pain. What was he to do? He was stuck. He could not move. How was he ever going to get out of here?

Where the car hung on this slope Bill could not be seen from the road. His only chance was if a car passed in the opposite direction and someone on the passenger side happened to look down over the edge. Even then they would not reach him but they could go and get help. But it was highly unlikely, especially at this quiet spot. Bill felt panic rising in his throat. He could not stay here. The pain was too much. He was losing blood. Would the car stay hanging where it was? What was to happen to him?

Even in his pain, Bill had assessed the situation correctly and, amazingly, a car passed the spot and the lady passenger looked down. It was not long before they had returned with help and he was hoisted out of the smashed car to the safety of an ambulance. Sirens blaring, he was rushed to the Vale of Leven hospital, some miles away.

When the doctors there saw Bill's arm and the shattered bones and joint, they took the decision to amputate immediately. It was as they were in the theatre about to begin the operation to remove his arm that a gentleman entered. He was a Glasgow surgeon who visited this outlying hospital periodically and this was the day of his visit.

Assessing Bill's case in front of him he offered his help and three hours later, Bill emerged from theatre with his arm intact, with the addition of two long steel plates and several screws.

From that moment on Bill knew an abundance of care from those around him. The extent of surgery on his arm made him something of a novelty, especially in this small hospital and he had medical students and personnel marvelling over him and his recovery. The nurses enjoyed caring for another nurse and there was always banter and fun. He was singled out as a celebrity too when the Matron from the Royal Hospital for Sick Children where he was studying came all the way to visit him with his pyjamas and slippers from his room in the Nurses' Home. When the Assistant Matron came to pick him up in her own car to take him back to Glasgow after several weeks, the Vale of Leven nurses refused to believe any more that he was merely a student there. Such high honour and preferment must single him out as a very important person!

Yet for all this special treatment, Bill felt very low. He was in a lot of pain and was completely incapacitated with an enormous plaster cast and he had no-one to help him. Back in Glasgow, he was all alone in the Nurses' Home while all the nurses were busy doing their own work. He felt forgotten and useless.

More distressingly, he knew that his chance of sitting his exams had gone and therefore he would not be returning to Congo in the immediate future. Through no fault of his own, he was letting people down and he could almost hear the devil's words in his ear: 'I've got you this time, Gilvear. What a mess you've made of everything. You're finished.'

Bill was very confused. He could not understand why this

should have happened to him. Why would God put him through all this pain? Why must it happen now, after he had worked so diligently all year to gain his Diploma? Did God not know that he found it hard enough without this added complication? Or did God not want him in Africa? Had he got it all wrong? Was he being forced down another path that he could not understand?

It was at this time that Bill received another blow when his friend with whom he had lodged, Tom Campbell, died. The Campbells had opened their home to him before he began his Diploma and although he now lived in the Nurses' Home, Bill had been accustomed to turning to them as he might turn to his family. Now he was bereft of this refuge too and he felt deeply for his widow left behind. It seemed the final straw in this dark and difficult time.

It was as he brooded over these thoughts, however, that more help arrived in the shape of a consultant at the Children's' Hospital. He was a Christian man who knew Bill and he was concerned to see him all alone at this time.

'Come with me, Bill,' said Dr Chalmers. 'I won't hear any excuses. We can't have you sitting here all pale and weak with no-one to look after you. You'll come home with me. My wife is a nurse and she'll take care of you till you recover from all this.'

So Bill was driven to Dr Chalmers' house, given a lovely bedroom, even given a bath, swathed in plastic bags to keep his plaster dry! Then he was given something to eat and put to bed. The doctor even placed a little bell on the cabinet beside him and told him just to ring it if he needed anything – 'as if I would dare!' thought Bill.

There was something Bill did require, however, and that was some means of contacting his Congolese friends who knew nothing of his accident and who would be expecting him any day. He must get word to them but he could write nothing with his right arm so immobilised. Yet this was no problem for the doctor either.

'I'm sure our lodger downstairs will know someone who can

come and act as secretary for you, Bill,' he said reassuringly. 'Don't you worry. We'll get you fixed up in no time.' And he was as good as his word. A few days later Bill's eyes widened when his friend from the Bible Club camp, Margaret Tennant, walked through the door. She was a close friend of the young student nurse in the Chalmers' flat, Katie-Anne McKinnon and she had offered to help Bill if she could.

It was not long before Bill began to wonder if he was perhaps discovering some reason for his accident after all and seeing God's hand in delaying his return to Africa! For immediately there was an affinity and closeness between Margaret and himself and they worked happily together in the painstaking job of writing his letters in Lingala, every word being spelt out meticulously.

Time-consuming as this was, Margaret stayed often after they were finished and their fondness for one another grew. Although they had known of each other vaguely as young people in the Tent Hall it was only during Bill's last spell at home in Glasgow that they had been thrown together more. Now Margaret looked back on the Bible Club camp in Brora the previous year as the time when she began to feel more for Bill and she had been shocked at the strength of her own feelings when she had heard of his accident.

Bill looked down at her dark head bent over the typewriter. She was like a tonic to him with her bright spirit and her ready, happy smile. He hardly dared to believe that after he had been through so much alone, there might be someone who would want to share it all with him. Yet as a full-time worker in a Christian association herself, Margaret understood so much of his desire for missionary work and his current frustrations at being unable to carry it out. It was wonderful to have someone with whom he could talk about these things at last.

It was awkward only seeing Margaret when she came to the Chalmers'. The doctor and his wife must have wondered just how many letters Bill needed to write! Yet where could they go?

Margaret felt strongly that she did not want any of her Bible Club youngsters to see her starting to go out with someone, especially when it was all so sudden. What if nothing came of it, she thought to herself. How could she explain to them? Bill too was aware that as two missionaries they had a responsibility to their employers and those who knew them. They did not want word to get back to any other workers there of a flowering relationship. They just wanted no-one to know but themselves. It all seemed so fresh and tentative. If everyone knew then it might all be spoilt, be trampled upon by people's well-intentioned interference.

So they attended the same meetings but avoided each other's gaze; they hid round corners when they were out if they saw anyone coming; Margaret even asked Bill to hide in a cupboard when someone called at her house while he was there!

But within four or five weeks both Bill and Margaret were certain of their feelings for one another. Never one to hold back or to hide his feelings, Bill soon spoke of marriage and although it all seemed very sudden, Margaret too was sure. But there was a complication. What about Bill's missionary work? He was due to sit in February the examination he had missed and return to Congo in March. He could not bear the thought of Margaret not going with him.

This was to be one of the biggest tests Bill had ever faced. Although he felt so sure himself about his relationship with Margaret, he knew that God must have a say in what was happening. Before they rushed ahead they must put him first and let God decide the next step. So they agreed that before they go any further, before they announced their engagement even, Margaret would have to be accepted independently as a missionary for Congo by the Unevangelised Fields Mission. That would be a sign that this was part of God's plan.

For some years now Margaret had been considering working abroad herself. She had been drawn particularly to Africa. Yet knowledge of Bill's work in Congo had discouraged her per-

versely from considering this country; she did not want anyone
to think that as a single girl going out to the mission field she had
any other motives than service in God's cause! Yet in his own
timing, God seemed to be opening the way for her to work in that
country.

The weeks and days waiting for an interview with the central
UFM Office in London were agonising. What would happen if
Margaret did not get through the interview – if she were not
accepted? Would UFM even consider a new missionary when the
country was in such turmoil? Would there be a problem with
Margaret being released from her duties with the Bible Club
Movement whose base was in America?

It was extremely difficult to think clearly about it all. And all
the time their love for one another had to remain a secret.

Finally, in December they were called down for interview at
the Central Offices of UFM in Ealing, London. Bill was asked to
wait upstairs while Margaret was taken in to the Conference
Room. Nobody knew how much Bill's future hung on what was
happening there downstairs.

He prayed fervently while he waited and tried to focus on some
words they had read in the Bible that morning: 'Listen, my
daughter, ... forget your people and your father's house'. What
could be clearer than that? Surely God was indicating his desire
for them to be together doing the work to which Bill longed to
return in Congo.

After an interminable wait, Bill was called downstairs. But
Margaret was nowhere to be seen! What had happened? Was no-
one going to let him know?

Inside, the questions were now put to Bill.

'Well, Mr Gilvear, what are your plans? What are you thinking
about the future?'

'As a matter of fact,' replied Bill, nervously, 'they are all tied
up with whatever you have said to that lovely lady you have just
been speaking to.'

His interviewers grinned. 'Put him out of his misery,' one demanded, and then Bill heard the news he was longing to hear: Margaret had been accepted as a candidate to work in the Independent Republic of Congo.

'Well, I can tell you exactly what my plans are now, sir,' grinned Bill, relief washing over his face. 'We are going over the way to Ealing Broadway to a wee jeweller's shop there and I am going to buy a ring and we will be engaged within the hour. Then I'll sit my exam in February, we'll be married in March and be ready for Congo in May.'

This sounded a rather whistle-stop itinerary yet such was Bill's certainty, not to mention his impatience to be gone, that his interviewers gave their blessing to his plans and he left. Bill met Margaret outside with the biggest grin she had ever seen cemented to his face. It did not come off all day, even when they telephoned Margaret's mother in Glasgow to tell of their engagement and Bill had to pour all the coins he had with him into the call-box, just to hear her weeping tears of joy down the line to them.

42

Joint Venture

The months which followed were extremely busy. Bill was studying for his Diploma in Child Health, while Margaret was continuing as Bible Club Missionary as a replacement was sought. In addition, she was taking day and evening classes to learn French and trying to absorb as much Lingala as Bill was able to teach her. The latter caused much hilarity: they could be the only couple in Glasgow they thought who were telling each other 'I love you' in an obscure African language! On top of all this they had a wedding to organise.

Neither Bill nor Margaret had money saved to spend on a lavish wedding, so they decided themselves that they would have the ceremony in the Tent Hall with just a short gathering with the two families afterwards.

'It makes sense, Bill,' Margaret agreed. 'And it's not as if we've got much time to organise anything bigger – what with you being in such a hurry to sweep me off my feet,' she added with a grin.

However when this was suggested to the Tent Hall leaders they would not hear of it.

'We will not have two of our missionaries married without a proper "do",' they exclaimed. And they promised to arrange a reception for two hundred guests in the Back Hall. All Bill and Margaret had to do was to name their guest list!

If this was not enough, Bill soon had other offers of help. A friend in the fellowship there was a policeman whose unusual hobby was cake-making. Years ago he had promised Bill that he would make his wedding cake one day and he stayed true to his

232

word. Another friend worked for the city's Parks Department and he offered to deck the Hall out in as much greenery and with as many flowers as they would wish. The Matron of the Hospital for Sick Children said that she would arrange a special guard of honour made up of his colleagues, for their (newly successful!) diploma student. Then there was the offer of a choir from one of Bill's supporting churches that they would come and sing. Even their honeymoon was gifted to them. It seemed as if everything was being provided for without even them having to ask.

And so the plans for their great day came together. Finally, standing at the front of the Hall with Margaret beside him, Bill could hardly believe this was happening to him. Only a few short months ago he had been dejected and discouraged, questioning his future as a missionary and even as a nurse with his terrible injury. In addition, he had felt lonely and isolated, for although he had many friends and supporters, there had been no-one close enough with whom to share his deepest concerns for his loved ones in Congo and his own worries for himself. As he had found on his return in '64, there had seemed no-one with whom to share his grief.

Now, however, everything was turned around and he looked at Margaret's glowing face beside him. She had all the vitality and warmth of spirit for which he had longed – and she shared his desire to serve Jesus Christ. At the ripe old age of thirty-nine, he felt he had been given the perfect companion with whom to share his life. And he would appreciate her all the more, he knew, because of what he had been through alone without her. Bill listened with overwhelming gratitude to the words of Mr MacBeath from the Bible Training Institute who had been asked to give the wedding address: 'Before you had telescopic vision, Bill. (He dropped the angelic nickname for the occasion!) But now you have binocular vision! You are not on your own. Now you will be able to see round a thing – see it from other angles.' And he continued to expound on the wonders of the guiding hand of God and his grace in using his servants to do his work on earth.

It was only during the last hymn that Bill and his new wife were made aware of the reason for the excellent singing which they could hear from the congregation behind them. For although the choir stood before them on the stage, there was a great volume of singing in the Hall. They were invited to turn round and Bill let out a great gasp – there in the main body of the Tent Hall were not just their own two hundred guests, but fifteen hundred visitors from all over the country who had come to share in their happiness with them! There were more there than came to the Saturday Night Rally. Bill could not remember seeing the place so full.

In addition, both Bill and Margaret's families who did not share their faith were amongst that number and during the service they had heard of God's great love and his desire for involvement in the lives of individuals and those far away from Him. Now they were witnessing clearly the abundant love which was being showered on Bill and Margaret by their many friends and saw it as something extraordinary indeed. It was a day that no-one, including the two families, would forget easily.

The weeks which followed were very busy. After their return from honeymoon in Southern Ireland there were goodbyes to be made, meetings to attend, families to visit, vaccinations to obtain and wedding gifts to pack for the long sea journey. With all the busyness of the final two months, Bill hoped the weeks of the voyage by boat from Antwerp to Matadi would be like a second honeymoon for them, away from the hectic farewells in Scotland and a lull before the work which lay ahead in Africa.

However, no sooner had they left the Belgian port than Margaret began to be sea-sick.

'I should have known, Bill,' she apologised. 'I've never been able to go "doon the water" to Greenock without feeling rough.'

So unwell was Margaret that soon she could barely leave the cabin. It seemed that she would never gain her sea-legs and throw off the sickness. It had been confirmed also that she was pregnant which, although this news made them very happy, did nothing to assuage the constant nausea.

By the time the boat approached the African coast, Margaret had lost a stone in weight and was desperate to leave the ship. The intense heat of the equator aggravated her weakness and it was decided that the Gilvears would have to fly the hundred miles to Kinshasa rather than continue by boat. Never had a passenger been so relieved to cross a gang-plank in her life!

However, in Kinshasa things got no better. Within days Margaret developed a kidney infection and had to be admitted to hospital there. Weakened from the voyage and in pain, Margaret wept in her hospital bed. What an arrival and what a start to her missionary career. Having scarcely suffered a day's illness in her life, Margaret was very frustrated at being so incapacitated and she knew too how expensive her stay in this government hospital would be to Bill and UFM. Perhaps worst of all was the problem of not being able to communicate with the staff. If they came to take her temperature or wash her face, she could not speak or even ask any questions. While discussions were held about her illness, she was kept in the dark. In a strange country with strangers all around talking in a strange, unintelligible language, Margaret felt quite intimidated and scared.

When Bill appeared she poured out her heart to him. Holding her to him and seeing the tired, uncharacteristic tears, Bill wondered what he had brought her into. He felt so responsible. Surely there was something he could do.

Bill could not make her better but he could make the language barrier less of a problem. He explained to the staff his wife's lack of the language and each time he visited, Bill brought her some flashcards. On each card he wrote a word or phrase in Lingala which Margaret might want to say, such as, 'May I have a drink?' or 'Can I go to the toilet?' And on the back he had drawn a little picture for Margaret to know what the card was for: a glass of water, or a bed pan or whatever. When the African nurses saw the cards they burst out laughing and called over all the other staff on the ward – no doubt to see this 'mad white couple' with their picture cards! Yet it was effective. Soon Margaret had a pile of cards with any number of phrases written on them so she could have quite long 'conversations' with those around her. It was not much but it helped to make the situation a bit more tolerable.

Once the infection had cleared the Gilvears were able to journey on to Kisangani which was to be their base. And here Margaret received a different impression entirely of the Africans. All she had known so far was the face of officialdom such as when they had tried to leave the boat in Matadi and were told initially that they were unable to take any of their belongings, including all their wedding presents into the country. This disaster having been averted, she had then experienced the uncommunicative and unfriendly attitude of the government hospital staff. Finally, however, in Kisangani she was experiencing the welcome and instant love that Bill had spoken of so glowingly. For his African friends in particular were overjoyed to see Bill and to discover that he had come back with a wife. Margaret enjoyed their outspoken congratulations: 'You should not have waited so long, Bwana William,' they insisted. 'Why were you so slow in finding your oh so beautiful wife? And now we will have a little Bwana William too!'

And when they heard how unwell Margaret had been there was not enough they could do to help. Bill watched happily as he saw Margaret's impressions change so immediately and to see such joy replacing all the uncertainty and wariness that had been there for the past weeks.

Having reached as far as Kisagani, Bill was eager to continue up to Bongondza. Not only did he want Margaret to meet all his friends there, but he knew that their need was still great, especially to carry out much of the medical work there. It seemed the obvious step to take next. On the first attempt, however, their truck broke down and they returned rather dejected but determined to try again as soon as possible. Yet before they could try, Margaret had again taken unwell. And it seemed that this was rather more serious than before.

43

Kisangani Days

It began suddenly with a severe pain on Margaret's right side of her abdomen. Immediately Bill could tell that this was different from the infection she had been hospitalised with previously and from the amount of pain she was experiencing something had to be done quickly.

In the local hospital Margaret was soon being examined by two American doctors working in Kisangani with the World Health Organisation. At least there was no language barrier here but the diagnosis they gave was not good.

'We believe you have a cyst there, Mrs Gilvear,' they told Margaret. 'We will have to operate and remove it. And,' they added, 'we are afraid you will probably lose the child you are carrying.'

The news was devastating. Bill and Margaret could only look at each other with helplessness and anguish.

'Oh, why can't we be home?' whispered Margaret. 'I wish I could be at the Queen Mother Hospital in Glasgow now. Not here.'

'It's a queer distance from here to Glasgow,' replied Bill, but he understood her concern. She wanted to be amongst her own folk at this time, to have her own mother with her, to be out of this alien environment where everything seemed to be going wrong. Now Bill was her only family. He must be the one to support and to comfort her. And yet he felt so devastated himself.

'Let's pray, Margaret,' decided Bill. 'This is too much for us. Let's tell it to Jesus and let Him help us.' And there in the hospital, Bill got down on his knees and poured out their troubles and distress to God.

Almost as soon as he stood up again, Bill thought of an idea.

He had known dramatic answers to prayer before but this was instantaneous! Now he remembered the Missionary Medical Centre at Nyankunde. It was a long way away – five days on rough roads – but Bill recalled that there was a Gynaecologist there whom he could contact by radio. If Bill explained Margaret's symptoms to her, she might be able to confirm or refute the diagnosis and advise Bill what to do. Quickly he rushed away to find a transmitting radio.

When he returned to Margaret he brought good news.

'I've spoken to the doctor, dear, and she says she knows exactly what's wrong. You'll need an operation still but the wee one will be all right!' Margaret looked up hardly daring to believe it. 'Yes, and you'll be going up by plane. Mind, I don't know how we're going to pay for it – in peanuts or bananas! But they are sending it down.' And for the first time Bill saw his wife's brow clear and she closed her eyes to rest.

Bill closed his own eyes too but to pray, for not only did he have no money to pay for the aeroplane which would cost a full $250, but he knew there was a long way to go before both Margaret and the baby were safe. Not only would the journey be difficult but the operation would be a dangerous one too.

Yet even the arrival of the plane was in God's timing, it seemed. Nothing was left to chance. Bill knew that the Missionary Aviation Fellowship planes were permitted to land at government airports only on national holidays, but as the next day was indeed such a holiday Bill and Margaret were whisked away out of Kisangani without delay. Soon his wife was in theatre at the mission hospital and instead of a cyst two fibroids were removed and they did not need to interfere with the baby at all.

Bill wished that this could bring them relief, yet it seemed that there was no let up to their worries. As soon as she began to recover, Margaret was struck by malaria. Weakened already by the journey to Africa, as well as the surgery, it hit her badly. Bill wondered just what could be next!

What happened next seemed the biggest hurdle of all. For although Margaret and the unborn baby had come through the surgery, the doctors had uncovered a complication. Margaret, it appeared, had a rare blood group known as Rhesus negative. Because Bill and probably the baby were Rhesus positive there could be problems with the birth – and certainly would be should they wish to have more children. This Rhesus incompatibility would mean that Margaret's antibodies in her blood would begin to attack the baby's bloodstream. There was a solution, they were told. A vaccine administered just after the birth would sort out the mixing of blood which would inevitably occur and would prevent the antibodies being produced. But – and this was the problem – there was none of this anti-Rhesus globulin to be found in Congo. Indeed, there was none in the whole of Africa!

It seemed that their worries would never be over. Together they puzzled over what could be done. On top of all this Margaret worried too because she was holding Bill back from getting on with work and from getting to Bongondza. She felt guilty at the burden she was being to him. Why did it have to be so complicated? Why should all this happen when all they wanted to do was get on with God's work?

Bill tried to reassure his wife: 'What seems complicated to us is not like that to God,' he tried to explain. Bill thought of all the 'why's' he had sent up to God before now: for his failed examinations, during his struggles in the Navy, for his failure to see his mother before her death, for the terrible happenings in Congo itself. Life had held many 'complications' for him. Yet he had been allowed to see the reasons for at least some of these seeming catastrophes, even if some still remained a mystery.

So Bill was able to comfort her honestly, from his own experience: 'God has a much bigger picture which we can't see. We have to pray that He will give us the faith to trust Him to have the overall view.' Many times he had said at meetings what had become almost a catchphrase for him: Our Dis-appointments are

His appointments. 'Perhaps He has something that He wants to show us or teach us through this,' he added, although it was hard to see the way out of this one. It was hard, he knew, to cling to this assurance when it seemed all so impossible, when so much depended on finding a solution.

Yet this was an occasion when Bill and Margaret were permitted to see just how much God was in control of every situation and how He was concerned with the intimate details of their lives. On discovering the blood problem, Bill had written immediately to a friend in Glasgow who worked in a Haematology laboratory there. She had written back saying that she had the vaccine but that it was too unstable to travel: they would have to get some from the manufacturers, a large chemical factory in Dublin. The London office of UFM then took over the hunt and having ordered it from Dublin, they arranged to pick up the flask containing the precious liquid at Heathrow airport. There, among the thousands of travellers in the world's busiest airport, the UFM representative who was collecting the flask 'bumped into' a young missionary bound on the next flight for Congo. The flask was then carried as hand luggage to Kinshasa, the capital, where the young missionary 'bumped into' a doctor leaving shortly for Nyankunde. Finally, it was handed over to Bill for safe keeping until Margaret was delivered of their child.

Bill had never believed in such outlandish coincidences and instead he simply praised God for His intervention. He clearly had the whole world in His control where every encounter and moment of time were known to Him. It was so exciting to see God intervening on their behalf. What better encouragement did they need as they prepared to embark on His work?

And so they prepared to return to Kisangani. It was advisable to travel by aeroplane again, yet Bill despaired still of paying for it. When finally the bill arrived for both flights he opened the envelope, full of trepidation – only to discover a receipt inside instead! The five missionary societies represented at Nyankunde had pooled their resources and had paid the flight fees on their behalf.

As soon as Margaret was able, Bill tried again to reach Bongondza. But each time something prevented him. First it was the weather. The rainy season began and the roads became a quagmire of mud and flood-water. Then malaria struck again and then it became too close to the birth. 'After the baby's born,' thought Bill, 'then we can go.'

Finally just before Christmas, young William Gilvear was brought into the world at the Kisangani government hospital. And as arranged, Bill had the vaccine ready and it was administered. It was a wonderfully joyful time with the Congolese celebrating with Bill and Margaret in their happiness. It was like an extended family at a time when it would have been so easy to miss their own families at home in Scotland. For Bill himself, whose own family life had been so fragmented and disturbed, to have his own family around him – his own wife and son – was a source of exhilaration and delight. No-one seeing Bill and the brilliant smile which seemed fixed to his face could have denied that they thought he was pleased!

And so to Bongondza – or so Bill thought. For once again he was prevented. As always the missionaries were under the direct control of the African church and its Congolese hierarchy. Whatever they decided on the missionaries' behalf had to be adhered to and it seemed a decision had been made for Bill. He was to remain in Kisangani and be ordained as a Pastor there. He would have responsibility for the North-East Province and would have seven evangelists under him whom he would teach and encourage.

Everyone was greatly shocked. It seemed a terrible shame to hold back a medical missionary when there was such need. And to be prevented from returning to his own people, as he thought of them, was a terrible blow. Had he not spent more than a year at home gaining the extra qualification in Child Health just so he would be of more use to all the needy children there? It seemed a hard decision to accept.

Yet Bill was unable to complain and he felt truly honoured when his ordination came about and he was appointed in his new role, even although he would rather have been a hundred and forty miles further north!

Slowly but surely, Margaret was learning the language. Now with young Billy with her she had the opportunity to have more to do with the local women and she was able to communicate quite well with them. There were still mistakes, of course. On one occasion Bill was called out of the house when he heard great shouts of laughter from outside. He stepped into the garden to find Margaret standing very perplexed, surrounded by a group of young people who were enjoying a good joke, obviously. It appeared that Margaret, instead of asking around in Lingala for a gardener (a word spoken with the last syllable raised), had asked instead most insistently for a drunken man (the same word spoken with the last syllable lowered)! Such were the pitfalls of learning a new language!

But Margaret's new abilities were put soon to good use as Bill saw the way ahead to begin a teachers' training course for Sunday Schools and Bible Classes. This is just what Margaret had been doing in Scotland and she threw herself into the task. It was so good to be useful again. Soon they had ordered material from home and had translated it.

And the Congolese Christians responded enthusiastically. Bill could hardly keep them away. They even turned up on his doorstep on Saturdays looking for extra tuition. And the essence of the course was to give them initial training in theory and then let them practise on one another. Together they made up quizzes, wrote their own choruses in Lingala, practised telling the Bible stories and giving their testimonies to one another. Finally, at the end of the course they held a big campaign for all the children. It was something which had never been attempted before and many

flocked to the meeting place, day after day. It was thrilling to see
so many young people so keen to share their faith and to see so
many willing to listen. And as Bill and Margaret watched, the Bible
Classes and Sunday Schools expanded and spread over other
parts of the city.

Bill too was encouraged by the work with the pastors in the
area. Every Monday they met together for study and worship and
often Bill travelled with them, conducting services and visiting
congregations in the more distant areas. This was the work he
preferred. Out in the bush he felt that he was having a direct impact
and was meeting the people face to face. And because he had been
working in Congo through the years of the rebellion, the Africans
knew that he understood their situations and had shown his
willingness to help in whatever way he could.

There was one drawback however with the travelling. Driving
on the rough roads in the bush put immense strain on Bill's arm
and he was often in pain with it.

'It's like driving on a scrubbing board like my Mammy used
to take to the Steamie,' he joked to Margaret. But it was hard to
remain jovial as the miles began to take their toll. Soon he could
get no relief from the pain. In Scotland he had never put his arm
to the test. Certainly nothing had prepared him for the constant
battering it took on the African roads.

Bill had never been discharged from hospital care entirely and
he had to have his arm checked every three months at the hospital
in Kisangani where they could take regular x-rays to monitor any
change. By the time for his visit in June 1971 he knew something
had to be done; he had even been passing out from the pain. And
the x-ray showed the reason for this. There had been a dramatic
change. One of the plates had come loose from its screw inside
his arm and was floating away from his elbow!

The doctors in the government hospital stared at the x-ray in
disbelief. Something needed to be done clearly, but no-one there
would tackle such a job.

'You must return to the surgeon who performed the original operation,' he was told, 'otherwise you will lose your arm for sure.' So urgent did they consider it to be that they organised immediately for his records and x-rays to be sent back to Glasgow.

Shocked and confused, Bill talked it over with Margaret. They knew it was no ten-penny bus trip to Glasgow: it would cost hundreds of pounds which they did not have. Even the mission which took some money from each monthly salary for return trips home had not accumulated enough in the Gilvears' 'kitty'. And how could they just dump everything as it was and rush off home? Bill had known the frustration of that only too well in the past.

That afternoon, however, they were shown without doubt that this was what they must do. A letter arrived from the London headquarters which knew nothing of the situation, informing them that a gift had been made to them of two hundred and fifty pounds. 'What would they like done with the money?'

'That's our flight home,' proclaimed Bill and immediately they booked their tickets. Within three days, without packing or preparing, Bill, Margaret and Billy Gilvear had left Kisangani behind and had set foot again on Scottish soil.

44

The Waiting Game

Having arrived back in Scotland, the Gilvears' first priority was to get to the surgeon about Bill's arm. The pain was intense and he could get no relief. And it transpired that their urgency was necessary for they turned up on the surgeon's last day before he left on holiday, so Bill may have missed the chance for his arm to be saved, had they delayed. When the surgeon opened it up he found that not only had one plate become dislodged but the whole arm was septic. It was in a terrible mess. No wonder Bill had experienced such pain!

There was little to be done but to remove the plate and clean up what they could. Bill was then plastered up from shoulder to wrist and given anti-biotics. They were not overly hopeful of success: 'We will just have to see if that will do the trick!' he was informed.

Bill was then incapacitated with the enormous plaster. It was hard to do anything: dressing himself, eating and even brushing his teeth became marathon tasks! But there were more important things to think about, for the Gilvear family had no home. Arriving back so peremptorily there was no provision made for them and Bill despaired how he would manage to find a roof over their heads.

Their first visit, however, was back to the Tent Hall to their friends there. Feeling tired and rather shocked by the suddenness of their departure from Congo and the abrupt surgery to Bill, they felt they needed to be amongst friends to share with them their present dilemmas. For they had no idea how long they might be forced to remain in Scotland. 'And I did not even stop to clear up the house!' protested Margaret.

Bill knew that there was a great shortage of council houses in Glasgow and however great was their need, it may be impossible to make contact even with the right people in the city's housing department. He was completely taken aback therefore when he found that the speaker in front of him that night at the Tent Hall was none other than a Glasgow house factor! After the meeting Bill approached the speaker and he was delighted to help.

'Just go up to the office on Monday,' he insisted. 'I'll tell them you're coming. Don't you worry.'

Duly on the Monday morning, Bill stepped into the office – only to be greeted like a long-lost friend! The man to whom Bill had been sent had heard Bill speak at his own church on a previous trip home and he was delighted to help. He could not do enough for Bill. As it transpired, just that morning a flat had become available and he offered it to Bill there and then for immediate occupation. As Bill left the office he felt like singing at the top of his voice! It seemed that God was going before them the whole way. Why should they worry when God was so obviously in charge?

The flat was a little room and kitchen near the centre of the city and it was empty except for a cooker standing in the kitchen and a telephone sitting on the floor. It had been lived in by an elderly couple for many years and it was in need of some repair and decoration. Looking at his arm, it was obvious that Bill could do very little but soon friends and family offered their assistance. Little pieces of furniture and carpet arrived, cushions and curtains appeared; a painter friend even left several pots of paint. The house was being furnished by the love of their friends, it seemed. Margaret enlisted two of her brothers to help and Bill looked on helplessly while it began to take shape around him. It took him all his time to hold little Billy on his knee and stop him diving headlong into the paint pots, far less starting on the DIY himself.

There was something he could do, however, and that was to look for some basic furniture. Without even a chair to sit on or a bed on which to lie, clearly something had to be done. And Bill had noticed that a large auction room was situated on the opposite side of the street. But he had very little money. Bill entered the auction rooms on the day of the sale with only thirteen pounds to his name. How could he decide on what to spend his money out of all the things he needed to buy?

As the sale progressed Bill waited anxiously for his chance. Never having bid for anything before he was nervous of what to do. But when a dining room table and four chairs were called he decided to enter the fray: 'Am I bid ten pounds?' came the cry ... 'Ten fifty' ... 'Eleven' ... 'Twelve' ... 'Twelve fifty', bellowed Bill, just as the hammer fell. It was only then that Bill realised that he had got not only a table and four chairs but a whole dining room suite: a dresser and carver chairs as well!

So shocked and bamboozled was Bill at what he had bought for his meagre twelve pounds fifty that he missed a couple of fireside chairs for which he was waiting. Undeterred, he found the manager after the sale and asked if he could buy them.

'You'll have to wait till next week,' he was told, abruptly.

Yet Bill would not be put off. 'Aye, but my need is a bit urgent, sir,' he explained and he told the man how he had just returned from Africa and he had nothing in his house.

'Nothing?' queried the manager. 'Oh, well, you can have the chairs for ten pence,' he conceded, generously. If he had hoped, however, that this would get rid of Bill he was mistaken for Bill saw that he was onto a winner: 'And we haven't got a bed either,' he added hopefully.

Margaret could hardly believe her eyes when Bill arrived back at their flat. For behind him was all the furniture they had been looking for, bobbing about in a long procession, carried by the young lads from the auction rooms. So close was the auction to Bill's house that he had talked them into not only giving it to him for next to nothing, they had even carried it across the road to the house.

'Oh, you're an awful man,' laughed Margaret, happily. 'How do you do it? You could charm someone into giving you their Granny if you put your mind to it!' And so they settled into their new home.

Margaret's brothers, although they did not share her faith, became used to seeing what they could only attribute to God's provision for the young family as they worked alongside their sister in decorating the house with all the materials that were given. Time and again they saw Bill and Margaret praying over some problem, only to find it solved in some unusual way. As young men who were spending their own money and energy on improving their own homes, they saw their sister's home appearing out of nowhere before their eyes.

It came down even to the most mundane of items. On one occasion the younger brother was laying a carpet (which had been gifted to them) round the fireplace and needed to trim a piece of the carpet away.

'Have you a piece of chalk, Margaret?' he asked, wanting to mark the area to cut.

'No,' replied Margaret. 'That is something I don't have. Where would I get chalk?'

He walked into the hall where his older brother was up on a ladder, whitening the ceiling. And there at the bottom of the ladder was a piece of chalk!

'Where did that chalk come from,' he demanded.

From the top of the ladder his brother looked down. 'I'm surprised you're even asking. It came from up the stair,' he said, lifting his eyes skyward.

Margaret's brother rushed back into the room. 'You tell your God He was only a minute late with that,' he exclaimed. And he shook his head in wonderment at what he was seeing happen around him.

But Bill and Margaret truly needed these signs of God's encouragement and nearness, for their lives were still very uncertain. Still employed by the Mission, as soon as he was able and despite the great, unwieldy plaster on his arm, Bill began to go round the country on deputation work. They were hearing constantly from Congo – or Zaire as it had just been renamed – so there was plenty to tell. And they received more help in this work in the way of an offer to carry out all Bill's correspondence (and pay for all his postage), and finally they received the gift of a car.

Yet the problem of being unable to see their future mapped out for them and the insecurity this brought was hard to take sometimes. It would be so pleasant, they thought, to be like other people now and again and live less of a day-to-day, hand-to-mouth existence. For although it meant their faith was strengthened, it also meant their faith was under pressure every step of the way.

Finally, after a year Bill visited the surgeon with raised hopes. He had been in plaster all this time and they had made tentative plans that if all was well when the plaster was removed they would ask leave to attend language school so Margaret could learn French properly. After the statutory nine months there they could then return again to the work in the new 'Zaire'.

But the news from the hospital was not good. The x-rays showed that although his arm was healing vertically, it was not healing horizontally or transversely. Still his forearm looked an ugly mess and Bill could see the pieces of bone and plate move about inside while he was being examined. The only solution was to perform another operation, taking a bone graft from Bill's hip and plastering him up again for another six months to a year.

Six months to a year! Bill could hardly believe it. Another year incarcerated inside that white monstrosity! And who knew if this would really work? He felt he had been of so little use for all these months already. And now they were expecting another child, Margaret would be left to do even more herself. It was in a gloomy frame of mind that Bill faced up to the impending surgery. In addition, they had the Mission to consider. Bill's first reaction was to resign as he felt he had strung his prayer and financial supporters along for long enough. Many had been extremely faithful with some even praying for him and supporting his progress since those days so far back in 1958 when he had travelled around the country with his Tent Hall 'loaves'. However, he was persuaded by the Mission to remain with them and they would supply work for him to do around the country as soon as he was able to take it up again.

However, the hip graft was not a success and after two years in plaster, Bill was no further to full recovery. Although the threat of amputation was gone, his arm would never be particularly stable and strong. Quite bluntly, Bill was told that there was no way he could return to a situation like Zaire with its bumpy roads and where he would be expected to participate fully in whatever work was required, heavy or otherwise. Indeed, he was informed that he would be unable to return to any form of nursing in this country either which would involve any lifting or physical work.

It was a terrible blow, yet one which they had begun to expect. It was clear that Bill's arm was not healing satisfactorily and there was no way he could return as a missionary when he could be more of a liability than as a genuine worker. Bill found himself reading some words from his Bible which could have been written just for him: 'I had it in my heart to ... but God said "You may not..."' (1 Chronicles 28:2, 3).

He looked back on his work as a missionary which had spanned twelve years and during which he had seen so much trouble and had experienced so much tragedy in one small part of the world. Even still there was turmoil in Zaire and it wrung his heart to think that he was unlikely to see any of his African friends again. Bill felt he was leaving a large part of himself out there in that land. He still wrote, of course. Indeed, they had sent a bicycle recently to help his dear friend Badi whose feet had been so badly burnt but who still travelled across the country with the Word of

God. Many months ago they had given up hope of ever seeing
their own belongings and many wedding presents again which had
been left behind so suddenly. But these things were immaterial
now. Now they had to look forward. God had shown that their
time there was over. They must learn to be at peace with His
decision. Now they had to be willing to see the next step. After
the past months in which he seemed to have been treading water,
waiting endlessly, Bill felt ready now to move on to whatever the
Lord gave him to do.

45

Do You Believe In Miracles?

The next step seemed, initially, to be a backward one, for Bill was asked to take charge for one year of the Glasgow Medical Mission where he had spent so much time as a teenager. Once again he was asked to do outreach work, knocking on doors in the high-rise flats in the Gorbals and speaking to the people about Christ.

This was work to which he was well-accustomed and Bill enjoyed the direct encounters with the people – even when they were less than complimentary about what he was doing! Every Monday he arranged to take students from his old college, BTI, with him and it was good to see them thrown in at the deep end, speaking for Christ and watching them learn in the process.

And yet Bill's heart was still heavy with the longing to be away in Zaire. It felt such a waste that he should have all his nursing qualifications and that he could speak French, Lingala, Bangala and Swahili and yet he had no opportunity to use any of these skills. It was when he felt lowest that he and Margaret received a visit in their home to encourage them. It was from an Irish couple, Eric and Anne McGowan. They had come to find Bill particularly because they wanted to tell him something of the effect he had on their lives. Mrs McGowan had heard Bill speak at a meeting in Armagh and had determined then to train as a missionary. Now she and her husband were preparing to go to Zaire to work with the young people there.

Similarly, a young student from BTI was encouraged by Bill. This was a dangerous thing to happen it seemed, for she too found herself working out in Zaire within a few short years! And so replacements were being found for the Gilvears. The work was not being left unattended: it would still go on. Yet even as they were thrilled for the Zairians and their new helpers, this too had its sadness for it was almost as if they were being left behind. They were no longer required, it seemed. It was a hard situation to accept.

It was after he had completed his work with the Glasgow Medical Mission that Bill received a visit from another representative of the past. This was a Commander Christopher Mather of the Royal Navy. Bill had no idea why such a lofty personage should be visiting him in his little room and kitchen in Glasgow but it transpired that the Commander had come with a request. Ever since his Navy days, Bill had kept in touch with the Naval Christian Fellowship and they had prayed for him during his time in Africa. Periodically he had led missionary meetings for them and the bond was still strong. Now as a member of the NCF he and Margaret were being asked to take up work with the Royal Sailor's Rest.

The Royal Sailor's Rest had been started in 1876 by a Miss Agnes Weston at the instigation of the Navy itself. It was begun by this Christian woman as 'a public house without drink' and the organisation had expanded ever since to provide a home from home for sailors across the country. Miss Weston had been honoured for her endeavours and even had been made a Dame of the British Empire for her work. But to the many sailors and WRENs who frequented them the homes were known still as 'Aggie Weston's' or even simply as 'Aggie's'.

Commander Mather and the other trustees' concern was for the Naval personnel at the Clyde Submarine Base at Faslane on the west coast of Scotland. Here there was no 'Aggie's' which could provide support for the Christians who came into the base and which could be the source of outreach there. Would Bill and Margaret be willing to take on this new venture of setting up a new Royal Sailor's Rest there and commit themselves to the work?

They knew this would be a huge undertaking. It would take a lot of energy and skill to begin such a project from scratch. As

Bill now had no work and there was little Catriona Gilvear toddling around as well as young Billy, it might have been easy to take this as just another job and to jump at the chance. Yet this had never been Bill's way and he and Margaret prayed earnestly over the days following that God would show them the way forward. Having decided finally to go ahead, Bill read in his Bible that first morning words of reassurance and support: "'Oh, that you would bless me ... Let your hand be with me, and keep me from harm" ... And God granted his request' (1 Chronicles 4:10). With this encouragement Bill began his new work.

A house had already been found for the new Rest and it stood at Shandon on the shore of the Gare Loch. This area held mixed memories for Bill: it was on this very road that his terrible accident had happened, effectively finishing his missionary work; but it was in Shandon too that he had experienced the wonderful and unexpected gift of the Fresh Air Fortnight, his only holiday as a child.

The house was a large, imposing building but as soon as Bill entered he could see that it required a lot of work. Vast renovations would have to be carried out. Soon they discovered it had dry rot, damp, a leaking roof, it needed to be rewired, painted, redecorated ... to be practically rebuilt, thought Bill! This was going to be an enormous task.

Yet almost immediately offers of help came flooding in from several sources, and each offer seemed uncannily relevant and timely. During this time Bill was conducting many services and meetings in the Strathclyde area. Usually he mentioned the work in Shandon although he seldom gave specifics of particular needs. Nevertheless it became a regular occurrence for people to come up after the meetings and offer their skills which would match exactly what Bill had been praying for, even as recently as that day. Thus he received the unpaid help of a joiner, a carpet fitter, an architect, a master builder, a signwriter, a gardener, a photographer, a fire protection officer – and so the list went on.

Bill stopped being surprised at the way God was providing all they needed – and just when it was required. It made the provision of their flat in Glasgow with all its furnishings pale into insignificance! And yet perhaps that had been a preparation for this great endeavour: God had shown then what He could do on the small scale; now He was demonstrating His much greater powers to them here in Shandon.

Those who did not share Bill's faith were equally astounded. One of the first jobs was to repair the roof and a firm of roofers was brought over from Dumbarton. When the boss saw what was required, however, he laughed out loud.

'You must be joking!' he mocked. 'Don't you know the weather we have down here at this time of year. We'll never get a big job like that done just now.' And he was ready to leave.

Undaunted, Bill replied, 'Listen, my friend, I believe in the God of Elijah, and I will ask Him to shut up the heavens so that you can come and get the job done.'

The roofer gaped at Bill as if he thought he was mad! 'He's away in the head', Bill could see him thinking. Yet for the whole duration of the job not a drop of rain fell on that roofer's head although the storm and rain clouds circled menacingly round the rest of the Gare Loch!

It was in these details of life that they saw God answer their prayers so directly. In the big house they set up a self-service dining room and kitchen for the sailors to use. The kitchen was fully fitted and gleaming. But to Bill's dismay he was informed that he had purchased one of the appliances incorrectly. Instead of a Ariston Fridge, he had bought an Ariston Freezer. Having received so much assistance for free, Bill, with traditional Scottish frugality, was upset that he may have wasted so much money on a mistake. He turned to a young officer who was with him that day and asked, 'Do you believe in miracles, son? Then stay here and pray while I 'phone the electrical shop,' and he rushed away to the telephone. The manager there was unhelpful, refusing to offer any exchange but he agreed finally that they could bring the freezer down to the shop.

Immediately Bill raced back to his young friend and between them they hoisted the unwanted freezer into the officer's van. Then they drove over to the shop, some miles away in Renfrew.

When they arrived Bill could hardly believe the sight. The manager was dancing about in the car park, waiting for them.

'You'll never believe this, Mr Gilvear,' the man exclaimed, breathlessly, as soon as they stepped out of the van, 'you'll never believe it but as soon as you put down the 'phone another customer rang saying she had bought an Ariston fridge instead of a freezer! So you can have a direct swap! Have you ever heard of anything so amazing in all your born days?' Bill and the officer looked at each other knowingly. They had heard of things just like this before – it was God answering prayer, just about every day of the week, it seemed.

Finally the home took shape and the work began for real. With such evidences of God's hand at work behind them, Bill felt sure that He was just waiting to bless the venture and these hopes were quickly realised. Bill was determined that there would be no 'Bible-thumping' of those who came. 'We would just get "thumped" right back,' he joked. So instead they opened their doors to all the personnel at the base, letting them come and spend time there, relax, use the facilities and enjoy the home. 'Let them see us living Christian lives,' Bill said, 'and then let God do the work.'

And that is what happened. Those who spent time there found themselves picking up Christian books from the bookstall, watching Christian films or just entering into conversation with Bill or the other Christians who happened to be there. And lives began to be changed.

Soon Bill was able to begin a Bible study at lunch-times and occasionally he would be accorded the special privilege of actually entering the high-security base itself and conducting a service to the sailors and WRENs. In addition, Margaret and he visited some of the families left behind in the married quarters to help them during their husbands' long periods of duty when they were alone and often lonely.

Those who were Christians in the base could not get enough of the fellowship and teaching which Bill and the Rest could offer. These men and women were away at sea often for weeks and months at a time and were isolated from other Christians and in a very hostile environment to their faith. Bill knew all about that: he had been in the same situation himself on one Mess Deck after another. When they arrived at an oasis like Shandon they took in as much as they could get.

This applied also to foreign sailors and Bill extended a warm welcome to all who came. Sometimes he would lay on a special sight-seeing trip for the visitors, guiding them round Edinburgh and Stirling to the famous Scottish landmarks. Sometimes he would organise a barbecue or, if they wanted, he would show them where to get the traditional Scottish fare – a fish supper in a newspaper poke!

To these boys and girls so far from home and missing their own churches and fellowships, Bill would offer to take them to church with him and the Rest even gave them tapes of church services and sermons to take away with them on the boat, all with their own tape recorder and headphones so they could get some peace in the cramped conditions of the submarine or boat.

Sometimes Bill organised special meetings at Shandon which either he would lead himself or ask a guest speaker to attend. On one occasion he had a very special speaker whom nobody could believe had agreed to come. He was the Commander in Chief of the Mediterranean Fleet, Admiral Sir John Hamilton. When he told the boys on the base they thought he was joking: 'Away you go, Bill,' they jeered. 'Pull the other one, it's got bells on!'

But Bill was quite serious for he knew that this man was a true Christian and he had dared to go up and ask him to interrupt his busy itinerary to speak at the home in Shandon.

Bill knew from past experience that although the Navy was full of rules and regulations about rank, so much so that a humble Sick Berth Attendant like himself dare not look an officer in the eye or even walk on the same path as him, when two Christians met together, whatever their status, all the gold braid and stripes were as nothing. They were 'blood brothers' in Jesus Christ. He would never forget times when he had ministered to the NCF and had been served at table by high-ranking officers who belonged to the Fellowship, and had even had his breakfast made for him by another Admiral of the Fleet.

So Bill had approached the Admiral who had been delighted to accept. Bill made sure he had the place full with as many unbelieving seamen and women as he could find. One of the Christians on the base was an Irish boy who was Quartermaster there. It was his responsibility to bring all the drunks and rogues before the officers and to look after them in the Naval jail. Much as Paddy disliked this tough and unpleasant job, it meant he had access to all the roughest men and women on the base. And he brought as many as he could along to hear Bill's Admiral speak.

And the evening was a revelation to many. For the Admiral spoke of how he had considered himself to be a Christian, doing all the right things like reading his Bible, going to church and even crossing regularly by motor-boat over to his chaplain on one of the other boats in his huge fleet to receive communion. But then he told of how he had sailed into Gibraltar and visited friends there, only to find that the daughter of the house, his own god-daughter, had become a Christian and she had started challenging him about his faith.

'And before my fleet left the Rock of Gibraltar,' he announced, 'my life was founded on The Rock – Jesus Christ.'

The room was deathly silent as the great man told this personal story. It was like nothing they had heard before, especially from as high ranking a man as this. He continued to tell them of the difference in his life now and that they too could have their lives turned around, whatever they had done or wherever they thought they were before God.

The impact of that night was felt for a long time and many of the listeners were disturbed and spiritually awakened by what they had heard. Bill enlisted all the Christians there to pray as they had never done before that lives would be changed as a result. It was only a few days later that Bill met one of the WRENs on the disciplinary list whom Paddy had taken along. She had been one of the most hardened and antagonistic and was on her last warning for drunkenness and disorderly behaviour. Now she came to tell Bill that her life had been changed radically since that night; she had trusted Christ to clean the past away and He had given her a new life, living for Him. She had just been down to the pub, she said, and had told her old drinking cronies what had happened and that they would never see her there again.

Perhaps the most surprising outcome of all from that night was when some time later Bill and Margaret were invited to a wedding: it was the marriage of this girl to her former Quartermaster, Paddy!

46

One Step Forward, Two Steps Back

So great and so obvious were the things which were happening up in Shandon that the Naval authorities became quite concerned. They sent chaplains who were unsympathetic to what Bill was doing to see him – to put out the fire! – but there was nothing they could criticise or condemn. Instead they tried to scatter the new Christians onto different vessels. Yet this only had the effect of sending out 'missionaries' throughout the Navy. And so popular was the home itself and so many seamen and WRENs crowded into it that it had to be extended to cope with them all.

Because of the antagonism in some quarters and because Bill expended so much of his energy, as was his way, in doing the job, there were times when they felt discouraged and tired. The nature of the work was to see people for only a short time usually, while their submarines docked at Faslane. So there were many good-byes to be made and constant new faces to meet. However, even when enthusiasm did wane temporarily, there were still times of excitement to be had such as Bill and Margaret's visit to the Queen's Garden Party.

Bill looked at the gilded invitation he had received and laughed out loud! Who would have ever thought that 'Oor Willie frae the Gallowgate' with his parish clothes and with his toes poking out of his dirty boots would ever be invited to meet the Queen – in her own back garden?

But they were indeed invited and went off to Buckingham Palace. The gathering was to celebrate the birthday of the Queen Mother and as soon as Bill saw her in the beautiful grounds he could not resist breaking with the protocol and he called out, 'Happy Birthday, dear!' as she passed, to which she responded,

'Thank you – and for coming so far to tell me,' for no-one could fail to recognise Bill's broad Glaswegian accent.

He even managed a conversation with the Queen for as she passed through the lines of guests she spotted Bill's uniform and soon he was telling her too of the great things that were happening at the base at Faslane. The many distinguished gentlemen in top hats and tails waiting for their turn were ousted by Bill and his talk of the Royal Sailors' Rest.

The latter years of Bill's time with 'Aggie's' were spent not at Shandon, but in travelling round the country, telling people of the work that was being done there. Others took over the day to day running of the home and of the new Rest on the east coast at the Rosyth Naval Base. Now Bill was back doing the public speaking at which he had become increasingly experienced and to which he brought his own style, full of anecdote and vivacity, expressing his excitement at what God was doing.

This change of emphasis necessitated a change of venue as the house in Shandon was to be occupied by the new RSR Missioner and Bill and Margaret would have to move out. But they were very concerned about finding a home. Even when the trustees of the Rest offered to cover half of his mortgage in buying a house, Bill knew this was beyond him. He was greatly moved therefore when he discovered that the many young people who came regularly to the home in Shandon and who could not help materially, had organised themselves to pray and fast unceasingly for forty days until Bill found somewhere suitable to live. In 'double quick' time he was delighted to be able to tell them that he had been offered a house through an assisted housing association. So prompt was the hand-over of keys, in fact, that the Gilvears moved into the brand new housing estate in Denny in Stirlingshire before it was properly finished – and they had the whole scheme to themselves for a month before anyone else moved in!

Within this new arrangement with RSR, Bill began to find that his working time was altered. Now his evenings were busier with meetings while he could arrange his preparation or travelling during the day with more flexibility. Therefore, in an attempt to keep his mind fresh and active, as well as to present himself with a new challenge, Bill was given permission by RSR to study two days each week at college towards gaining some 'O' grade qualifications. Was he being courageous or foolhardy, he wondered, for not only was it many years since he had been at school, he had rarely been there in the first place! And after his struggles with nursing and language exams he thought he would never put himself through such torture again!

Nevertheless, Bill revelled in the learning environment of college. He joined the Christian Union and made many friends among the young folk: he loved their vitality and genuineness; they loved him for the happiness he exuded and for the transparency and straightforwardness of his faith and life. And Bill managed even to pass his exams. This, he thought, would equip him better to help Billy and Catriona as they approached secondary school. Perhaps their old Dad would not be such a 'duffer' after all!

It was during Bill's time as a travelling representative for the Royal Sailors' Rest that the Argentinian Navy invaded the Falkland Islands, precipitating the Falklands' War of 1982. Great numbers of ships and submarines were sent at short notice to the South Atlantic, carrying hundreds of men. For those whose loved ones had gone and who had no information of their whereabouts, it was an extremely trying time. For those sailors in the direct firing line with the Task Force, the stresses were enormous.

As he travelled around the country, Bill often came into contact with the families of those at sea and as time went on, with those who had returned. He heard tales of great loneliness, of terror during missile strikes and air attacks, of camaraderie built up over weeks of tension, of the constant proximity to death forcing questions from the most toughened campaigners. It reinforced to Bill the reality and relevance of his faith and he heard many times of the peace which was accorded those who loved the Lord as they faced starkly their own deaths. No man-made delusion or belief could give someone that lack of fear, even boldness, in these circumstances as experienced by these Christian folk.

One of the things which Bill was able to do was to arrange for the distribution of hundreds of Bibles in the vessels of the Task Force. In addition, the recording of a talk given by Bill in Edinburgh was distributed all over the country. On it he told many stories of the conflict which he had heard direct from survivors themselves of situations turned around by prayer as well as new depths of understanding of God's Word coming from these times of crisis.

There was one halt to Bill's busy itinerary with the Rest, however. That was the birth of their second daughter, Judith. Never had Bill been so surprised than when Margaret had announced to him that she thought she might be pregnant! They thought that their family was complete with Billy now ten and Catriona eight. And at fifty Bill joked that he looked more like a grandfather than a new parent! But in the hospital, gazing down at the little bundle in his arms, Bill's delight was unmistakable.

'Well, I've no idea where she came from, Margaret,' he quipped, 'just a surprise package from heaven.' But they both agreed that she was all the more precious because she was so unexpected!

As Bill travelled round the country there were several times when he was approached about taking up other work. Yet nothing tempted him to leave the work with the Navy personnel and the Royal Sailors' Rest until finally Africa was again brought into the equation: Bill was approached by the African Inland Mission, asking him to join their Scottish team.

The longing to return to missionary work had never been removed completely. And whenever the vast continent of Africa was mentioned Bill would prick up his ears. Even after more than a decade since his return to Scotland, the pull of Zaire and her sister countries was strong.

However, both Bill and Margaret were unsure. Recently, it was true, they had begun to think that it was time to finish work with RSR. Bill felt it needed a fresh impetus from someone new. But during their times of Bible reading and prayer they both felt that they were being pointed in another direction: 'Be at peace,' God seemed to be saying, 'Stand Still.' Various Bible verses cropped up in this connection and there was a growing conviction of God's desire for their willingness to rest and wait upon Him.

Conflicting with this, of course, were worries over the family. 'Stand still?' How could Bill do that? He was no longer young. Would he be able to find another job? And surely it would be irresponsible with a young family to give up one job and turn down the immediate chance of another? Could AIM not be the answer – the way in which God was pointing?

So eager were they to grasp the African connection that it was easy to listen to the latter argument. For were they not in service for God? Surely He would be happy enough with that?

So Bill began work with the African Inland Mission. He was to be a travelling secretary with them and would be responsible for a variety of tasks, from leading missionary meetings to interviewing prospective missionary candidates, to even visiting the several countries where the Mission had personnel. He would not be on the mission field as before but at least he would be able to be involved from the home side of the operation.

Bill approached this new venture with real excitement. This was a chance, he felt, to get stuck into Africa again. God had called both Margaret and himself to Africa before. That memory had remained with them ever since and the abrupt nature of their departure had left many desires for work there unfulfilled. Forgotten was the word from God to put Africa behind them and step forward. Now, thought Bill, is my chance to set the record straight.

Immediately Bill was thrown in at the deep end with a varied and heavy workload. Soon he found himself travelling vast distances leading, attending and organising meetings; he visited local support groups, encouraging them and informing them of current AIM work; he chaired and organised large Annual General Meetings as well as various missionary training sessions and weekend seminars; he arranged speaking itineraries for missionaries home on furlough, often escorting them and supporting them at meetings; he maintained regular contact with them while they were abroad; he interviewed and assessed candidates for missionary work and students for medical electives, and arranged their placements abroad; and all within so tight a timetable that there were not enough hours in the day in which to complete the work or even to be in as many places as he was expected. On top of this, although he was so seldom able to be at home, he extended hospitality to any African visitors in the country. It was a hectic assignment he had been given.

Much as Bill enjoyed the contact with people and communicating the needs and challenges of the African work, it became apparent quickly that the organisational side of his job did not come naturally to him. So much was alien: so much was beyond his knowledge. Bill may be able to hold an audience enthralled at meetings, yet, in the office, looking at lists of venues, dates, times, costs and schedules, Bill just felt his head spin!

Margaret went into the office whenever she could to use her secretarial skills to help him and Bill appreciated her presence there. For it was hard to own up to simple problems in the office when he felt he should be able to cope. Everyone else seemed so efficient and knowledgeable. Bill quickly began to feel inadequate and frustrated at the growing evidences of his lack of skills.

There was a need also to become accustomed to the change of organisational style which came with Bill's new job. AIM was such a huge missionary society compared with the Royal Sailor's Rest that inevitably the job was very different and brought much greater responsibilities. Paradoxically, however, Bill was surprised to feel increasingly isolated in his own particular role. He lacked people with whom he could share the day to day problems and to whom he could delegate effectively: the London office seemed too remote and sometimes distant from the Scottish work. Yet with all the responsibility there was not the same freedom to carry a project through from start to finish as he saw fit: now there was a number of others to whom he had to answer. And there was so much of which to keep on top, so many details to work out; he had to keep a finger in so many different pies. In addition, there was always so little time; there were always a dozen more jobs waiting to be done as well. Therefore, although the work itself had a larger audience and greater impact, Bill was more alone than he had ever been before.

Nevertheless, Bill knuckled down. He put in the many hours and struggled with the administrative tasks which he found so irksome. He would settle in, he told himself. These were merely teething troubles, perhaps. He would soon get used to it all, he hoped.

Yet as the months passed, it became no easier. The meetings and public speaking, he could handle: but the arranging, the organising, the planning he could not. Slowly and insidiously, Bill's confidence in his work began to ebb away. The small frustrations and feelings of inadequacy mounted up, nagging at him and making him worry.

In addition, it seemed that the job was simply not working. However many hours he put in, Bill saw little in the way of results. Although this could not be his only yardstick, in terms of personal relationships and in the promotion of missionary work, it was not going well. With a sense of his own responsibility in this, Bill made himself work harder and harder. For in the back of his mind was the worry about his own eagerness to take this job with AIM. Perhaps God had wanted to show them other plans He had for them. Had they been too impatient and rushed ahead with what they had wanted? More than anything Bill wanted to be in God's will. Now he wondered if perhaps he had strayed out of it.

As these pressures mounted, Bill did not know whether to be pleased or not when he was asked to go on a visit to some of the Mission stations in Africa. Although he was desperately keen to go back to Africa, he was concerned that there would be a pile-up of work to do on his return. However, the trip itself seemed worthwhile as it would be an opportunity to meet the missionaries in their own situations and encourage them, as well as deal with any concerns they may have.

As with work at home, the trip was busy with a full itinerary. Beginning in Nairobi, Bill travelled widely throughout Kenya before moving on to Uganda, Tanzania and Zaire. Much of the travelling was done in the tiny Missionary Aviation Fellowship aeroplanes which could land in the most inaccessible places and reach the furthest outposts. As Bill flew over the deep African bush and looked down on the vast jungles or the stretches of empty savannah country, he could feel his heart thrill and quicken just with the fact of being back again. The intense heat, the deep and vibrant colours all around him, and the generosity of the welcomes extended to him, made him yearn to be part of it all again.

'If I didn't have Margaret and 'the brood' back in Denny,' he thought to himself, 'you wouldn't find me on a flight back home.'

Yet Bill had come to do a specific job and what he discovered on some of the stations made this very difficult for it distressed him greatly. On some stations he found the living conditions for the missionaries extremely poor, even below local African standards of hygiene. Bill was appalled, never having seen anything like it on the mission field and he could see that if nothing was done the missionary families would all be extremely ill.

Elsewhere Bill encountered relationship difficulties across the cultures, similar to that which he had witnessed at Bongondza. Having experienced the damage this could do, Bill was worried about what might be the result of these rifts.

In another area Bill discovered chronic overwork and stress among mission staff. Looking at it from the perspective of a missionary himself, Bill could see that something must be done.

He came back to Britain therefore and presented these findings in his report. At least now something could be done to improve these situations, he felt. The missionaries were relying on him to do something to sort out these problems.

To Bill's intense concern, his report was not interpreted as he wished. His recommendations were not taken on board and it seemed that he was considered to be too extreme in his assessment of the situations. Bill worried continually about it all. Had he misread the problems? Had he been scaremongering, even? Or had he failed to communicate his concerns properly in his report: the written word had never been his strong point?

And so it preyed on Bill's mind. Nobody at home seemed to appreciate the extent and seriousness of the problems he had witnessed. And there was no-one to whom he could turn. He felt out on a limb and increasingly responsible. The missionaries were relying on him to alleviate their problems and he was letting them down. In addition, Bill was sure that the work of the Mission and the furtherance of the gospel would be seriously damaged if these situations were allowed to continue.

Sadly, it was with grief and with a terrible sense of failure, that Bill watched helplessly from Scotland over the subsequent months as each of the catastrophes he had predicted and of which he had warned, came about.

With his confidence at a low ebb and with frustration mounting as steadily as his workload, Bill continued with his job. Indeed, he worked harder than ever, trying desperately to make it all work. But there was an emptiness about what he was doing. Now the day to day anxieties of the organisational work began to affect his more public responsibilities. He felt as if he were operating under some heavy cloud.

For Bill found it increasingly difficult to lead meetings and be able to offer something to say there which would be encouraging and motivating. Meeting people constantly became more of a strain and he was very tired. His sleep was disturbed with worries about all he had to do and anything he may have forgotten to arrange or omitted to organise. He felt he had hundreds of things in his mind all clamouring for attention. It was all getting out of control. And he was finding it increasingly hard to pray. He felt distanced from God. Partly his time was so pressurised there was always something else intruding on prayer time. But even when he sat down to it, he would flounder, hardly knowing where to start. It was as if anything he prayed was hitting the ceiling and not getting through.

Bill knew there was something badly wrong when he was leading one of the many conferences he had organised over the past two years for AIM and he found himself physically unable to take part. He gave out the opening hymn and prayer and then sat down. When the time came for Bill to fill his fifteen minute slot, he begged his companion who had been playing his violin during part of the evening to take over. Bill could only sit immobile while his friend filled the time. He played 'Rest in the Lord', perhaps especially for Bill. But at present that was something Bill seemed unable to do.

47

Picking Up the Pieces

The final straw came at home. It had been an encouragement to Bill and Margaret that although their commitment to God's work had meant that they had moved from Africa, to Glasgow, to Shandon and finally to Denny, the family had seemed unaffected and had settled well. They liked the church too and they were so pleased when Billy became a member there at thirteen and was involved in the youth work, going on young people's Christian holidays and attending other groups for Christians of his age.

However, by the time he was sixteen, Billy had other priorities. He had plans for his life and it was as if there was a sudden need to be free, to make his own decisions, and most of all to get away from home. And so began the first of many battles.

Billy decided that he wanted to join the Army – at once. Bill and Margaret were bewildered by this sudden demand. At sixteen they considered him far too young to be committing his life to several years of military life. Did he know what he was letting himself in for? How could he look after himself? Why not wait a year or two? It all seemed so sudden and such a dramatic step to take.

Because he was underage, Billy needed his parents to sign his draft papers on his behalf but Bill and Margaret refused. A tense and resentful stalemate ensued. Bill found it increasingly hard to come home exhausted and find this unpleasant atmosphere. And because he was away from home so much, Margaret had much more of the animosity and frustration with which to contend.

Finally, Billy had had enough. He had heard all the arguments but nothing could change his mind. He wanted out. And what about church – and God – and faith? All these were to be abandoned too in his need to be his own person and to have an identity of his own.

'I know what you and Mum believe,' he yelled at Bill, 'and I don't want any part of it. It's not for me.' And with that he hurled his Bible across the room. 'Here's my Bible! Have it!'

As he looked at the pages lying twisted and fluttering on the floor, Bill knew that this could not go on. Every barrier they put up was just driving Billy further and further away. Maybe it had gone too far already. The time had come to let go. They must sign the papers. Billy would leave.

The immediate relief from this climb-down was immense. Suddenly Billy was happy. The frustration was gone. He was their normal, loving son again.

'We must let him go,' Bill said to Margaret, 'like Moses' mother when she let go of her son. We must just entrust him to God's care.' But this was not some impersonal situation he was discussing. This was about his own son and by the day of Billy's departure, the cracks in Bill were beginning to show. It was as if this was too much after all the strain of work and he was being pushed to the edge – to the very limit of himself. Worried by it all, he felt in a panic, he could not think straight, he could get no sleep, tears were never far away.

Bill was very concerned for Margaret as she wept bitterly for her son who was still so young. Feeling helpless himself, Bill called the minister and doctor to see her. However, he too needed this help and soon he was sitting nervously in the doctor's waiting room himself. He had no idea what he would say. The doctor, he knew, was a Christian herself. But there seemed too much to explain, and he was so confused himself.

When he entered her room, however, and began to relate his problems and the symptoms he was experiencing, Bill broke down completely. For the first time in years he wept openly and loudly. He could not stop. It was as if the concern he felt for Billy was unravelling all the pressure and loneliness of the past two years.

The doctor could see that Bill needed more help than she could give. However, she gave him some medication to help him sleep and relax and promised to arrange for someone to see him. Then with great thoughtfulness, she let Bill out of the surgery by a side door so that he would not have to walk through the waiting room with the tears running down his face and the great sobs still catching in his throat.

Soon Bill received an appointment from a specialist. Bill was worried that after this consultation he would be taken away to a Mental Hospital: he felt so unable to cope that he thought he must be going mad. However, he was treated at home for depression, although all the cocktail of drugs seemed to do was to dope him up. They left him feeling groggy and he could tell from those around him that he was being unresponsive. Yet it was easier to feel like this rather than to be so out of control.

Throughout all this, Bill was trying to carry on with his work. It was desperately hard and he thought sometimes his head would burst from the strain of trying to hold onto all its different strands. But there was no relief from the hectic schedule of meetings and engagements. There seemed no way out.

During this time, Bill and Margaret received a visit from a friend of Margaret's called Adam Hannah. He was a doctor on the west coast of Scotland in Ayr. Knowing that Bill was unwell, he was very interested in his condition and tried to encourage Bill to speak about his feelings.

'It's like there are lots of different rooms inside my head,' explained Bill, struggling to describe it all, 'and all the doors are banging.'

Adam discussed with him what this meant, along with his other symptoms. 'This is a perfect description of your kind of depression,' he explained. Everything Bill was doing, apparently, was being absorbed by his conscious mind without time for it to slip into his sub-conscious as usually happens. Therefore it was all getting jumbled up and he got no respite from the bombardment of information that resulted.

Bill found it helpful to speak to this young man and it was good to know that there was someone willing to understand his situation and who could offer some explanation. For as Bill could see no relief from the heavy cloud under which he was struggling, many friends did nothing to help. Indeed many did more harm than good.

'You shouldn't be depressed – you're a Christian,' they insisted. 'Snap out of it!' He was accused of selfishness and melodrama, of malingering and self-pity. And each accusation and admonition sent him deeper into the dark, bottomless hole out of which he was trying so frantically and ineffectively to escape.

From time to time, Bill would be touched by the effort made by some to comfort him. On one occasion a Christian family travelled to visit him from nearby Falkirk. They were gifted singers and they sang to Bill there in his sitting room and prayed with him. Although they were strangers to him, they had heard Bill speak previously at their church and were distressed to hear that he was unwell. And because they made no demands of him and he was not forced to respond, just listen, it was a time of encouragement to him, full of peace and healing.

Yet there was no easy way out of his situation and Bill despaired of ever feeling normal again. For Margaret to see her fun-loving, larger-than-life husband so low and bowed down by this invisible illness was terrible. Bill had spent most of his life encouraging others and knowing just how to reach people who were in distress: now he was in desperate need yet she felt so unable to help. It was like watching him slowly drown but not being able to pull him out.

As the situation deteriorated and Bill continued to struggle on with his work, AIM became keen to help. As the months went by it was recognised that Bill's troubles were work-orientated and they were concerned to do all they could for him. From the first visit to his doctor, Bill had offered to resign from AIM, but the Mission were reluctant to lose him and instead had persuaded him to stay on. Now they provided the opportunity for Bill to receive Christian advice and help: he and Margaret were to spend some days at a Centre in the Borders which was specifically for Christian workers who were in need of a place of rest and recovery.

This Care Mission in Duns was run by a Dr Michael Jones and his wife. It had individual cottages where visitors could stay and have complete peace and solitude during the day. In the evenings the doctors held interview sessions in the main building, providing an opportunity to discuss and talk with their guests through their individual problems.

This place of retreat was of immense benefit to Bill, offering as it did a complete release from the ubiquitous pressures under which he was struggling, as well as a chance for a skilled professional to probe into his situation and assess his needs, pointing the way towards recovery. Night after night, Bill was questioned at length about his life, about his past and about his current situation. Gently yet persistently they probed him for answers. Bill would come away exhausted as so much of his past spilled out and the situations of these years were uncovered. For Bill had experienced from his earliest days as a boy and then as a teenager, to his Navy days and then the various trips to Congo, much that was very traumatic and distressing. For some people one such event might be enough to unbalance them; yet Bill's life had been full of many tragic and shocking circumstances. Finally he had been pushed to extremes in his present situation so that he could not cope as he had done before. It was as if he was continuing to give out, yet was not able to receive from others or, more importantly, from God.

Because the help given at this Centre was from a Christian perspective and the doctors were Christians themselves, Bill felt he could share many of his needs which were spiritual in nature and which were not understood by other doctors to whom he had spoken. Without fear of sounding like a fanatic, or of seeming to betray his God by admitting to spiritual struggles, Bill was able to discover the burdens he was carrying without even knowing it and so clear the way towards a more untrammelled relationship with Christ.

Specifically, he was able to discuss his current situation and his growing fears that he had raced into AIM without seeking God's blessing on it. Was he now incurring God's wrath with this depression or, at least, perhaps God's intervention to stop him in his tracks?

Together with the Jones', Bill was able to look constructively at his own skills and those required by his job. It appeared that although some overlapped, many did not. Instead his weaknesses were being emphasised and exposed while leaving many of his undoubted abilities untapped. Thus his own sense of worth was being steadily diminished.

Dr Jones pinpointed clearly with straightforward clarity to Bill how this related to his own lack of assurance of being in God's will. It confirming his own doubts.

'If God has called you to a task,' the doctor concluded, 'you may not *seem* suited to it, but God will equip you for it. But if He is not equipping you, you have to ask, "Has He called you?" '

At the end of this time of retreat, Bill was given a report on himself which detailed his condition and which pointed to the various peaks and troughs in his experience. It traced his skills and strengths too as well as his weaknesses and showed clearly how his present job was unsuited to him.

Having shown the creation of his depression, the report also indicated Bill's need to relinquish the present stresses in his life so that recovery could take place. Therefore Bill took it to the Mission headquarters and again offered his resignation. Once more he was offered help and assistance but Bill could see it was no use. He had struggled on for seven months under medication and could see no improvement. The time had come to make the break. And if he was out of God's will then this was the first step to rectifying matters. Thus, it was with a mixture of relief and disappointment, as well as fear for the future, that Bill resigned.

Although Bill received help from his time in Duns and from the various others who were concerned with his recovery, it was a long time before any progress began to be made. Many months went by and Bill could do little to respond to what was happening around him. Margaret would watch him sitting huddled in the armchair, looking barely half the man she knew him to be. It felt sometimes with little Judith chattering or Catriona talking about school, that he was only partly hearing what was going on. At times he could hardly bear to have people round him. His head would ache and he felt a terrible need to escape from any company. Even the noise of talking voices could prove too much.

Margaret tried to understand and to help, yet it was hard to know if Bill was taking in what she was saying. As they discussed it over and over, Margaret likened Bill's situation to that of a prophet in the Old Testament.

'I feel we've been like Jonah,' she sighed, struggling to find the words which might reach into Bill's locked thoughts. 'You know, Bill, how the sailors on his boat tried everything to save the situation – rowing harder, throwing out the excess baggage – but the storm was too fierce. Nothing worked because they were going in the wrong direction. God had to intervene dramatically to turn things around – to make Jonah stop and take stock – to Stand Still.'

She reiterated the words which they felt had been given to them more than two years previously but which they had largely ignored. Gently, she continued, 'Perhaps, Bill, this has been God doing the same thing for you – stopping you in your tracks – making you stand still.'

Bill lifted weary eyes then to hers: 'So this is me in the belly of the whale then, is it?' He smiled but there was no humour in his face. 'And how long will my three days and nights there take to pass?'

It seemed they were to last for many months, yet gradually Bill did begin to improve. The despairing, drawn look began to lift from his face and he seemed more responsive and relaxed. There was a letting go of the stresses, little problems were not so insurmountable, conversation became more natural: slowly he was returning to his normal self.

The catalyst to these great changes was a visit one evening from a group of elders in their church. Previously Bill had been too ashamed to ask for their help. However now they prayed with Bill and cried to the Lord for his recovery and while they were there Bill knew that he had been touched by the Lord. From this point he began to see some light for which to aim after being stumbling around blindly in a dark, deep labyrinth for so long.

And as he began to recover, Bill found he could talk again with his God. For he knew he needed to come humbly before God. Although his illness had never been of his own making, his own honesty demanded that if he had gone contrary to what God wanted, then he must admit it and seek God's forgiveness. Human pride could have no place.

There was humility required too as Bill began to face the world again. Many had known Bill for many years as a powerful Christian leader and evangelist, a role model for those seeking to be whole-hearted and sincere in their Christian lives. Yet now he had experienced the stigma associated with mental illness, especially for a Christian. In addition, however much it cost him in the eyes of the world, he had to admit to his mistakes. For nothing was more important than being close to his God. Having known a time of distance from God and the feelings of isolation that had brought, Bill never wanted that channel of communication blocked or broken again. Just to be able to speak with God again and know His nearness was a continual source of joy.

Bill discovered during this time how wrong many of those had been who had blamed him for his own depression. How ashamed they had made him of himself and of this illness to which they said he should not have succumbed. How guilty they had made him feel. Now Bill was finding that even great men in the Bible had suffered in this way, like the prophet, Elijah. One day Elijah had been working wonders for the Lord, Bill read, and the next he was running away from a woman, wishing he were dead! Yet whatever mistakes Elijah may have made in the past or whatever he said to God during this time, God had still treated the prophet gently and with compassion. It seemed that some of Bill's so-called friends had a lot to learn.

When he attended his next appointment with the specialist, Bill had made great progress, not showing the withdrawal effects from the drugs which might have been expected and coping well without them. Most of the symptoms seemed to have left. He was more of the happy, trusting man with the direct gaze and uncomplicated outlook he had been before. Finally, it seemed, there was hope: he was coming through it at last.

48

Back To Work

As soon as he was declared fit enough for work, Bill set off for the local Employment Agency. Almost two years had drifted by without Bill being able to take an active part in the running of his family or in contributing to its upkeep. He was eager now to put that right.

Yet for all his enthusiasm, there was not much on offer. Indeed, after a few weeks of regular appointments there and a couple of unsuccessful interviews, it was politely suggested to Bill that perhaps he need come down only every few months – just to keep his name on the books.

'Hey, what are you on about?' queried Bill. 'What are you telling me?' But he had to admit that he was not a very inviting prospect to a future employer: he was fifty-eight, he had a bad arm and he had just been off work for two years with depression. He could understand if they were not queuing up to enlist his services!

'So it looks like I'm just "on the burroo",' he told Margaret and they sat down together to figure out what to do. Catriona was now reaching the important stage of Higher examinations and Judith was only seven. Someone would need to be at home to care for them. But if Bill was to be at home anyway, perhaps Margaret should try to get a job instead?

Although she had trained as a secretary and then worked as a youth leader with the Bible Club Movement, Margaret felt that these skills were very rusty and she would need to retrain. And so it was decided that Margaret should go to college and gain some qualifications. As her elder daughter was thinking of Higher examinations, so would Margaret.

This left Bill with the house to run and so began his further education too. Like many men of his generation, he had not taken much to do with the running of the household. Now, however, he became a dedicated house-husband, learning the new skills of cooking and ironing, shopping and cleaning – and the many other mysterious chores which he discovered needed to be done. The kitchen, however, was the greatest revelation with many hidden pitfalls for the unsuspecting novice. Even boiling potatoes was a new experience – as was eating burnt ones! Many were the culinary disasters which were inflicted on the Gilvear family during those days and although he did improve, Bill could not claim to enjoy it.

It was good, however, to spend more time with Catriona and Judith and be on hand to hear all their news from school and all about their friends. It was a time of discovery for him when he became closer to his daughters than ever before and it brightened his otherwise mundane days. With Catriona this was especially important for Bill. She had experienced more than Billy or Judith the trauma of Bill's illness: Billy was only home periodically on Army leave while Judith was too young. Catriona, however, was at home and old enough to understand something of what had been wrong. She knew certainly that her father had not been himself. Now Bill wanted to put that terrible time behind them both and devote himself to being the parent she had missed effectively during those years.

And he thoroughly enjoyed getting to know his little live-wire of a younger daughter too. Together he and Judith would sit down for a snack after school and chat about the day, or Bill would help her with her homework. This, however, was not always so simple for having missed so much of school himself, Bill was disconcerted to discover how little he knew, even with his extra 'O' grades. Sometimes they would give up and Margaret would take over when she came home.

By the end of the year, Margaret had completed her course and having sat three Highers, was thrilled to find that she had gained two 'A' passes and a 'B'.

'If I had known you were as clever as all that I would have sent you out to work long ago,' laughed Bill, delighted at her success. As a result, Margaret quickly got a job while Bill remained at home.

Shortly afterwards Bill saw an advertisement for a job. It had been sent by his cousin Ken who had seen it and suggested it to Bill. It was for a representative for the Scripture Gift Mission, a Christian organisation which sought to publish and distribute Christian literature in the form of tracts and books. The Mission were looking for someone to travel the country, introducing the literature wherever possible and giving churches the opportunity to use it as they tried to spread the gospel. This, thought his cousin, would be just right for Bill.

When Bill read the job description and saw the application form, however, he thought otherwise. They were looking for a man aged between thirty and forty-five who was a minister and who could type. Bill just did not fit! He discovered also that all his predecessors had belonged to another denomination: this could not be the job for him, he decided, and he threw the form away.

However, Margaret was not happy in her work at this time and when SGM was suggested to Bill again he decided to apply. The job interested him, definitely. There seemed such an opportunity for Christians to be involved by just offering a friend or colleague something to read. And he knew the recipients would be challenged by having God's Word and gospel presented to them. He was even offered as a referee for his application an acquaintance who was a Professor in Mathematics in Glasgow University.

'That'll impress them, don't you think?' laughed Bill, 'until they discover I can't even help my wee daughter with the sums in her homework!'

Not expecting any results because of his seeming unsuitability and the troubles of recent times, Bill was amazed to be offered the job. They knew all about him, so it was a boost to his confidence to know that this group of Christians was ready to employ him. Yet it was frightening too. He would have a travelling job with similarities to his last position where it had all gone so sadly wrong. It was a real test to trust God that He would not let this happen again.

Soon Bill was thoroughly immersed in the work. The tracts and literature were used largely as aids in evangelism and this had been the main focus of Bill's life since his own conversion. Now he was in a position to provide resources for others to do the work and to enthuse church members to share their faith with those around them. In addition, Bill was often called to speak at meetings to which many unbelieving people had been invited and he spoke with such directness and relevance that his words reached into many lives and situations. He was thrilled once again that he was being used to direct and lead people to Christ.

Bill recalled his colleague in Congo, Kinso and his wife Alice. They had begun a work with literature in Kisangani. Seeing Congo become more literate, they had opened a Christian bookshop in the city and had toured the bush also with a van full of books. They had been very excited to see how God was using this means of spreading knowledge of Him and the Christian message. And they had been amazed at the quarters into which their books had reached. Now Bill could enter into that enthusiasm in his own situation in Scotland.

The work with SGM involved a lot of travelling and Bill found himself driving to areas he had never visited before. There was a great variety in the types of churches to which he was invited. There were Brethren Assemblies and Baptist churches, Independent fellowships, Charismatic groups, and Reformed churches of every persuasion. Yet these diverse churches had a desire in common – to see God's Kingdom grow and extend. It was a source of encouragement to Bill to see this focal centrality even within widely divergent traditions. Nevertheless it was useful also to always remember where he was!

Coming as a stranger into many meetings, Bill was thrown often into situations which he thought were beyond him. This had happened many times before. Years previously in Edinburgh, he had been confronted with a number of learned professors in his audience. Grabbing the minister, James Fraser, he had protested: 'I can't preach to them! What can I say that they don't already know?'

Mr Fraser replied calmly, urging Bill into the pulpit: 'In the Free Church College they may be professors. Here they are just my elders. Now get up and speak!'

Now on a return to that same church, Bill was introduced as 'Reverend Bill Gilvear' to the congregation. Invitations had even been printed with the same misnomer. Afterwards Bill took the person who had promoted him in this way to task.

'I must be the most irreverent Reverend you ever had in this church! What did you mean by that?' But Bill found the response as cheerful and supportive as it had always been for Rev Douglas MacMillan replied cheerfully, 'You come into the College tomorrow and I'll ordain you, after what I heard tonight!" '

Not long after Bill began work with SGM, there was a time of outreach across the country involving nearly every denomination. It was the occasion of Dr Billy Graham's return to Scotland for the first time since 1955, when Bill had served as a counsellor and helper round the country. Many venues were involved and Bill was very honoured to be asked to join the evangelist on the platform in his home territory in Glasgow.

Standing there in Celtic Park Football Ground, Bill spoke to the people gathered there of a little of the turnaround there had been in his own life. And he could sense an appreciation of his words. These were his own people. Many could relate to the experiences of his life. Bill gazed round at the thousands gathered there who were just like him – and just like him they needed Jesus Christ. Later he watched the hundreds upon hundreds of people flooding onto the pitch to learn more and to find Christ. It was so exciting to be part of it all. He looked down at his Bible which Billy Graham had inscribed for him with the verse: 'May Christ be always first in your life' (Psalm 16:11). All those years ago in the Tent Hall he had made a decision which some were making now before his eyes in Celtic Park. Bill had proved the value of these words since that day – putting Christ first. There and then Bill prayed that God would lead on these new Christians as He had always done for him.

As Bill continued to travel round the country after this event, he met up with many who had been present at various venues during Mission Scotland 91 and who had been changed forever from that time. There was even a young boy in Bill's own street in Denny who had been touched by God that night. Just as in the campaign in 1955, this was an occasion which would have positive spiritual repercussions for many years to come.

49

All For Him

Shortly after this time Bill was asked to be involved in a project which forced him to take a retrospective look at himself. He was approached by the BBC and asked if a programme could be made about him by their Religious Affairs Department. It would be part of a series entitled 'Moment of Truth' which was focusing on various people who had experienced some spiritual encounter. Bill had been chosen to be one of these subjects.

The producer, Stuart Millar was a Christian himself and was sympathetic to Bill's position so Bill trusted him to deliver the truth in the programme. And so filming began.

Bill was taken back to as many of the old Glasgow streets and tenements as were still standing and he showed on camera the places and haunts where he had run with his friends as a boy. He showed the games they had played and the mischief he had got up to. He described too his gang days and his liberation from that life by Christ. Standing thereafter in the now dilapidated Tent Hall which held so many memories for him was very moving, yet sad. The work there had stopped many years before and the building had been left to decay. But it seemed that so much of his life had circulated around that simple place.

Bill laughed when old film footage of him was used to depict his work in Congo. The Africans had been right: he could see that he had been balding even then! But throughout the programme Bill was able to speak of God's hand on his life and of the dramatic difference God had made to him. It was all too obvious that his whole life had been shaped by God's intervention so many years before. Never one to 'pull any punches', Bill told his story with all the directness and vivacity for which he was known, and to his delight it was all included in the final programme.

When it was shown, the film had a great impact and Bill was given more opportunities than ever to speak for God. In particular, he found himself speaking increasingly in meetings to people who did not know God and he was able to point them in the right direction towards Him. For this had always been his greatest and most treasured gift.

It was useful sometimes to have the memory jogged, Bill thought, although the memories recalled could be good and bad. If he thought of one young lad who had left the gangs behind like himself and who had ended up in the Salvation Army, there was always the recollection of another who had been incarcerated in Barlinnie Prison and had indeed been executed there. For the fond memories of family and the close bonds as children, there was also the fragmentation of their relationships as adults and even for Bill the pain of conducting the funeral service of his own sister. For the happy recollection of Congolese friends and of continued contact with them, there was also the knowledge of M'bongo's recent death and the gradual severance of ties in this way.

On his travels Bill often came across acquaintances from his past and he discovered many whom he had known before they had become Christians, only to find them as leading lights in churches where he was asked to speak! Sometimes he was called to meet needs of those with whom he had lost touch many years before and on whom he had not known he had had any effect. One such man was Joe McCarvill. Bill and Joe had worked together in Oakbank and had become friendly because Joe had a motorbike. On many occasions he had given Bill a lift to Dennistoun where they both lived.

Bill was called many years later to Joe's hospital bed where he lay dying. Although as a Roman Catholic Joe had been attended by his own priest, both he and his wife had been desperate to find Bill. They remembered Bill's faith and that he was a man who knew God. Although they had not seen him for

almost thirty years, they tracked him down and called on him now.
When he arrived Bill barely recognised the man in the hospital bed.
But he took hold of Joe's hand and was able to lead his old friend
to Christ.

As time for Bill's retirement approaches, he feels encouraged
by these signs from the past. Although he knows he can see only
a tiny part of his own life at one time, God is clearly in charge of
the whole. God can see the beginning from the end, such as
knowing when was the right time for Bill to be able to reach out
to Joe after all these years.

For this reason Bill feels confident to leave his concerns for
his own family in God's hands. As Billy left the Army and took
up new work, Bill continued to commend him to God, as with
Catriona in the Police and Judith still at school. Each of them has
filled him with great pride in what they have achieved and he is
comforted that God knows the plans He has for them in the future.

But as Bill does look to the future and retirement, it is not with
the thought that this is the end of his work.

'God is never finished with us,' Bill has said and he has proved
this through the various times of hardship as well as in the times
of success and achievement. It is natural then that he anticipates
that the rest of his life will be committed to God, just as God has
shown that He is committed to Bill. It is this partnership and
closeness to God which is so transparent in Bill and which shines
through him – usually onto his broad, irrepressible grin.

So of the future then? 'We only have one life to live for God,'
Bill is certain. 'All the rest is dross and is worthless. So it has been,
and will be, all for Him – and when we get to see Him,' Bill adds,
'we will wish that we had done much more.'